Introduction to Agent-Based Economics

Introduction to Agent-Based Economics

Edited by

Mauro Gallegati
Antonio Palestrini
Alberto Russo

ACADEMIC PRESS
An imprint of Elsevier

Academic Press is an imprint of Elsevier
125 London Wall, London EC2Y 5AS, United Kingdom
525 B Street, Suite 1800, San Diego, CA 92101-4495, United States
50 Hampshire Street, 5th Floor, Cambridge, MA 02139, United States
The Boulevard, Langford Lane, Kidlington, Oxford OX5 1GB, United Kingdom

Notices

Knowledge and best practice in this field are constantly changing. As new research and experience
broaden our understanding, changes in research methods, professional practices, or medical treatment
may become necessary.

Practitioners and researchers must always rely on their own experience and knowledge in evaluating and
using any information, methods, compounds, or experiments described herein. In using such information
or methods they should be mindful of their own safety and the safety of others, including parties for
whom they have a professional responsibility.

To the fullest extent of the law, neither the Publisher nor the authors, contributors, or editors, assume any
liability for any injury and/or damage to persons or property as a matter of products liability, negligence
or otherwise, or from any use or operation of any methods, products, instructions, or ideas contained in
the material herein.

Library of Congress Cataloging-in-Publication Data
A catalog record for this book is available from the Library of Congress

British Library Cataloguing-in-Publication Data
A catalogue record for this book is available from the British Library

ISBN: 978-0-12-803834-5

For information on all Academic Press publications
visit our website at https://www.elsevier.com/books-and-journals

Working together
to grow libraries in
developing countries

www.elsevier.com • www.bookaid.org

Publisher: Candice Janco
Acquisition Editor: J. Scott Bentley
Editorial Project Manager: Susan Ikeda
Production Project Manager: Julie-Ann Stansfield
Designer: Miles Hitchen

Typeset by VTeX

Contents

3. AD-AS Representation of Macroeconomic Emergent Properties

Luca Riccetti, Alberto Russo, and Mauro Gallegati

4. Heterogeneity in Macroeconomics: DSGE and Agent-Based Model Approach

Federico Giri

Part III
Macroeconomic ABM: Perspectives and Implications

10.   A Networked Economy: A Survey on the Effect of Interaction in Credit Markets

Ruggero Grilli, Giulia Iori, Niccolò Stamboglis, and Gabriele Tedeschi

Contributors

Leonardo Bargigli, University of Florence, Florence, Italy

Alessandro Caiani, Marche Polytechnic University, Ancona, Italy

Ermanno Catullo, Marche Polytechnic University, Ancona, Italy

Eugenio Caverzasi, Marche Polytechnic University, Ancona, Italy

Fabio Clementi, University of Macerata, Macerata, Italy

Annarita Colasante, Universitat Jaume I, Castellón de la Plana, Spain

Mauro Gallegati, Marche Polytechnic University, Ancona, Italy

Lisa Gianmoena, Marche Polytechnic University, Ancona, Italy

Federico Giri, Marche Polytechnic University, Ancona, Italy

Ruggero Grilli, Marche Polytechnic University, Ancona, Italy

Giulia Iori, City University, London, United Kingdom

Antonio Palestrini, Marche Polytechnic University, Ancona, Italy

Luca Riccetti, University of Macerata, Macerata, Italy

Alberto Russo, Marche Polytechnic University, Ancona, Italy

Niccolò Stamboglis, City University, London, United Kingdom

Gabriele Tedeschi, Universitat Jaume I, Castellón de la Plana, Spain

Foreword

The financial meltdown of the years 2007–09 and the global great recession have initiated a search for new perspectives in economics. This holds true for conventional macroeconomics, for standard DSGE models, for traditional Keynesian, and for New Keynesian thinking. This book, with its contributions by well-known scholars in the field of agent-based modeling, takes a new and refreshing perspective in many economic issues. It offers a new paradigm of how decentralized decision making is organized, how decentralized matching mechanisms work in economies with limited information agents, how complex and nonlinear dynamics can evolve, and what potentials of destabilizing mechanisms exist. The book proposes a fundamentally new perspective, worked out through sophisticated new technical tools.

Willi Semmler
The New School, New York, United States

Part I

Introduction

Chapter 1

An Introduction to Agent-Based Computational Macroeconomics

Mauro Gallegati, Antonio Palestrini, and Alberto Russo
Marche Polytechnic University, Ancona, Italy

> *Economic research frontier of the XXI century has entered the post-neoclassical era. Although most of the textbooks still refers to the orthodox neoclassical theory, this does not reflect the way of thinking of those economists who work at the frontier of the discipline, including those who consider themselves mainstream. The domain of the neoclassical orthodoxy is over, and the discipline to its more advanced levels is looking for an alternative.*
>
> David Colander

The recent global crisis has challenged the mainstream approach. The economic crisis has indeed produced a crisis in macroeconomics. Not just because it was not able to predict the arrival of the crisis itself (a very doubtful possibility in social and complex disciplines, but that for Friedman [12] is at the root of the "as if" methodology), but rather because such a massive decrease of output cannot even be imagined by the dominant economic theory, obsessed as it is by the straitjacket of equilibrium. Like a physician "specialized in healthy patients," mainstream economics seems to work only when things are going well.

Blanchard [3] published a paper with an at least improvident title "The state of macroeconomics is good," though he provided a correction a few years after maintaining that until the 2008 global financial crisis, mainstream U.S. macroeconomics had taken an increasingly benign view of economic fluctuations in output and employment; the crisis has made it clear that this view was wrong and that there is a need for a deep reassessment [4]. Blanchard asked whether these models should also be able to describe how the economy behaves in crisis, and the answer he gave was both disarming and ingenious: when things go well, we can still use the DSGE; but another class of economic models, designed to measure systemic risk, can be used to give warning signals when we are getting too close to a crisis and evaluate policies to reduce risk. Trying to create a

Introduction to Agent-Based Economics. http://dx.doi.org/10.1016/B978-0-12-803834-5.00002-3

3

model that integrates both normal and crisis times (and thus suitable for all seasons) is beyond the conceptual and technical capacity of the profession, at least at this stage. As economists, we can only aspire to a model that explains how the sun rises and another that explains how the sun sets. Science is different: Earthquakes are always attributable to the movement of tectonic plates, regardless of whether they have a magnitude of 0 on the Richter scale (eight thousand a day) or a magnitude of 9 (one every twenty years).

The crisis of mainstream economics is well documented by academic works (see, for instance, [16], [17] and [18], [21]) and central bankers' contributions ([23], [24]). In our opinion, a fundamental feature of macroeconomic modeling resides in the ability to analyze evolutionary complex systems like the economic one. What characterizes a complex system is the notion of emergence, that is, the spontaneous formation of self-organized structures at different layers of a hierarchical system configuration. Agent-Based Modeling (ABM) is a methodological instrument—that can be usefully employed by both neoclassical or Keynesian economists, or whatever theoretical approach—which is appropriate to study complex dynamics as the result of the interaction of heterogeneous agents (where a degenerate case would be a "representative agent" model in which the degree of both heterogeneity and interaction is set to zero, which is a situation that reduces holism to reductionism in a hypothetical world without networks and coordination problems).

For the past couple of decades, ABM have seriously taken to heart the concept of economy as an evolving complex system [2,22,5]. Two keywords characterize this approach:

1. *Evolving*, which means the system is adaptive through learning. Agents' behavioral rules are not fixed (this does not mean that it is not legitimate to build ABMs with fixed rules, for example, to understand what the dynamics of an economic system would be if agents behaved in a certain way), but change adapting to variations of the economic environment in which they interact. As explained in Chapter 6, the traditional approach, which assumes optimizing agents with rational expectations, has been and is a powerful tool for deriving optimal behavioral rules that are valid when economic agents have perfect knowledge of their objective function, and it is common knowledge that all agents optimize an objective function, which is perfectly known unless there are exogenous stochastic disturbances. If agents are not able to optimize, or the common knowledge property is not satisfied, then the rules derived with the traditional approach lose their optimality and become simple rules. Moreover, they are fixed, that is, nonadaptive. In an ABM individual adaptive behavioral rules evolve according to their past performance: this provides a mechanism for an endogenous change of the

environment. As a consequence, the "rational expectation hypothesis" loses significance. However, agents are still rational in the sense that they do what they can in order not to commit systematic errors. In this setting, there is still room for policy intervention outside the mainstream myth of optimal policies. Because emergent facts are transient phenomena, policy recommendations are less certain, and they should be institution and historically oriented.

2. The expression *complex system* is just as important. It implies that the economic systems have a high level of heterogeneity, indirect and above all direct interactions that can generate *emergent properties* not inferred from the simple analysis of microeconomic relations [14]. This is the key point of the aggregation problem: starting from the microequations describing the (optimal) choices of the economic units, what can we say about the macroequations? Do they have the same functional form of the microequations? If not, what is the macrotheory derived from? What characterizes a complex system is exactly this notion of emergence, that is, the spontaneous formation of self-organized structures at different layers of a hierarchical system configuration. Mainstream economics conceptualizes the economic system as consisting of several identical and isolated components. If we make N copies of the optimizing agent, then we obtain (under the specific conditions of perfect aggregation) aggregate dynamics. This implies that there are no emergent properties, apart from the ones encapsulated in the microrelations. In economics we know that there are emergent properties not evident from the microlevel. Famous old examples are (i) [19] *segregation problem*, in which a small preference for same-colored neighbors may produce complete segregation and not a small segregation as one may think from microanalysis, and (ii) the [6] *game of life*, in which very simple local rules of movement in a two-dimensional grid of square cells produce very complex emergent dynamics.

From this point of view, ABM models take the microfounded approach seriously because they do not assume that microeconomic dynamics always have the same properties of aggregate dynamics [11]. The dynamics of the "evolving agents" are aggregated without requiring special conditions for perfect aggregation and a dynamic always in equilibrium, which in traditional analysis lead to mistakes, perhaps negligible in normal economic situations, but to badly wrong analyses in situations of crisis like the present one.

As mentioned before, another point that differentiates the ABM approach used today is the possibility of considering in the former approach also nonequilibrium dynamics. The equilibrium of a system in an ABM no longer requires that every single element be in equilibrium by itself, but rather that the statistical distributions describing aggregate phenomena be stable, that is, in "[...] a state of macroscopic equilibrium maintained by a large number of transitions in opposite directions" [10]. In other words, one of the objectives of an ABM simulation (but not the only one) is to make the joint distributions of economic agents converge in a suitable space of distributions. Even when fluctuations of agents occur around equilibrium, which we could calculate using the standard approach, the ABM analyses would not necessarily lead to the same conclusions. This is because the characteristics of the fluctuations would depend on higher moments of the joint distribution and often on the properties of the tails, or three kurtosis of the distribution [13].

ABM is a methodology that allows us to construct, based on simple (evolving) rules of behavior and interaction, models with heterogeneous interacting agents, where the resulting aggregate dynamics and empirical regularities, not known a priori and not deducible from individual behavior, are characterized by three main tenets:

- there is a multitude of objects that interact with each other and with the environment;
- the objects are autonomous, that is, there is no central or "top down" control over their behavior; and
- the outcome of their interaction is numerically computed.

We can further characterize the methodology by enumerating a number of features that, although not necessary to define an agent-based model, are often present. These are: Heterogeneity, explicit description of the space of rules, local interaction, bounded rationality, nonequilibrium dynamics, micro-meso-macro empirics. The meso analysis means that you do not have only the micro and the aggregate level, but you can also investigate different levels of aggregation. Differently from Keynesian economic policy, which theorizes aggregate economic policy tools, and mainstream neoclassical economics, which prescribes individual incentives based on [15] but ignores interaction, which is a major but still neglected part of that critique, the ABM approach proposes a bottom-up analysis. Generally what comes out is not a "one-size-fits-all" policy since its effectiveness depends on the general as well as the idiosyncratic economic conditions; moreover, it generally has to be conducted at different levels (from micro to meso to macro). Furthermore, nonlinear dynamics far from the equilibrium is characterized by an evolutionary process of differentiation, selection, and amplification, which provides the system with novelty and is responsible for its growth in order and complexity, whereas the mainstream approach has no such a mechanism to endogenously creating novelty or generating growth in order and complexity.

This micro-meso-macro possibility does not complete the novelty introduced by the ABM models. As stated before, the moments higher than the first and the tails of joint distribution are often decisive in explaining the aggregate dynamics. Agent-based models have shown a high ability to explain statistical properties of empirical distributions and of stylized facts of the economic and financial cycles [8]: from debt/asset evolution to bankruptcies; from the size and variances of business cycles to their comovements; from industrial dynamics properties, such as growth rate and firm size distribution, to income distribution [9], the probability of exit, and still others.

As mentioned before, results of the ABM model are new because they take into consideration a very important element of economic systems: the networks of direct and indirect interactions, which are often extremely complex and not approximated by simple graphs such as random graphs. Real economies are composed by millions of interacting agents, whose distribution is far from being a simple transformation of the "normal" one. As an example, consider the distribution of the trade-credit relations among firms in the electronic-equipment sector in Japan in 2003 [7]. It is quite evident that there exist several hubs, that is, firms with many connections: the distribution of the degree of connectivity (the links) is scale free (power law, Pareto distributed), that is, there are a lot of firms with one or two links, and a few firms with a lot of connections. Let us assume that the Central Authority has to prevent a financial collapse of the system or the spreading of a financial crisis. Average connectivity is much less important compared to the tail analysis of degree distribution.

Such an interaction network may give rise to *autocatalytic systems*. The existence of an autocatalytic process implies that looking at the average behavior of the constituent units is nonrepresentative of the dynamics of the system: autocatalyticity insures that the behavior of the entire system is dominated by the elements with the highest autocatalytic growth rate rather than by the typical or average element [20]. In presence of autocatalytic processes, a small amount of individual heterogeneity invalidates any description of the behavior of the system in terms of its average element: the real world is controlled as much by the tails of distributions than by means or averages. We need to free ourselves from average thinking [1].

Summarizing, the ABM approach can offer new answers to new and old unsolved questions, although it is still in a far too premature stage to offer definitive tools. This book shows that this new tool has already yielded interesting results and also that this approach does not say different things in simple situations where the comparison with the standard models is possible. It enables analysis of complex situations that are difficult to analyze with the models most in use today.

Research is still far from being complete, above all, where empirical verification of aggregate models is concerned, but it is already more effective in explaining reality than what has been done so far and continues to be done by the DSGE models that dominate the economic scene. Although ABM certainly do not constitute a panacea for the crisis, it is indisputable that they provide suggestions of economic policy unknown in traditional models (network, domino effects, resilience and fragility, etc.). Freed from the straightjacket of equilibrium and representative agent hypothesis, which only works with a single good and a single market, we can finally dedicate time to investigate the potentiality of interactive agents and their emergent properties.

The book collects a series of contributions showing the advancements in agent-based macroeconomic modeling and simulation, experimental economics, network analysis, the empirics of agents' distribution, and so on, proposed by the research group located in Ancona and its connections in Italy and worldwide. The book is divided into three parts: After this Introduction, in Part II the focus is on agent-based computational macroeconomics. Part III proposes further perspectives and implications related to ABM.

In particular, Chapter 2 proposes a synthetic introduction to agent-based macroeconomic modeling by tracing the roots of this approach, outlining its main characteristics, and presenting an overview of the literature. Then, the chapter focuses on a recent contribution, the so-called "Modellaccio," by explaining various theoretical and technical aspects related to the particular modeling approach applied in its development and which aim at representing a new paradigm in macromodeling.

In Chapter 3, it is shown how to build the aggregate demand and supply curves from the bottom up in an agent-based macroeconomic model. A computational exercise is presented in which the authors calculate the notional quantity of individual demands and supplies corresponding to a set of different good prices introduced as a shock to the price emerging from the model simulation. In this way, the chapter provides a simple visualization of complex macroeconomic dynamics, similar to that proposed in the mainstream approach. Therefore, the authors discuss the similarities and differences between the mainstream and the agent-based frameworks, trying to understand the role of heterogeneity and interaction in shaping aggregate curves and macroeconomic equilibria.

The aim of Chapter 4 is to provide an introductory overview on the problem of heterogeneity in economics with a special attention to the macroeconomics discipline. Starting from the classical representative agent Real Business cycle model, the survey presents several possible alternatives in order to introduce heterogeneity into a standard macroeconomics model and finally discusses the role of agent-based modeling as a way to deal with heterogeneity and complexity.

Chapter 5 tries to answer to the question whether is it possible to anticipate a crisis, and then it wonders if something more can be done to respond to a crisis. In this chapter, the author illustrates an agent-based simulation model in which crises emerge endogenously, in particular, during expansions, the combination of high levels of leverage and high degree of credit network concentration may create the conditions that may lead to huge output downturns. The chapter suggests that some early warning measures for crises can be derived by using the signal technique, where macro-variables variations are conceived as signals that are valued according to their capacity of anticipating crises avoiding false alarms.

Chapter 6 focuses on the necessity, for economists and economic analysts, to understand agents' behavioral rules. In this respect, optimization with rational expectations is simply a way to derive these behavioral rules, but the perfect rationality assumption could be too strong to produce a reasonable representation of actual behavior. The chapter then tries to explore an alternative based on the ABM approach within the adaptive expectations tradition.

Chapter 7 proposes a review at the crossroad between Behavioral/Experimental Economics and Agent-Based Models. Though different in their approach, the two disciplines share a common feature: the analysis of the individual behavior by discarding the neoclassical assumptions, so that the two kinds of analysis can complement each other. The chapter explains what an experiment is and how does it work, showing that experiments can be used to validate and/or calibrate Agent-Based Models. Three different applications are presented to show how to calibrate/validate an ABM based on experimental data.

Chapter 8 reviews the recent developments of the agent-based literature with respect to empirical estimation by highlighting that the main methods employed in the literature include Bayesian estimation, simulated minimum distance, and simulated maximum likelihood. The chapter focuses parameter calibration as a useful approach for Agent-Based Models (ABMs), which typically presents a large parameter space. Then the chapter shows the possibility of replacing ABMs with a metamodel, that is, a statistical model linking the value of parameters to a set of model outputs, which might be used for a variety of purposes, including estimation. In particular, we focus on sensitivity analysis and on the problem of parameter identification.

Chapter 9 elaborates a new parametric model for the joint distribution of income and consumption. The model combines estimates for the marginal distributions of income and consumption and a parametric copula function to capture the dependence structure between the two variates. Using data from the Bank of Italy's Survey on Household Income and Wealth for the period 1987–2014, we find that the proposed copula-based approach accounts well for the complex dependence between income and consumption observed in our samples.

The chapter also points to further developments that are specific to the field of welfare economics

Finally, Chapter 10 reviews the literature on credit market models by emphasizing the mechanisms able to generate financial crises and contagion. Starting from the theoretical microeconomic literature up to network theory and agent-based methodology, we illustrate how these different approaches investigate the (in)stability of financial systems. Although very different, these methodologies emphasize the importance of a careful analysis of the interaction among heterogeneous agents recognized as the key element to explain real and financial cycles.

REFERENCES

[1] P.W. Anderson, Some thoughts about distribution in economics, in: Santa Fe Institute Studies in the Sciences of Complexity – Proceedings Volume, vol. 27, Addison-Wesley Publishing Co., 1997, pp. 565–566.

[2] W.B. Arthur, Complexity and the economy, Science 284 (5411) (1999) 107–109.

[3] O. Blanchard, The state of macro, Annual Review of Economics 1 (1) (2009) 209–228.

[4] O. Blanchard, Where danger lurks, in: Finance & Development, International Monetary Fund, September 2014, pp. 28–31.

[5] L.E. Blume, S.N. Durlauf, The Economy as an Evolving Complex System, III: Current Perspectives and Future Directions, Oxford University Press, 2005.

[6] J. Conway, The game of life, Scientific American 223 (4) (1970) 4.

[7] G. De Masi, Y. Fujiwara, M. Gallegati, B. Greenwald, J.E. Stiglitz, An analysis of the Japanese credit network, Evolutionary and Institutional Economics Review 7 (2) (2011) 209–232.

[8] D. Delli Gatti, C. Di Guilmi, E. Gaffeo, G. Giulioni, M. Gallegati, A. Palestrini, A new approach to business fluctuations: heterogeneous interacting agents, scaling laws and financial fragility, Journal of Economic Behavior & Organization 56 (4) (2005) 489–512.

[9] G. Dosi, G. Fagiolo, M. Napoletano, A. Roventini, Income distribution, credit and fiscal policies in an agent-based Keynesian model, Journal of Economic Dynamics and Control 37 (8) (2013) 1598–1625.

[10] W. Feller, Probability Theory, vol. I, 1957.

[11] M. Forni, M. Lippi, Aggregation and the Microfoundations of Dynamic Macroeconomics, Oxford University Press, 1997.

[12] M. Friedman, Essays in Positive Economics, Chicago University Press, 1953.

[13] X. Gabaix, The granular origins of aggregate fluctuations, Econometrica 79 (3) (2011) 733–772.

[14] W. Hildenbrand, A.P. Kirman, Equilibrium Analysis: Variations on Themes by Edgeworth and Walras, vol. 28, North-Holland, 1988.

[15] R.E. Lucas, Econometric policy evaluation: a critique, in: Carnegie–Rochester Conference Series on Public Policy, vol. 1, North-Holland, 1976, pp. 19–46.

[16] N.G. Mankiw, The macroeconomist as scientist and engineer, The Journal of Economic Perspectives 20 (4) (2016) 29–46.

[17] P. Romer, The trouble with macroeconomics, 2016.

[18] P. Romer, The trouble with macroeconomics, update, 2016.

[19] T.C. Schelling, Dynamic models of segregation, The Journal of Mathematical Sociology 1 (2) (1971) 143–186.

[20] S. Solomon, Complexity Roadmap, Institute for Scientific Interchange, Torino, 2007.

[21] R. Solow, The state of macroeconomics, The Journal of Economic Perspectives 22 (1) (2008) 243–246.
[22] L. Tesfatsion, Agent-based computational economics: modeling economies as complex adaptive systems, Information Sciences 149 (4) (2003) 262–268.
[23] J.-C. Trichet, Reflections on the nature of monetary policy non-standard measures and finance theory, 2010.
[24] J.L. Yellen, Macroeconomic research after the crisis, 2016.

Part II

Macroeconomic Agent-Based Computational Economics

Chapter 2

Decentralized Interacting Macroeconomics and the Agent-Based "Modellaccio"

Alessandro Caiani and Eugenio Caverzasi
Marche Polytechnic University, Ancona, Italy

2.1 AGENT-BASED MACROECONOMICS: AN INTRODUCTION

2.1.1 Roots and Characteristics of an Innovative Approach

Agent-Based (AB) models are often regarded as a novelty when applied to macroeconomics. However, their roots date several decades ago. Due to the required computing power, the surge of this methodology followed the technological progress in the advent of computers. For example, [46] trace the intellectual lineage of AB models back to contributions in the field of computer science (in particular, [102]) and to their application in the study of social sciences by Thomas Schelling. In [94], he used a *cellular automata* (a grid of cells that evolves as each cell follows a set of rules related on the states of neighboring cells) to study segregation phenomena. The model was fairly simple. Two types of agents are placed randomly on the grid, each agent has a preference on the minimum number of units of their same kind living in their neighborhood, and if this threshold parameter is not reached, then the agents move to another area. The key outcome of the model was that segregation phenomena could arise even with low thresholds. In the words of the author: "What is instructive about the experiment is the "unraveling" process. Everybody who selects a new environment affects the environment of those he leaves and those he moves among. There is a chain reaction" [95, p. 151]. What Schelling was describing is an example of *emergence*: the phenomenon for which macrostructures emerge starting from simple adaptive micro behaviors. As we will see later on in the chapter, the presence of emergent proprieties is one of the characterizing elements of AB models.

Other authors, referring in particular to the application of this approach to macroeconomics, identify other precursors. According to [4] and [87], [81]

Introduction to Agent-Based Economics. http://dx.doi.org/10.1016/B978-0-12-803834-5.00004-7

15

stands as a seminal contribution to AB macromodels. Guy Orcutt initiated a new methodology, *microsimulation*, for socioeconomic studies that bears key features of nowadays macroeconomic models: "This new type of model consists of various sorts of interacting units that receive inputs and generate outputs" [81, p. 117]. This new methodology had been made possible by technological innovation. Indeed, the invention of computers "such as the IBM 704 or the UNIVAC II" (*ibidem* 1957) provided with the computing power required for simulation-based models. With the availability of the necessary technology and the pioneering contribution by Orcutt the path for the development of a *microsimulation* approach was traced and followed by [7] and [44]; however, it did not succeed, at least in its aftermath, in giving rise to a well-established macromodeling framework. [7] presented a simulated model (completed in [6]) with six different firms, one financial intermediary, and a bank. Almost concurrently, [44] presented a microsimulation model of the Swedish economy. The model MOSES (Model of the Swedish Economy), then developed in [45], is a complex of macromodels enclosing, among other features, numerous sectors and industries, innovation dynamics, units' entry–exit, and different kinds of goods produced.

Albeit these first examples, it was only recently that AB models are regarded as a possible new paradigm in macroeconomic modeling (see, e.g., [51,25]), substantially different from existing approaches. In particular, standard mainstream macroeconomic models (i.e., DSGE) rely on a microfoundation based on the *representative agent* (RA). This approach is an extreme version of *methodological reductionism* and makes the microeconomic and the macroeconomic level of analysis coincide: a single agent, a utility maximizing individual, represents an entire sector, which may be, for instance banks, consumers, or firms. Much has been said on the limits of the representative agents, and an extensive review of the critiques goes beyond the scope of this chapter. See [67] and [34] (among many others) for a thorough analysis of this issue.

AB models rely on a different kind of microfoundation, based on the *complexity theory*. According to [98], a complex system is characterized by the presence of two key elements: (i) interacting units and (ii) *emergent properties*. The key outcome is that in a complex system the whole is more than the sum of its parts. Accordingly, AB models conceive the economies as a complex adaptive dynamic system, in which a multitude of heterogeneous adaptive agents, interacting locally (at microlevel), generates macro regularities, which in turn influence the microbehaviors of the units, and so on. This chain of feedbacks determine an evolving network of interactions that makes the micro- and macrolevels interdependent.

This methodology juxtaposes the microfoundation of AB models to the representative agent. "Complexity arises because of the dispersed and non-linear interactions of a large number of heterogeneous autonomous agents. While we can naturally observe and measure macro outcomes [...] aggregates could not be deduced directly from an examination of the behavior of a typical individual in isolation" [31, p. 14].

Next to their distinct type of microfoundation, AB models have other characterizing features. In fact, the definitions of AB models are diverse. Here we refer to Epstein ([48, p. 1588]), who, building on [46] and [47], lists the following key elements:

- *Heterogeneity:* units are explicitly modeled and can differ one from another for their endowment, preferences, local network, and whatever characteristic the modeler considers important. It is important to notice that heterogeneity is both one of the starting assumptions of the model and the results of the dynamics of the system.[1]
- *Autonomy:* there is no central controller, and regularities emerge autonomously from the interaction of the agents.
- *Explicit space:* the space in which units act and interact (both one with another and with the system) is explicitly modeled. This allows us to define the concepts of "local" and "neighborhood" (just as in the example of the segregation model by Schelling).
- *Local interactions:* the actions of the agents are local since they do not interact with the totality of the system, but only with their neighbors, which may be referred to their spatial, economic, or social position.
- *Bounded rationality:* agents base their decisions on heuristics since they are not endowed either with perfect information of the functioning of the system where they live or with unfettered ability to process available information.
- *Nonequilibrium dynamics:* equilibrium is not treated as a natural state of the system. Nonequilibrium dynamics are of central concern; in many cases, model dynamics are not ergodic because of relevance of initial conditions and path dependency. This allows us to focus on the process rather than on the final state and therefore to analyze systems in which equilibria may not even exist.

This approach is very flexible and can be used to study different issues in social sciences. It has indeed found many applications in economics. Most of the literature analyzes single market dynamics; a good example is represented by numerous contributions in the study of the financial markets (see [98, Ch. 17]). Conversely, in this chapter, we focus on the strand of the literature devoted to the study of the economy as a whole. Applying this methodology to the

---

1. There is increasingly awareness on the importance of heterogeneity for macroeconomics (e.g., see [105]), as this allows us to cope with crucial issues such as distribution.

study of macroeconomic issues raises nontrivial difficulties. The flexibility of the framework and the lack of imposed equilibrium dynamics or optimizing behaviors leave with numerous degrees of freedom. This, from the point of view of the modelers, has pros and cons. Whereas they can rely on more realistic assumptions, they are also left with less landmarks. According to [72], AB macromodels, in order to be useful, must meet three criteria. First, they need to rely on a realistic (i.e., empirically grounded) taxonomy of units and categories. The economy can be divided into different sectors as real, financial, or public. Each sector can include different industries buying, producing, and selling different kinds of goods and services. Not to be lost amid this multitude of possibilities, the modeler needs to ground its choice on data and empirical observations. Second, models should be robust to scaling. The number of units populating the system is a modeler's choice; however, a model is always a simplified abstraction of the reality, and as such it requires an assumption on the scale. This choice has important theoretical implications, for instance, the number of participants to a market determines the type of competition in the market. Third, models need to be empirically validated. [49] underlines that validation consists of two different blocks. On the one hand, the robustness of the results must be accounted for. That is to say, it is necessary to perform a sensitivity analysis to test weather the results hold when the values of the parameters change and when different stochastic elements are included (this last step is usually performed through *Monte Carlo* simulations). On the other hand, models need to be validated with respect to empirical data, both in its inputs (i.e., *calibration* of the model) and in its outputs.

2.1.2 Agent-Based Macromodels: An Overview of the Literature

Up to this point, we presented an overview of the precursors and initiators of this approach; we then sketched the main characteristics of Agent-Based macromodel. We now move forward and review some of the main contributions in the literature. This review has no ambition to include a complete nor exhaustive list of contributions. Our goal is to provide with an overview of the state-of-the-art in AB macromodeling with a focus on the contributions offered by our research group and by those groups following a similar path of research. As shown before, albeit the roots and the first examples of AB macro models date back in time, it was only recently that this approach surged as a possible new macroeconomic paradigm. A possible explanation for this relies on the fact that these models are seen as an alternative to the current mainstream. Their fortune appears to be attached to the dissatisfaction with the state of macroeconomics and macroeconomic modeling. If that is the case, then it does not come as a surprise that the AB modeling literature recently has been flourishing, in particular, after the financial crisis, which started in the 2007 in the subprime mortgage market and then hit the world economy. A crisis that came unexpected for the great majority of economic practitioners (see [12]) and toward which existing macro models appeared to be ineffective (e.g., [100]).

AB models proved to be particularly fit in reproducing key destabilizing dynamics taking place in the financial sector. A particularly interesting example is represented in [36]. The paper presents an AB model with three sectors: households, banks, and corporate; the latter is made of downstream firms, producing consumption goods, and upstream supplying intermediate goods to the other firms. The model, based on previous works by the same authors [35,37], is characterized by the presence of an endogenously evolving network of credit and epitomizes some of the advantages of the AB framework linked, for example, to network dynamics and local interactions. The paper applies the AB modeling approach to the theory of the *financial accelerator* [8–10], which up to that moment was developed relying on the representative agent. It offers an original contribution to the literature. The authors show how through a cascade effect even idiosyncratic shocks can progress and lead to major distress at the aggregate level. Furthermore, the effects of the shock can propagate at different speeds impacting certain units more than others.

Two of the main groups working on AB macroeconomics are involved in the aforementioned works: the Ancona group, working with Mauro Gallegati of the Marche Polytechnic University, and the Cattolica group, working at the Catholic University in Milan with professor Domenico Delli Gatti. The fruitful collaboration between these two groups has originated numerous works. For instance, [32,33] have focused on the role of scaling effects and power-law distributions in the business cycle. In particular the latter encloses an agent-based model with two sectors (firms and banks) and two markets (goods and credit). Once simulated, the model succeeds in reproducing numerous empirical evidences in terms of distribution, as the frequency of firms' entering and exiting from the market, or the bankruptcies and consequent bad debts, or the distribution of profit.

Independently, these two groups have produced numerous important works in the field of AB macroeconomic modeling. [85] and [89] build on [36] to deepen the AB analysis on the financial accelerator. The former, including multiperiodal debt and a "dynamic trade-off theory" [52], analyzes the role of leverage on financial stability and on the effectiveness of monetary policies. The latter investigates the role of the stock market in the propagation of financial distress. Firms experiencing a negative shocks on their output face a decreasing capitalization on the stock market and a higher interest rate on loans.

A particularly important contribution put forward by the Ancona group is the model presented in [85,87], the *Modellone*. The paper represents an important evolution toward the development of the framework presented in the second part of the chapter and toward the realization of a benchmark model. The *Modellone* includes three kinds of agents (individuals, firms, and banks) and four markets (goods, labor, credit, and deposit). Its characterizing feature is a common decentralized matching process for all markets, working as follows. In each period in each of the four markets, units on demand side are divided into random ordered lists. The first unit of the list observes a random subset of the whole supply side of the market and chooses the cheapest counterpart. Then there comes the turn of the second agent on the demand side, which observes a new random list on the supply side. The process continues until either all demand is satisfied or no more matching is feasible, that is to say, the lowest price on the supply side exceeds the highest price that the remaining units on the demand side are willing to pay. This decentralized matching mechanism can be applied to any market. The model, albeit including important aspects of sophistication, such as bankruptcy of both firms and banks and firms' financial structure based on the "dynamic trade-off theory," is fairly simple in its structure ("minimal" in the words of the authors) since it was conceived to represent a flexible starting point to be enlarged and enriched in following researches. Indeed, it was later developed in numerous contributions. [91] analyzes the impacts on the economy of increasing inequality and in particular of the consequent rise in credit to consumption. The authors show how this financial practice presents a tradeoff for the economy. On the one hand, it sustains demand and GDP, whereas, on the other hand, it makes the economy more prone to crisis. [88] addresses financialization, here represented as a rise in firms' dividend. The simulation results show how this phenomenon has major effects on macroeconomic dynamics, as it worsens financial stability and income distribution. The impacts on growth are mixed: whereas consumption is boosted due to wealth effects, the low level of retained earnings can worsen banks' balance sheet and ultimately lead to credit rationing. Banks are also at the core of [1], which focuses on the destabilizing role of banks in Minsky's Financial Instability Hypothesis, and [63], where a network analysis is applied to the credit market showing how interbank linkages may become a channel for the propagation a crisis. Another interesting contribution to the AB macroliterature, developed by the Ancona group, is represented by [20], one of the very first multicountry AB macromodels. The model reproduces the functioning of a currency union with a perfectly integrated goods markets and national labor and capital markets and test for different fiscal policies. The simulations show that the leverage is procyclical and that restrictive fiscal regimes may increase inequality between countries and determine a rise in systemic vulnerability. Finally, [18] is a recent contribution aiming to study the relationship between income and wealth inequality and economic development, building on the "benchmark" Agent-Based Stock-Flow Consistent Model presented in [17]. This model, which came to be familiarly called the AB "modellaccio" to honor a famous econometric model of the Italian economy developed in Ancona by Giorgio Fuà, and its later versions will be extensively discussed in the remaining of the chapter.

As regards the Cattolica group, [2] introduces a methodology to build a bridge between the aggregate and the microlevel of the analysis. Whereas [3], building on [31], presents a model, dubbed by the authors CC-MABM (Macro-Agent-Based Model with Capital and Credit), with four sectors: (i) households, (ii) firms producing consumption goods, (iii) firms producing capital goods, and (iv) banks. The results of the simulations show how the interconnections between investment and the credit market are at the core of the rise of idiosyncratic shocks into a full-blown crisis. The model, due to the uniform productivity of labor and capital and the lack of R&D, is described by the authors as being simpler than other works in the literature on the same topic; that is to say, AB growth macromodels with investment goods and capital market. They refer in particular to two other families of AB macromodels. One originates from the European project EURACE, and one is centered around the model *Schumpeter Meeting Keynes* presented in [42]. The former has been developed separately by two groups: (i) the *Genova group*, working with Silvano Cincotti and Marco Raberto at the University of Genova and with Andrea Teglio at University Jaume I in Castellón; (ii) the *Bielefeld group* working with Herbert Dawid (EURACE@ Unibi). The latter is the cornerstone of the AB macromodels developed by the group working at the Sant'Anna School of Advanced Studies (Pisa) with professor Giovanni Dosi.

The Pisa group roots most of its models on the literature on evolutionary models. [79,42] present a model, Schumpeter meeting Keynes (SK), with consumers/workers, public sector, and two kinds of firms: those producing heterogeneous capital goods and those producing consumption goods. The model introduces endogenous innovation: through R&D, firms create new more and efficient technologies, which are then adopted by competitors, hence leading to the diffusion of the innovation. The results of simulation show how both technological innovation and demand affect economic growth both in short and long runs. The SK model has been further enlarged in the following publications. [40] adds the credit market. Minsky "joins the meeting" between Schumpeter and Keynes as the interactions between credit dynamics and economic fluctuations enter the picture. The model is then used to test different fiscal and monetary policies under different conditions of income distribution. [41] enriches the KS model with the heterogeneous banks and tests different combinations of monetary and fiscal policy, showing the negative outcome of *austerity* policies.

The EURACE model [30,24,84] and EURACE@Unibi [28,101] stand out from the rest of the literature for their size. They are indeed very large-scale models conceived as a policy tool at European level and aiming at reproducing the functioning of the European economy. The models are very complex and sophisticated in both their real and financial sides, including numerous assets and kinds of agents. At the best of our knowledge, EURACE was the first stock-flow consistent model (more on this in the remaining of this chapter).

A further contribution to the literature is represented by [69]. The model (Mark I CRISIS) builds on [31] and reproduces an economy consisting of three sectors: firms, banks, and households, which can be either workers or firm owners. Banks are subject to capital requirement and can go bankrupt. The model is used to test three different crisis resolution mechanisms, that is, policy interventions in case of banks bankruptcy. "Purchase & assumption" [...] (P&A) is a resolution mechanism that allows for transferring the troubled bank's operations to other, healthy banks. [...] Bail-out: A bail-out usually describes providing funds to a financially distressed institution or country that is deemed healthy enough to survive after recapitalization. [...] Bail-in: As opposed to a bail-out, a bail-in forces the creditors of the troubled financial institutions to bear some of the financial burden [69, p. 146–147]. The results of the simulation show that performances of the three mechanisms depend on the state of the economies.

Finally [73], like [87], proposes a benchmark AB macromodel. The economy is highly stylized and consists exclusively of two kinds of agents, namely firms and households. This contribution has a particularity in the time treated. Each single period of the simulation represents a day, which will then sum in weeks and months. Different actions take place in different time intervals. The model, albeit being simple, is able to reproduce numerous realistic dynamics and to show the possibility of butterfly effects, small shocks at the microlevel having impacts at the aggregate level.

2.2 THE "MODELLACCIO"

2.2.1 An Agent-Based Stock-Flow Consistent Paradigm?

In the late 2013s, a collaboration started between the research group of Prof. Mauro Gallegati at the University of Ancona and the nascent research group of Prof. Stephen Kinsella at the Kemmy Business School of the University of Limerick. The objective of this joint research effort was to realize a merge between the bottom-up perspective characterizing the Agent-Based approach to macroeconomic modeling [31] and the accounting-based modeling logic of the Post-Keynesian Stock Flow Consistent (SFC, hereafter) framework [59]. This AB-SFC research program was funded by the Institute for New Economic Thinking (INET), being part of Prof. Joseph Stiglitz's task force on macroeconomic efficiency and instability. The task force aimed at developing alternative tools for macroeconomic analysis after the financial turmoil of 2007 and the ensuing Great Recession had risen serious doubts on the plausibility and efficacy of standard ones, in particular the class of DSGE models.

Among the fathers of the SFC framework, two economists in particular gave a fundamental contribution: James Tobin, who in his later works in the 1960s tried to connect the Keynesian theory with the flow-of-funds accounts [15], and Wynne Godley, who picked up Tobin's legacy and his flow-of-funds approach [58] giving a fundamental push in formalizing the methodology [56,59]. At the base of their work, we find the idea that real and financial flows and the stocks on which they impact are closely interrelated with each other and in a social accounting perspective must always satisfy given accounting identities. Indeed, every financial flow will be recorded at the same time as an inflow for some sector (or agent) of the economy and an outflow for some other sector, so that from the system viewpoint they must always sum to zero. In turn, these flows affect the end-of-period values of stocks held by agents, so that these latter can be also seen as the sum across time of inflows and outflows, whereas they also concur to generate new flows (e.g., a flow of interest payments on a given stock of loans). Since the nature of every financial stock is that of being an asset for someone and a correspondent liability for someone else, their sum has to be zero at the whole economy level.

Accounting-based models thus employ specific social accounting matrices to track the flows arising from sectors' and agents' transactions and the variations of stocks they generate, ensuring that all these accounting entries are mutually consistent through the adoption of a quadruple-entry, rather than double-entry, book-keeping logic: "because moneyflows transactions involve two transactors, the social accounting approach to moneyflows rests not on a double-entry system but on a quadruple-entry system. Knowing that each of the columns and each of the rows must sum to zero at all times, it follows that any alteration in one cell of the matrix must imply a modification to at least three other cells. The transactions matrix used here provides us with an exhibit which allows to report each financial flow both as an inflow to a given sector and as an outflow to the other sector involved in the transaction." ([26] quoted in [59]). In this way, SFC models aim at providing a comprehensive and fully integrated representation of the economy, linking real and financial transactions and ensuring that there are no black holes in the representation of (real and nominal) stocks and flows, acting as a "conservation of energy principle for economic theory," using Godley's [58] words. To help the reader to understand the quadruple-entry principle employed in the social accounting matrices of SFC models, Table 2.2 shows the Transaction Flow Matrix of the economy depicted in [17] in its initial simulation period. The upper section of the matrix displays flows taking place during a period of the simulation, whereas the bottom section shows how these flows determine the variation of financial assets, thus providing a full integration between the Balance Sheet matrix and the Transaction Flow Matrix of the economy displayed in Table 2.1 and Table 2.2 respectively. Stock-Flow Consistency implies [59] that the rows and columns of the Transaction Flow Matrix sum to 0, whereas a similar condition holds for the BS matrix where sectors' net worth acts as vertical balancing item, with the only exception of real assets (here represented by capital and inventories), which are not a liability for anyone, their value being thus equal to the total net worth of the economy.

Accounting-based methods can be of great help in spotting possible buildups of financial fragility and the possible emergence of real and financial imbalances between sectors (or countries, or agents'), which can jeopardize the resilience and stability of the system. Using flow-of-funds accounts to analyze the US economy at the turn of the century, Godley [57], Godley and Wray [60], and Godley and Zezza [61] recognized that households' indebtedness was pushing assets' inflation and leavening systemic risk under the surface of the alleged stability of the early 2000s.[2]

Though accounting-based models, such as Stock-Flow Consistent models,[3] have found fertile soil in the Post-Keynesian tradition (see [38] and [22] for a literature review), in recent years they gained more and more interest also outside this community. In 2011, the Bank of England used a similar approach to analyze the mechanics of financial instability. [5] advocates the diffusion of macroeconomic approaches that stress the importance of balance sheet linkages. On a similar ground (though in a general equilibrium framework), [43] revisits Tobin's efforts to understand financial-real linkages, and proposes a modeling framework for analyzing households' flows-off-fund jointly with consumption. Finally, the Bank of England has recently presented a Stock-Flow Consistent Model to perform scenario analysis on the UK economy [16].

---

2. In particular, [57, p. 2] identified seven unsustainable processes associated to the economic growth pattern experienced by the US during the nineties: "(1) the fall in private saving into ever deeper negative territory, (2) the rise in the flow of net lending to the private sector, (3) the rise in the growth rate of the real money stock, (4) the rise in asset prices at a rate that far exceeds the growth of profits (or of GDP), (5) the rise in the budget surplus, (6) the rise in the current account deficit, (7) the increase in the United States's net foreign indebtedness relative to GDP."

3. However, it must be stressed that the SFC approach cannot be limited to a set of accounting rules. Whereas accounting rules are fundamental, they are not sufficient to ensure an exhaustive representation of complex financial systems and their interaction with the real side of the economy. In his Nobel lecture, Tobin [99] identified five defining features underlying the innovative character of his work with respect to existing macromodels: precision regarding time, a complete tracking of stocks accumulation, the incorporation of several types of assets with different rates of returns, the modeling of financial and monetary policy operation, and finally the compliance with **** Walras' law, as a result of the macroeconomic adding-up accounting constraints discussed above. These properties are common to most SFC models as well. To these points, we add a further defining feature of most, if not all, SFC models: a realistic representation of the process by which private and legal money are created, injected into the monetary circuit of the economy, and destroyed.

TABLE 2.1 Aggregate Balance Sheet (Initial Situation)

	Households	Cons. firms	Cap. firms	Banks	Government	Central Bank	Total
Deposits	+80,704.1	+25,000	+5000	−110,704	0	0	0
Loans	0	−52,194.4	−1298	+53,492.5	0	0	0
Cons. goods	0	+2997.4	0	0	0	0	+2997.4
Cap. goods	0	+53,863.6	+500	0	0	0	+54,363.6
Bonds	0	0	0	+38,273.5	−66,838.1	+28,564.6	0
Reserves	0	0	0	+28,564.6	0	−28,564.6	0
Advances	0	0	0	0	0	0	0
Net worth	+80,704.1	+29,666.6	+4202	+9626.4	−66,838.1	0	+57,361

TABLE 2.2 Aggregate Transaction Flow Matrix (Initial Situation)

	House-holds	Cons. firms CA	Cons. firms KA	Cap. firms CA	Cap. firms KA	Banks CA	Banks KA	Govt.	Central Bank CA	Central Bank KA	Σ
Consumption	−32,971.4	+32,971.4	0	0	0	0	0	0	0	0	0
Wages	+36,800	−25,000	0	−5000	0	0	0	−6800	0	0	0
Dole	+1280	0	0	0	0	0	0	−1280	0	0	0
CG on inventories	0	+22.3	−22.3	+3.7	−3.7	0	0	0	0	0	0
Investments	0	0	−5375	+5375	0	0	0	0	0	0	0
Capital amortization	0	−4974	+4974	0	0	0	0	0	0	0	0
Taxes	−7084.7	−484.8	0	−68.7	0	−39.3	0	+7677.4	0	0	0
Dep. interest	+200.3	+62	0	+12.4	0	−274.7	0	0	0	0	0
Bonds interest	0	0	0	0	0	+95	0	−165.9	+70.9	0	0
Loans interest	0	−388.5	0	−9.7	0	+398.2	0	0	0	0	0
Advances interest	0	0	0	0	0	0	0	0	0	0	0
Profits	+2367.6	−2208.4	+220.8	−312.8	+31.3	−179.1	+71.7	0	0	0	0
CB profits	0	0	0	0	0	0	0	+70.9	−70.9	0	0
Δ Deposits	−600.8	0	−186.1	0	−37.2	0	+824.1	0	0	0	0
Δ Advances	0	0	0	0	0	0	0	0	0	0	0
Δ Reserves	0	0	0	0	0	0	−212.6	0	0	+212.6	0
Δ Gov. bonds	0	0	0	0	0	0	−284.9	+497.6	0	−212.6	0
Δ Loans	0	0	+388.5	0	+9.7	0	−398.2	0	0	0	0
Δ Total	0	0	0	0	0	0	0	0	0	0	0

AB models may thus greatly benefit from an integration with the SFC accounting framework. Indeed, whereas the disperse interactions among heterogeneous agents are capable of generating complex, unexpected emergent properties, as stressed by the AB literature discussed above, complex behaviors and sudden transitions also arise from the economy's financial structure as reflected in its balance sheets, as pointed out by [11]. Furthermore, by looking at the evolution of aggregate intersectoral flows and stock-flow norms, we can then get a first clue of the emergence of imbalances in stocks accumulation between sectors, eventually leading to crisis if not properly tackled. Finally, the adoption of an AB-SFC framework based on rigorous micro- and macroeconomic accounting rules provides a powerful tool to check the internal theoretical consistency of the model, as we extensively argue in [17]. The integration of an SFC accounting framework can thus also represent an expedient to discipline AB practitioners, thus partially responding to the common criticism regarding the arbitrariness of agents' behavioral specification. A fusion of the two approaches can thus help AB macroeconomic modeling to set itself as an alternative paradigm to DSGE New Keynesian and RBC models, as originally advocated by [51,34].

Conversely, AB models can help to overcome several drawbacks affecting the SFC approach [65]. For example, SFC models are traditionally highly aggregated, dividing the economy into major institutional sectors, typically households, banks, firms, and the public sector. This perspective usually abstracts from tracking intrasectoral flows and does not allow us to analyze the causes and effects of agents' heterogeneity emerging within and across sectors. This limits and, in some cases, impedes the possibility of studying phenomena that are deeply connected to agents' heterogeneity and agents' disperse interactions, such as self-organization processes within markets or industries, the generation of financial bubbles, and diffusion/contagion processes, such as the diffusion of financial disease through balance sheets contagion or the diffusion of innovations through industry spillovers and imitation.

By combining the AB and SFC methodology our project thus aimed at adding a new complexity layer besides that referring to the role of agents' interactions in shaping individual and aggregate behaviors: in a monetary economy, agents are closely interrelated through a complex network linking their balance sheets, where decisions undertaken by each agent and resulting in a variation of his balance sheet also affect the balance sheets of other agents both directly and indirectly.

Admittedly, this objective of combining the AB and SFC methodologies was shared with some other projects. In particular, our work showed several points of convergence with the philosophy of the EURACE model (see [30,24, 84,27,28,101]), already discussed above. As previously mentioned, EURACE is a massively large-scale economic model, first developed in 2006 and implementing in its various versions many hyperrealistic features, such as day-by-day interactions, asynchronous decisions, geographical space, and a huge variety of agents, including international statistical offices concurring to affect the "sentiment" of entrepreneurs and bankers. Our objective was somehow complementary in that we aimed to develop a relatively simpler and flexible benchmark AB-SFC model, rather than moving toward a large-scale one-to-one matching of real economic systems. Other examples of AB-SFC models are [66,87,96], though in these contributions the merge between the AB and SFC approaches is realized at the expense of several simplifying assumptions (e.g., uniperiodal loans, lack of investment in capital accumulation, stylized financial sector) that limit the advantages of having an SFC framework. During the last years, the awareness of the importance of a rigorous handling of financial flows and stocks in macromodeling has been growing within the AB community, and efforts have been made to embed an SFC accounting in popular preexistent AB macromodels.

Yet, fully fledged AB-SFC models are still a minority not only in the macroeconomic literature in general, but also within the AB subbranch, their diffusion being hampered by the lack of a common set of concepts, rules, and tools to develop, analyze, and validate these models. Besides these methodological issues, also technical reasons concur to narrow the diffusion of this type of models. In particular, AB-SFC modeling still suffers the lack of adequate computational techniques to handle the heterogeneity of stocks held in agents balance sheets and to track their variations across time. Filling these deficiencies was one of the main objectives of the AB-SFC research program at INET.

More precisely, the project had a twofold aim. First, developing a "benchmark" AB-SFC model, that is, a model characterized by a relatively flexible and general structure susceptible of being refined or augmented along different aspects, according to one's needs. For the model to represent an actual "benchmark," we were also aiming to provide a set of general and replicable rules to (a) calibrate the model in an SFC manner, (b) analyze its results, and (c) validate it by checking its actual consistency and assessing the model ability to give account of major empirical regularities. All these aspects related to the benchmark model, the so-called AB "modellaccio," have been discussed in details in [17].

Secondly, the project also aspired to provide a technical support for scholars interested in this field of study. Whereas the model can be replicated in different programming languages, its original implementation was realized using a brand new programming tool suite that we explicitly designed for AB-SFC models: the Java Macro-Agent-Based (JMAB) simulator. The platform exploits the logic of the object-oriented programming paradigm to provide a flexible and highly modular computational framework embedding general procedures to ensure and check the model stock-flow consistency at the macro-, meso-, and microlevels. It has the potential to implement a wide variety of models and a number of crucial features of modern economic systems. The platform has been released under Beta-version and is freely available online with introductive documentation explaining its structure and its main classes.[4] In the next section, we will briefly present the programming logic, main features, and advantages brought by JMAB.

2.2.2 The JMAB Tool-Suite

Many, if not most, AB macroeconomic models are developed according to the logic of "procedural" or "functional" programming. According to this approach, the model is represented by a loop iterating on a sequence of mathematical expressions, which define how each variable is computed as a function of some exogenous parameters and some other variables of the model. Ideally, each variable is represented by a vector. These vectors represent specific attributes or endowments of agents (e.g., net worth, deposits, loans obtained or granted, prices offered, wages demanded, etc.). Therefore, they have the same dimension of the population of agents to which they pertain. In this approach, agents have no autonomous representation in the program. That is, they are not treated as separated objects, being instead identified implicitly by their position in the vectors. The ith element of these vectors will always represent a property of the ith agent. Similarly, it is also possible to represent simple network relationships, for example, credit relationships between firms and banks, by employing vectors where the ith element contains the numerical index (or a vector of indexes, in case agents have multiple links with others) identifying the agents to which the ith agent is linked. Alternatively, we can use matrices instead of vectors where the element occupying the $\{i, j\}$th position indicates the presence (indicated by either 0 or 1) or the strength of the link between the ith agent of the population represented in the rows (e.g., households) and the jth agent of the population represented in the columns (e.g., banks where households hold their deposits).

At its bottom line, the model thus reduces to a set of matrix equations, which are numerically solved in a sequential way. Just as a matter of example, the computation of interests accruing from deposits held by households at banks can be expressed as follows: $int = rd * Dep$, where int is defined as a vector of dimension N^H (the number of households), representing interests earned by households, rd is a vector of dimension N^B (the number of banks), representing the interest rates offered by banks on deposits (one for each bank), and Dep is

---

4. The platform, the installation guide, and related documentation can be found at: https://github.com/S120/jmab.

a matrix of dimension $N^B \times N^H$, representing the amounts of deposit held by each household in each bank.[5]

Admittedly, this programming and modeling approach provides several advantages: first, this way of representing agents is very memory efficient from an engineering point of view as each agent uses only a few bites of memory. This allows for fast execution, thus making possible the simulation of very large number of agents. Furthermore, since behaviors of agents are directly represented through matrix equations, the interpretation of the code is very intuitive. Finally, this programming method allows for a simple and fast display and analysis of results, not to say that software employing this programming paradigm usually come with powerful statistical and graphical packages.[6]

However, this modeling technique also severely constrains the construction of models in some important respects, in particular, related to the timing and frequency of economic processes and decisions by agents and to the heterogeneity of real and financial stocks. More precisely, the "matrix-based" programming approach briefly discussed above complicates and, in some cases, prevents the possibility of having agents holding multiple heterogeneous assets (liability) with multiple liability (asset) counterparts, having different durations, ages, and time to maturity. Similarly, the fact that agents' attributes (i.e., variables) are updated at once when the correspondent mathematical expression is executed sensitively limits the possibility of modeling agents' taking decisions in an asynchronous way and different durations, or frequencies, of economic processes (e.g., monthly versus day-by-day investing). Given these technical difficulties, in most models, loans are assumed to be completely repaid at the end of the period (see, e.g., [34,85,87,39]), or when the uniperiodal duration assumption is softened, other simplifying assumptions are employed in its place; for example, that the financial sector is composed of a single giant bank, or that the credit network of firms-banks is predetermined once and for all in the simulation setup phase [87,34,39,3].

For the same reason, in most applications, the physical capital is assumed to have a constant and equal duration, when not also the same productivity, production usually takes place within a single period regardless the type of good produced and consumption, and investment (real or financial) decisions are characterized by the same time frequency.

Whereas one may be prone to argue that these latter assumptions on real stocks homogeneity and real economic processes synchronicity represent a reasonable price to pay for tractability, not compromising the generality of results,

---

5. For further clarifications about this modeling approach, we refer to the textbook [19], which provides several examples and applications designed for newcomers in AB modeling.
6. This is the case, for example, of MathLab, R, or Mathematica.

the case of financial stocks, and in particular of loans, is different. Indeed, a loan (a similar reasoning may also apply to many other financial stocks) represents a long-term commitment both for those who hold it as a liability, the borrower committing to pay interests and repay the principal, and for those who hold it as an asset, bearing the risk of default by the borrower. This implies that loan projects that appear to be safe and remunerative today, at current economic conditions, may turn risky and possibly result in a bad debt after a while, as the experience of the Great Financial Crisis of 2007 dramatically demonstrated. Having loans granted and repaid within the same period thus prevents to grasp this very crucial aspect of the credit–debt relationship. Furthermore, this also implies that the very concept of leverage, which played a crucial role in many AB models of financial disease, looses much of its meaning: at the end of each period, either the leverage of firms is 0 (as loans have been completely repaid), or firms have defaulted. Finally, this also means that at the end of each period, all private money issued by banks through credit has disappeared since this credit has been already repaid [62] and only legal money remains in the system.

All these assumptions, rather than being motivated by theoretical or empirical reasons, are hence due to the technical difficulties in handling the multiplicity and heterogeneity of agents' stocks and to the rigidity in defining the sequence of events in the model: in fact, embedding these aspects using procedural programming would require an exponential increase of the number of vectors and matrices employed in coding, thus complicating the development of models while narrowing the advantage in terms of computational efficiency.

2.2.3 Object-Oriented Programming and Dependency Injection

To overcome the above limitations, our Java Macroeconomic Agent-Based (JMAB) tool suite adopts a different programming paradigm. In an attempt to provide the most general and flexible framework, JMAB was written in Java, that is, an Object-Oriented Programing (OOP) language.[7] OOP indeed provides a natural way of programming agents (see [76] and [55]). Agents populating an AB model can be conceived and constructed using "objects," that is, program structures holding "data" (representing agents' information and attributes) and "methods" (representing agents' heuristics) to update this data, take decisions, and perform actions. These agents/objects are created from templates called "classes," which specify the composition of the agent, the attributes and data it can hold, and the methods it uses (for example, pricing/production strategies, investment behaviors, portfolio functions, etc.). All the objects instantiated from

---

7. JMAB has been developed on the top of another simulation tool suite: JABM, a high-performance auction simulator [82,83] to develop AB models of financial markets.

the same class inherit its methods and data and thus represent similar classes of agents.

Classes can be arranged in a hierarchy, with subordinate classes inheriting the methods and data from superior classes, but adding additional ones, or replacing some of them with more specialized substitutes. In this way, we can create a number of specific classes of agents starting from generic templates. For example, there is a generic class firm in JMAB called *AbstractFirm*, which contains methods and attributes that can be reasonably considered to be common to most firms, regardless their type, such as a list of employees, the amount of inventories held and the price to offer, and (the signature of) methods to hire and fire employees, set prices, determine output levels, and so on. This *AbstractFirm* class can then be extended into specialized firms such as capital-good producers and consumption-good producers. Each of these extensions (subclasses) inherits the fields and methods of the parent class, but also has its own specific methods and attributes (or modify those inherited), for example, methods to perform R&D or methods to choose between alternative sources of financing.

Therefore, OOP provides a practical way to manage heterogeneity among agents within an economic model. Furthermore, OOP leads naturally to a useful "encapsulation" as every agent instantiated from a class is a separated, autonomous, and clearly distinguishable object, having its own memory and features. This helps to store and preserve all the information regarding the evolution of both micro- and macrovariables.

Finally, besides being a natural way to implement multiagent simulations, OOP is also a convenient technology for building libraries of reusable software since modelers can start to build models by directly instantiating useful classes from preexisting libraries or specialize them, adding new variables and methods via inheritance.

The modularity allowed by OOP is enhanced by the particular architecture of JMAB, which has been conceived as a system of relatively independent functional blocks, communicating and interacting with each other through "Abstract Classes" and "Interfaces." Each functional block takes the inputs to operate from other blocks, elaborates them, and sends its output to some other functional blocks that can use it as an input.

The functioning of each block does not need to know how other blocks work. The only thing that matters is that these functional blocks agree to a "contract" that spells out how they interact with each other. In OOP these contracts are called "Interfaces." This allows us (a) to change the features of each functional block without having to intervene on the others and without compromising the functioning of the system as a whole and (b) to develop each block without the need to know how the other blocks operate.

Different AB are usually characterized by a high degree of heterogeneity in modeling agents' behaviors, such as their pricing, investment, financing purchasing, and credit rationing. To allow modelers to implement a high variety of different behaviors without having to change, we kept the definition of these strategies separated from the definition of the classes of agents that employ them. That is, agents and their strategies are two independent blocks communicating thorough interfaces, each representing an abstract type of strategy, which can then be implemented in different ways by the concrete classes representing specific behaviors. For example, we can create an interface "InvestmentStrategy" to determine firms' investment, which defines the general method "computeDesiredCapacityGrowth." This interface and the method it defines can be then implemented by different concrete classes, representing different possible investing behaviors, for example, a strategy that computes firms' desired capacity growth as a function of expected sales, or a function of firms' profit rate, or a weighted average of the two, or whatever.[8] In this way, the classes representing firms only need know that firms have an "InvestmentStrategy" but need not know how this strategy is implemented in practice. This means that if we want to analyze a new behavior by an agent, we only have to develop a concrete class representing the new strategy, without being forced to intervene in the class representing the agent that uses that strategy. The only thing we need do is to inject the new strategy into the agent initialization through a configuration file. This can be done by employing a special programming protocol, which represents a further advantage of JMAB and which is called "Dependency Injection" [54]. Dependency Injection allows models developed in JMAB to be easily analyzed under a wide variety of assumptions concerning agent behaviors and the model specification.

Roughly speaking, the logic of Dependency Injection implies that the construction of the general attributes of classes and instances of agents is maintained separated from their configuration, so that we can easily switch agent strategies or modify the initial conditions of the simulations (endowments, behavioral parameters, etc.) without having to modify anything in the code of the model. That is, the definition of agents and their possible behaviors is made in the code (through classes, abstract classes, and interfaces) representing the model, but the initial configuration of their attributes and strategies is defined in a separated **.xml** configuration file, which is then read by the software and injected into the objects composing the model. In this way, we can write the code representing agents without having to make any assumption regarding how the properties

---

8. The same can be done for other general types of strategy: a "FinanceStrategy" defining the method "computeCreditDemand," "WageStrategy" defining the methods "setAskedWage," "TaxPayerStrategy," "SupplyCreditStrategy," "SelectWorkersStrategy," "SelectSellerStrategy," etc.

representing agent attributes are initialized, and we can reexecute the model under different configurations without having to change the code. In particular, Dependency Injection allows to:

- Reconfigure simulations by changing the behavioral equations of agents (expectations formation or learning mechanisms, routines, etc.) without having to rewrite the code representing the underlying model of the agents themselves.
- Express the configuration of the model, including its statistical properties, declaratively: reexecute the simulations many times under different setups of initial conditions and parameters without making any modifications to the code representing the model itself. This feature is particularly relevant since AB models are usually executed as Monte Carlo simulations to check the robustness of results and perform sensitivity or scenario analysis.

All in all, the adoption of the object-oriented programming paradigm, of a modular structure based on interfaces and abstract classes, and the employment of dependency injection sensitively enhances the flexibility and generality of JMAB, making it suitable to develop a wide variety of different models.

2.2.4 Event-Based Approach

As explained above, most AB models are conceived and implemented as a set of matrix difference equations, to be executed in sequence. The sequence of actions taking place within each period of the simulation is thus defined by the order in which these expressions appear in the script. In most cases, this sequence reflects the modeler's particular vision of how the economy works, that is, his theoretical approach. Different modelers thus usually have different sequences of events in mind when writing the code of their models.

A crucial feature for a platform aspiring to provide a general, flexible, and nontheoretically biased tool should then be the neutrality regarding the definition of the sequence of events. That is, the modeler should be allowed to easily change the order and the frequency of actions performed by agents, which may be agent interactions, expectation formations, or any other decisions. For this reason, in JMAB, we adopted a different approach to manage the sequence of actions during each period of the simulation, based on the use of particular objects called "events." We divide each period of the simulation into a series of subperiods called "ticks," each of them being represented by an "event" object.

These objects can be conceived as "messages" sent to a particular set of agents, the event "subscribers" who "listen" the events, telling them that the simulation has reached a certain point. Every event is characterized by a particular index identifying the event and its position in the intraperiod ordering of events, decided ex ante by the modeler. Agents listening to these events will react to these messages through their methods, taking decisions, and performing actions based on the information they possess and/or the information passed to them by the message contained in the event sent to them. For example, a hypothetical event "investment decision" identified by index 13, which is the 13th tick of a simulation round, will trigger the computation of the demand for real capital for firms investing in physical capital, whereas it will not trigger any reaction by households. Similarly, a hypothetical tick "households consumption," identified by index 17 will tell to households buying consumption goods to choose a seller and buy the required amount of goods, this amount having been possibly defined earlier as a response to another event, for example, a "consumption demand" tick event. Each event can also contain further information, for example, the subset of seller with whom the buyer is allowed to interact during the current round of the simulation.

In this way the sequence of events is not imposed by the platform, but it is maintained up to the modeler. In addition, this approach brings about several advantages, vis à vis the traditional equation-based ordering. First, the definition of the order of events is kept separated from the definition of the agents' methods, that is, from the equations defining agents' behavior. Therefore, we can easily change the ordering of events without having to touch the blocks of the program defining agents' behaviors.

The separation between the definition of the events sequence and of agents' behavior also simplifies the modeling of economic processes with different frequencies: an event, such as one asking agents to take a portfolio decision, can be called several times during a single round, without having to rewrite every time the block of code defining agents' portfolio function. Furthermore, it allows us to implement different latency response to events. Indeed, an agent may receive only one message out of four while others receive all messages. This might be particularly handy, for example, in modeling High Frequency Traders vs. traditional investors.

A further possible advantage brought about by the use of OOP combined with an event-based approach is the possibility of dealing with asynchronous decisions by agents, though this aspect has not been explored yet at the current stage of development. As already mentioned, in models developed as blocks of matrix equations, agents act together. For example, in each period, every firm will decide together how much to invest in capital accumulation. Given the matrix form of the model, it is extremely complicated to consider the possibility that firms decide to invest in two different ticks of a certain period. This drawback does not apply in principle to our event-based approach: once the event is sent, it is up to the single agents' to decide how to react to it through their specific methods. An important further advantage of our event-based approach is that the very firing of a particular event can be easily endogenized, that is, linked to the occurrence of specific economic conditions, rather than being scheduled once and for all through a rigid ex ante definition of the sequence of ticks. However, this possibility also has not been developed yet.

2.2.5   Stock Matrix Approach to Agents' Balance Sheets

The very core of our new platform lies in the representation of stocks held by agents, which is crucial to ensure the Stock-Flow Consistency of the models developed with JMAB.

In JMAB, all stocks that agents can hold are instantiated from classes that are derived from the abstract class "Item." This class is then specialized by the concrete classes representing specific types of stocks, such as capital goods, deposits, loans, etc., providing the templates with the fundamental features of each type of stock. Every object referring to a real stock contains generic and specific information regarding, for example, its owner, its producer, its price, its age, the scheme of amortization, or its productivity if it represents a productive factor. Similarly, objects referring to financial stocks, for example, to a loan, contain information about the agents who hold it as a liability (e.g., the borrower) or an asset (e.g., the bank granting the loan), plus further information pertaining to the specific type of stock considered. As a matter of example, a loan object will have a set of attributes such as the interest rate, the duration, the original amount, the outstanding value of the principal, and so on.

A first advantage of describing stocks as objects is that OOP, as already explained, represents a very flexible and efficient tool to store information and manage heterogeneity. Starting from the general classes defining the fundamental features of a certain type of stock, we can easily generate new more specific subclasses modifying some features or adding new ones.

The other crucial component of our approach to ensure the SFC is represented by the concept of "Stock Matrix," with which every agent of the model, may it be of the type household, firm, bank, government, or whatever, is endowed since the beginning of the simulation. The stock matrix is inherited from the root class "SimpleAbstractAgent," which represents the common superior template of all types of agents. In a nutshell, the stock matrix is a table in which all the stocks owned by an agent are stored and divided into assets and liabilities. Hence, each financial stock is stored at the same time on the liability side of the stock matrix of the liability holder and on the asset side of the stock matrix of the asset holder. Real stocks are instead stored on the asset side of their owner, for example, in the "inventories" slot if they represent firms' unsold goods, until they are eventually transferred to the asset side of another agent in case a transaction takes place. This transaction, in turn, is cleared by the concomitant exchange of a given financial asset (e.g., deposit transfer, cash) for the agreed value.

The structure of the Stock Matrix is the same for all agents. Each type of stock is identified by a specific position (or ID). Some of these slots can remain empty if the agent does not hold the related kind of stock: for example, household and banks will generally hold no productive capital, and the corresponding slot in the transaction matrix will then be empty.

The stock matrix is then deeply related to the representation of agents' balance sheet, though being a broader concept.[9] In fact, we can easily access the accounting value of the various stocks, aggregating them for each type of asset/liability and then summing them up in order to derive the balance sheet values of assets and liabilities, with the net wealth as balancing item.

This representation of the stock matrix helps to ensure the Stock-Stock consistency. Indeed, since every financial item is stored as an asset for one agent and a liability for another agent, the platform does not allow for leakages. The only source of net wealth accumulation for the economy as a whole comes from the accumulation of real assets (houses, machines, etc.).

Whereas this ensures the stock-stock consistency of the model, the Flow-Flow and Stock-Flow Consistency are guaranteed by specific objects that are responsible of handling the exchange of financial and real assets underlying each transaction, ensuring the accounting consistency. These objects are called "transaction mechanisms," and they are part of the programming structure by which we define markets. In JMAB, a market is composed of two populations (buyers and sellers), a mixing mechanism determining which agent is being activated (a specific buyer or seller) and specifying who are the counterparts with whom the activated agent is allowed to interact (the potential sellers or buyers), a matching mechanism that selects one of the counterparts according to the specific strategy followed by agents (e.g., lowest price, lowest price with a random switching probability, best quality, etc.), and finally, a transaction mechanism that supervises the exchange between the activated agent and its selected counterpart.

The transaction mechanism first verifies whether the chosen supplier has enough supply to satisfy agents' demand and whether he is willing to satisfy it. In the opposite case, we have a supply-constrained transaction, and the transaction is realized for a lower amount or may not take place at all. In the case of a purchase of a good or financial asset, first, the mean of payment accepted by the supplier is identified (e.g., cash or deposit transfer). The transaction mechanism assesses whether the buyer has enough liquid resources to pay the seller.

---

9. Indeed, the Stock Matrix contains the very objects representing a stock, whereas the Balance Sheet just refers to their financial value.

Otherwise, the transaction ends up to be financially constrained. In the case of a loan application, the transaction mechanism first checks the amount of credit the selected creditor is willing to grant to the borrower and then creates both the loan and deposit items connecting the creditor's balance sheet with the debtor's one.

Finally, the transaction mechanism updates the Stock Matrices of agents' (e.g. sellers' inventories and buyers' stock of that good, sellers' and buyers' cash and deposits) ensuring that the flows stemming from the transaction respect Copeland's quadruple-entry principle.[10]

As a result of this representation of agents' balance sheets, we obtain a dynamic network of agents' balance sheets evolving through time as transactions occur between different agents.

2.2.6 Fully Scalable View of Model Dynamics

Besides being a convenient solution to ensure the Stock-Flow Consistency of the models, our stock matrix approach leads to a further crucial improvement regarding the display and analysis of models dynamics: the possibility of having a fully scalable view of the model.

Starting from the information stored in the objects representing the stocks, we can easily draw a network linking liability and asset holders for each type of stock; for example, we can plot the network linking borrowers to lenders in the credit and bond markets, banks to the Central Bank through cash advances, or a network linking customers to suppliers in a specific good market. In other words, our approach provides a comprehensive representation of the complex network linking the balance sheets of different agents. This network, evolving over time as the simulation goes on, can then be analyzed using the tools developed in the field of social network analysis. As a matter of example, Fig. 2.1 displays the evolution of the community structure of the banks–firms directed credit network of the "modellaccio" presented in [17], from the initial symmetric situation—where firms are assumed to have the same number of links (i.e., loans) to the same number of banks, and banks have the same degree—to the final period of the simulation. The need to analyze economic networks structure arises from the fact that, in decentralized economies, most economic processes are shaped as local interactions. The topological structure of these relationships affects agents' behavior in many ways, and it can be of topical importance to understand the resilience of the economic system: for example, how a shock in a node (e.g., a default by an agent) propagates to other nodes (agents linked

---

10. The transaction mechanisms further ensure total Stock-Flow Consistency by updating reserves of banks when modeling a deposit transfer between tow agents having their deposits at different banks.

FIGURE 2.1 Credit Network Community Structure: arrows point from liability holders (firms) to asset holders (banks).

to the defaulted agents through financial, commercial, working relationship), possibly leading to economic instability. Analyzing the global (e.g., degree distributions shape, average path lengths) and local (e.g., clustering, transitivity, support, neighborhoods of nodes, nodes centrality, nodes influence) patterns of economic networks often represent the key to understand the complexity of our economics systems (see, e.g., the growing literature on network-based early warning indicators [21]).

In addition to this micro-meso depiction of agents' balance sheets and transactions evolution, our approach also allows us to move to the aggregate level, summing up individual agents' balance sheets and transactions at the sectoral level in order to derive the overall balance sheet and flow-of-funds of the economy. In AB artificial economic systems, just as in free-market economies, agents interact in a decentralized way on different markets. Since these economies lack of any coordinating mechanism supervising agents' and sectors exchanges, to ensure a balanced growth of inflows and outflows across sectors, agents' autonomous interactions may and generally do lead to significant changes in the sectoral distribution of real and financial stocks. This in turn affects the stability of aggregates stock-flow norms: when some sectors accumulate increasing liquid resources at the expense of another, who experiences a drain, we eventually go into a crisis. Combining the insights from the micro-meso analysis of the system with a more traditional SFC aggregate analysis can then greatly help to assess the state of the economy and anticipate its future evolution.

Our approach based on stocks representation as "objects" thus allows the researcher to browse through all the possible levels of aggregation according to his needs, providing a fully scalable vision of the functioning of the simulated economy.

2.2.7 The AB "Modellaccio"

In [17], we presented the "benchmark" AB-SFC model developed with JMAB. As already discussed, we aimed to characterize the model with a relatively flexible and general structure, susceptible of being refined and augmented along different directions, according to one's needs.

Our artificial economy is composed of the following five sectors: a consolidated public sector with Government and Central Bank, two productive sectors, consumption and capital goods producers, a financial sector composed of commercial banks, and a household sector which collectively owns firms and banks. All agents are boundedly rational and follow simple heuristics in a context of incomplete and asymmetric information. Each period of the simulation corresponds to a quarter.

The model considers an economy in which agents interact on five markets:

- A consumption goods market: households interact with consumption firms;
- A capital goods market: consumption firms interact with capital firms;
- A labor market: households interact with government and both types of firms;
- A credit market: firms interact with banks;
- A deposit market: households and firms interact with banks.

As for models discussed in the previous sections, also the "modellaccio" gives particular importance to the role played by agents decentralized interactions in driving the dynamics of complex macrosystems. This aspect is modeled by assuming that agents on the demand and supply sides of each market interact through common matching protocols, similar to those adopted, for example, by [87] and [34]. In a nutshell, when a market interaction is triggered, "demand" agents are allowed to interact with a random subset of potential suppliers, comparing their offers and assigning to each supplier a synthetic measure of its attractiveness. In most cases, this index coincides with the price (or interest rate) offered, or its opposite, according to whether the price represents a disbursement (e.g., purchase of a good or loan application) or generates an inflow (e.g., in the deposit market, where depositors receive an interest) for the demander.

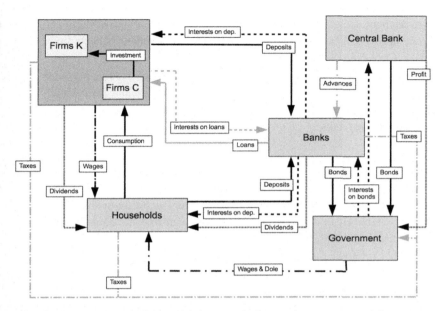

FIGURE 2.2 Flow diagram of the model. Arrows point from paying sectors to receiving sectors.

The flow diagram of Fig. 2.2 presents the structure of the economy and the flows originating during each period of the simulation.

The economy is thus composed of:

- A collection Φ_H of households, selling their labor force to firms in exchange for wages, consuming and saving in the form of banks' deposits. Households own firms and banks proportionally to their wealth and receive a share of firms' and banks' profits as dividends. Unemployed workers receive a dole from the government. Finally, households pay taxes on their gross income.
- Two collections of firms, consumption (Φ_C) and capital (Φ_K) firms. Consumption firms produce a homogeneous consumption good using labor and capital goods manufactured by capital firms. Capital firms employ labor only (with constant productivity) to produce a homogeneous capital good characterized by given productivity and capital–labor ratio. Firms can apply for loans to banks in order to finance production and investment. Retained profits are held in the form of banks' deposits.
- A collection Φ_B of banks, collecting deposits from households and firms, granting loans to firms, and buying bonds issued by Government. Mandatory capital and liquidity ratios constraints apply. Banks may ask for cash advances to the Central Bank to restore the mandatory liquidity ratio.

- A Government sector, which hires a given number of public workers and pay unemployment benefits to households. The government collects taxes and issues bonds to cover its deficits.
- A Central Bank, which issues legal currency, holds banks' reserve accounts and the government's account, accommodates banks' demand for cash advances at a fixed discount rate, and possibly buys residual government bonds not purchased by banks.

2.2.8 Agents' Behaviors

In what follows, we sketch out agents' heuristics in a discursive way for space reasons and not to overwhelm the reader with too many technical details. However, readers interested in the details of the model can find the equations describing agents' behavioral rules in [17].

As already explained, agents follow simple adaptive rules. A clear example of adaptive heuristic is represented by the expectation formation mechanism that follows a very traditional simple adaptive scheme according to which the expectation for a generic variable z, marked by the superscript e, at time t can be computed as $z_t^e = z_{t-1}^e + \lambda(z_{t-1} - z_{t-1}^e)$.

A similar adaptive rule is also followed by households who increase or decrease by a stochastic share the level of their reservation wage, the minimum wage at which they are willing to work, according to their past employment condition (i.e., the number of quarters over the last year in which they have been unemployed) and the aggregate rate of unemployment. This latter condition proxies the fact that workers' bargaining power is affected by the level of unemployment. Unemployed households interact with firms willing to hire workers on the labor market through the common matching protocol described in the previous section with firms choosing first cheaper workers.

In addition to wages, households also receive interests paid by banks on their deposits and dividends from firms and banks, which are distributed proportionally to the net worth of each household. Wages, interests, and dividends determine households' income, which is then taxed according to a flat tax rate. Unemployed workers also receive a tax-free dole from the government, equal to a given share of households' average net income. Households then consume with fixed propensities out of real net income and real net worth, saving the remaining in the form of deposits.

Households then interact with consumption firms to choose their consumption goods supplier and with banks to select their deposit bank. For this sake, they compare the prices and interest rates offered by a random subset of consumption firms and banks, respectively, through the usual matching protocol.

On the firms' side, production depends upon sales expectations. What cannot be sold is stored by firms as inventories (evaluated at their cost of production). Firms are assumed to hold a certain amount of real inventories, expressed as a given share of expected sales, as a buffer against unexpected demand swings [97] and to avoid frustrating customers with supply constraints [70].

Capital–good suppliers produce their output out of labor only, firing or hiring workers according to their planned level of output and to workers' (constant) labor productivity.

Consumption firms instead produce a homogeneous consumption good using both workers and capital goods purchased from capital suppliers. The two productive factors are employed in the production process with fixed coefficients. Therefore, consumption firms' demand of workers depends upon their planned level of output, capital goods productivity, and the capital–labor ratio. The productivity of capital and the capital–labor ratio, and so also labor productivity, are assumed to be exogenously fixed in the simplest version of the model without technological change.

Both types of firms set their price as a nonnegative markup over (expected) unit labor costs, here coinciding with unit variable costs. This markup is the crucial competitive variable of firms since households interacting with firms in the consumption goods market look for cheaper consumption goods. Firms then adaptively revise the markup from period to period according to whether their inventories were higher or lower than desired, that is, according to whether they were able to attain their sales target or not.

Investment by consumption firms is demand driven, given that firms' desired rate of productive capacity growth is determined as a function of two variables: the profit rate and the expected rate of capacity utilization, which depends on firms' demand expectations. The number of capital goods demanded by consumption firms is thus a function of their desired productive capacity and their current stock of capital (net of vintages reaching their technical obsolescence), given the (exogenous) productivity of capital goods. Capital goods last 20 periods (i.e., 5 years) before being scrapped. Their financial amortization scheme has the same duration.

Finally, production and investment by firms can be financed using both internal and external resources. More precisely, in accordance with the "pecking order theory" of finance [75], according to which firms' resort to external finance only as a residual resource, its costs are usually higher due to capital market imperfections. However, we depart from the rest of the AB literature assuming a similar behavior in that we assume that firms do not completely exhaust their funds before resorting to credit, but rather want to hold a certain amount of deposits, expressed as a share of their total outlays for wages, as a buffer stock to reduce the risk of liquidity problems in the event of unexpected swings in their revenues.

In each period, firms can apply for a loan to banks. They interact with banks on the credit market through the usual matching protocol and compare banks according to the interest rate on loans they offer. We assume that loans are repaid with a fixed principal amortization scheme in 20 periods. Hence firms have collections of loans with (possibly) different banks, having different ages, different interest rates, and different original and outstanding values. This very important feature was facilitated by the employment of JMAB, as explained in Section 2.2.2.

Firms' profits are then computed, and taxes are paid to the government according to a flat tax rate. A constant share of dividends is then distributed to households, whereas retained earnings are stored in deposits at banks, which are chosen through the same matching protocol between households and banks on the deposit market discussed before.

On the supply side of the deposit and credit markets, banks operate following simple adaptive heuristics as well. Banks are subject to mandatory capital and liquidity constraints, but, at the same time, they also have common endogenously evolving capital and liquidity ratios. For simplicity reasons, these are assumed to be equal to the sector average. Then banks modify their interest rates on deposits and loans to attain their target ratios. More precisely, when a bank's capital ratio is above the target level, the bank aims to increase its credit supply and consequently decreases the interest rate on loans to make them more attractive to customers. In the opposite case, they increase the interest rate making their loans less attractive while at the same time increasing their profit margin. Similarly, when the liquidity ratio is below the target, banks increase the interest rate on deposits to attract depositors and cheap reserves, whereas in the opposite case they decrease the interest rate on deposits to reduce their costs. However, the interest rate on deposits has an upper bound represented by the interest paid by banks to the Central Bank when asking for cash advances. These cash advances can be demanded by banks when needed to satisfy the liquidity constraints. Cash advances last one period for simplicity reasons and yield a constant interest rate to the Central Bank.

As reserve of banks held at the Central Bank do not yield any interest, banks use reserves in excess of their target to buy newly issued government bonds, which last for one period and yield a constant interest rate, the possible residual part being purchased by the Central Bank.

Banks' behavior is then completed by the inclusion of a sophisticated credit rationing mechanism according to which banks try to estimate the expected internal rate of return associated with each loan application they receive. The expected rate of return estimated by banks depends on the interest rate offered and the applicant's collateral value (i.e., capital hold by consumption firms) and also on the estimated probability of default of the borrower. This in turn depends negatively on the applicants' net operating cash flows (i.e., cash inflows minus cash outflows, including payments related to loan already obtained by borrowers) and positively on the flows of payments (interests and principal payments) arising from the loan project under evaluation. Banks may also decide to grant a loan for a lower amount in case the expected return of the loan project is negative for the amount originally demanded but turns positive for a lower amount.

Firms and banks may go bankrupt when they run out of liquidity or if their net worth turns negative. Defaulted firms and banks are bailed in by households and depositors, respectively, thus maintaining their number constant: in the case of default by a capital firm, the loss induced by the associated nonperforming loans is totally borne by banks since capital firms do not have any collateral. In the case of a consumption firm, creditors can recover part of their outstanding loans through fire sales of the firm's physical capital to households, that is, the owners of firms that thus allow defaulted firms to restart. The financial value of assets sold through fire sales is lowered by an exogenous share.

Banks default when their net wealth turns negative. We assume that depositors bear the loss associated to the default. To restore a positive net wealth, deposits are lowered up to the point the bank's capital ratio equals the minimum capital adequacy requirement (6%), as it happens in a bail-in procedure. The total loss borne by depositors is distributed proportionally to their deposit amount.

Finally, the government hires public workers whose amount is a constant share of total workers, pays a dole to unemployed people, collects taxes, and issues bonds to cover possible deficits. The other public institution is the CB, which accommodates banks' requests for cash advances, hold banks' reserves, and the government account, buys bonds not purchased by commercial banks, and redistributes all its profits to the government.

2.2.9 Calibration Procedure

A further contribution our work aimed to make to the nascent AB-SFC literature was related to the calibration of the model initial stocks and flows in an SFC manner. Calibration is always tricky. Admittedly, whereas very sophisticated techniques have been proposed to calibrate the model parameters, less attention has been devoted to the procedures to determine initial values of stocks and flows. In the AB-SFC approach, calibrating the model is even more difficult since the values of stocks and flows should be mutually consistent since the beginning. Furthermore, the model being an approximation of reality, the relative size of different types of stocks should be also set at reasonable levels. Third, given that AB models require a "burn-in" period, agents should also have sufficiently high initial buffer stocks (e.g., capital, deposits, reserves) to face possible strange or extreme dynamics originated in this initial periods and to avoid a general collapse before the model exits the "training phase." Besides determining the values of aggregate flows and stocks, calibration must also specify how these values are distributed between microagents and then how the age, time to maturity, and original and outstanding values of each specific stock in the balance sheets of agents are determined. Finally, calibration will also define how the balance sheets of agents are initially connected, that is, who are the liability and asset holders of each specific stock in the economy.

To address these challenges, we proposed a detailed procedure based on the derivation of an aggregate stationary state with positive (exogenously given) inflation. For this sake, we treated sectors as aggregate units rather than focusing on individual agents. Then, we numerically solved the steady state by setting exogenously the values of some behavioral parameters, stocks, and stock-flow norms. These were parameters whose empirical counterparts were easily observable, or parameters acting as numeraire (e.g., the value of labor productivity, the initial nominal wage), or parameters that we wanted to control exogenously. Having determined the aggregate values of stocks and flows of each sector (and the values of the parameters involved in the steady-state definition), we then distributed them across agents in a way such that agents of the same type all started with similar initial conditions. This defined the outstanding financial values of each type of stocks in agents' balance sheet. Finally, for stocks having a duration higher than one (i.e., loans and real capital), this outstanding value was then divided between different stocks whose features (e.g., the original and outstanding value, the real value, the age, and time to maturity) were determined taking into account the amortization scheme, the duration, the real stationary state condition (i.e., each stock has the same original value, net, of inflation), and the nominal rate of inflation. Finally, we drew the links between asset and liability holders for each of these stocks ensuring that every agent had the same number of links of his peers.[11]

2.2.10 Analysis and Validation of Results

We then ran 100 Monte Carlo simulations under the baseline scenario for 400 periods, corresponding to 100 years.

The analysis of the artificial time series, obtained by averaging the trends across the 100 Monte Carlo simulations (see Fig. 2.3), highlights that the model first experiences a succession of expansionary and recession trends, as a consequence of the complex dynamics of prices, wages, profits, and credits arising

---

11. Also the details of the calibration procedure summarized in this section can be found in [17].

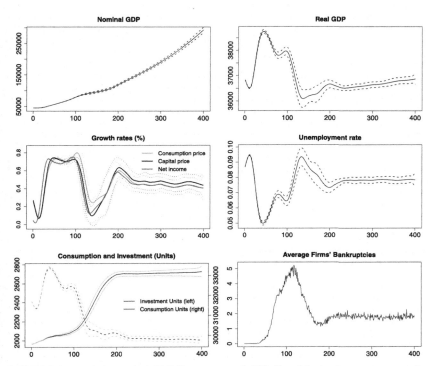

FIGURE 2.3   Top left: nominal GDP. Top center: real GDP. Top right: net-income, consumption prices, and capital prices rates of growth. Growth rates of prices have been computed using average market prices (weighted for firms' market shares). Bottom left: Unemployment. Bottom center: Investment (continuous) and consumption (dashed) in real units. Bottom right: number of firms' bankruptcies. Continuous lines are mean trends over Monte Carlo simulations. Dashed lines are standard deviations of trends across Monte Carlo runs.

from agents' decentralized interactions. Then, in most cases the model converges to a relatively stable configuration of the economy in which main real aggregates fluctuate around stable values and nominal aggregates grow at similar rates, fluctuating around a steady level. We refer to this situation as a "stochastic steady-state" or "quasi-steady-state" (quasi-SS), whereas the previous time span could be identified with the transition phase of our artificial economy.

After having checked the actual accounting consistency of the model over the whole simulation time span, we proceeded to analyze and validate the model against empirical evidence, employing for this sake a collection of stylized facts collected from the empirical literature.

Results seem to suggest that the model is capable of replicating and explaining a significant number of empirical regularities at both the micro- and

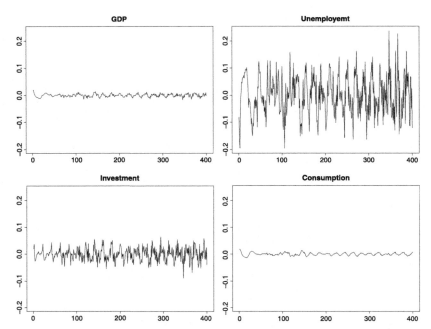

FIGURE 2.4 Cyclical components of simulated times series for Real Output, Unemployment, Investment, and Consumption.

macroeconomic levels, ranking among the most sophisticated models in the literature.

As a matter of example, Fig. 2.4, displaying the cyclical component of the artificial time series for GDP, unemployment, investment, and consumption (each normalized by the trend), shows that our artificial data provide a good approximation of the relative standard deviations of main real aggregates: **(1)** the investment and unemployment volatility are significantly higher than real GDP volatility, whereas the consumption is slightly less volatile than output; similarly, **(2)** Fig. 2.5 shows that the autocorrelation structure of artificial (de-trended) times series up to the 20th lag looks remarkably similar to the autocorrelation function observed in real data[12]: the same happens for **(3)** the cross-correlations between the cyclical component of real output at time t and of real output, unemployment, real investment, and real consumption at time $t - lag$ (the right panel of Fig. 2.5), whose shape, dimension, and peak position (indicating whether the variable is lagged, coincident, or leading) provide a very good fit to their empirical counterparts.

---

12. With the only exceptions of the 20th autocorrelation of investment and unemployment, which are significantly higher than real-world ones given our assumptions that capital goods last for 20 periods, which embed a cyclical component in real investment.

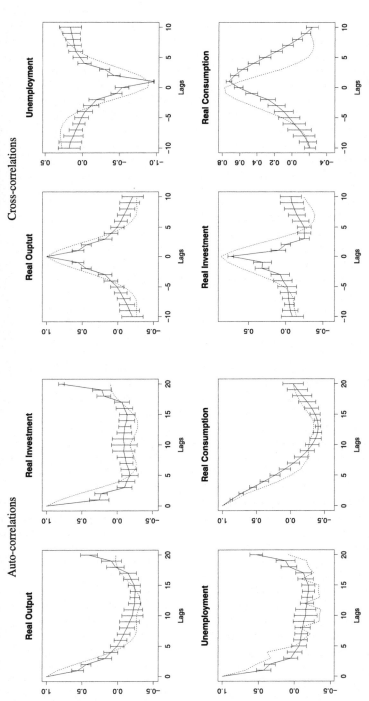

FIGURE 2.5 Left panel: Average artificial (continuous) and real (dashed) autocorrelations of the de-trended series up to the 20th lag. Bars are standard deviations of Monte Carlo average auto-correlations. Right panel: Average artificial (continuous) and real (dashed) cross-correlations between the cyclical component of real output at time t and of real output, unemployment, real investment, and real consumption at time $t - lag$, with lag ranging between -10 and 10. Bars are standard deviations of Monte Carlo average cross-correlations.

The model also reproduces several other important macroeconomic stylized facts observed in reality. In accordance with the empirical evidence on business cycles, **(4)** inflation is procyclical and lagging (tending to build up during expansions and fall after the cyclical peaks), whereas **(5)** mark-ups are countercyclical and lagging; see [13] and [90]. In addition, the model results are also in line with the empirical evidence presented in [68] regarding the **(6)** frequency of price adjustments and the frequency of price decreases over total price changes.

Results also show that **(7)** changes in inventories are procyclical, whereas **(8)** the inventories/sales ratio is counter-cyclical as it happens to be in reality [14].

Banks' leverage **(9)**, defined as total loans over banks' net worth, appears to be procyclical, as expected. Furthermore, its correlation with real GDP (0.25) and its relative standard deviation (1.69) **(10)** are both consistent with the correspondent statistics provided by [80].

Firms' leverage and firms' total debt are procyclical **(11)**. The procyclicality of firms' total debt is another well-known stylized fact [74,71], whereas the empirical evidence on firms' leverage is more controversial and varies across countries and industries.

Finally, real output growth rates generated in the model show the well-known tent-shaped leptokurtic distribution **(12)** (with excess kurtosis ≈ 0.70) observed in real world [50].

The model also reproduces several important stylized facts at the microeconomic level. Despite agents within each class are almost perfectly homogeneous at the beginning of our simulations, heterogeneity emerges during the simulation **(13)**, first as a consequence of the inherent stochasticity affecting agents' interactions and adaptive behaviors, and then as the result of the path-dependent/cumulative effects arising from agents' competition on real and financial markets. The selection processes affect the evolution of market structures, from an initial situation in which firms' market shares are all equal toward a more concentrated market. As observed in reality, also market shares in the model are characterized by a high degree of heterogeneity across firms and by high persistency, both for consumption and capital firms **(14)**.

The distributions of firm sizes appear to be right-skewed and fat-tailed **(15)** for both capital and consumption firms, regardless the measure used (i.e., real sales or firms' productive capacity). The fat-tailed and right-skewed nature of firm size distribution, with upper tails made of few large firms, is well known since Gibrat's seminal contribution though the shape of the distribution may vary considerably across countries and industries.

In addition, a certain degree of lumpiness in investment at the microlevel **(16)**, as observed in real world, emerges from the model complex dynamics, where investment is not smoothed over the time span but rather displays successive spikes, followed by periods in which investment is significantly lower, or even null.

As far as the financial sector is concerned, both credit and degree distributions of banks have positive skewness and excess kurtosis suggesting the presence of fat tails (**17**), in line with the (not conclusive) empirical evidence available [29]. Fig. 2.1 discussed in Section 2.2.6 displays the evolution of the community structure of the banks–firms directed credit network from the initial symmetric situation, where firms' are assumed to have the same number of links (i.e., loans) to the same number of banks, and banks are assumed to have the same degree, to the final period of the simulation. The figure also shows another important property: the average degree of firms is significantly lower than that of banks (**18**).

Finally, the distributions of firms' bad debts and firms' bankruptcies broadly reflect the properties observed in the empirical counterparts, both being right-skewed and characterized by positive excess kurtosis (**19**).

2.2.11   Robustness Checks and Sensitivity Experiments

To check how a different parameterization of investment and credit behaviors affects the transition phase, the properties of the economy in the long run, and the robustness of the cyclical properties employed to validate the model, we performed sensitivity experiments on selected parameters referring to: (a) banks' risk aversion in assessing consumption and capital firms' credit worthiness; (b) the weights given to the profit rate and to the capacity utilization rate in consumption firms' desired capacity growth function (i.e., investment); (c) the share of firms' precautionary deposits, which affect their quantity of credit demanded. Each sensitivity analysis was performed through a parameter sweep in a plausible range of values. For each configuration, we ran 25 Monte Carlo repetitions. The figures and tables summarizing the results of the five sensitivity experiments can be found on the platform web page referring to the benchmark model.[13]

Results confirm that all the cyclical properties of our artificial time series hold under all the scenarios investigated, suggesting that changes in the parameters employed for the sensitivity do not subvert the structural interdependencies between its main variables. Hence, the model ability to fairly approximate the properties of macroeconomic time series is not circumscribed to the baseline parameterization.

---

13. At the link https://github.com/S120/benchmark. After having logged-in to github, figures and data can be accessed and downloaded following the path benchmark/paper/Benchmark Model—Simulation Results/Sensitivity.

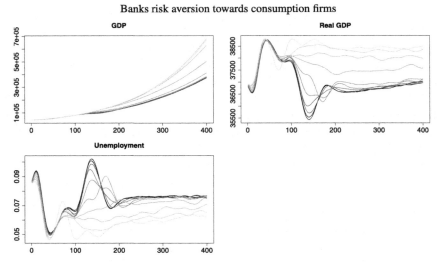

FIGURE 2.6 Nominal GDP, real GDP, and unemployment (trends). Lighter gray lines correspond to higher values of the parameter.

However, changes in the parameters can affect both the transition phase and the properties of the long-term quasi-SS in a significant way.

As a matter of example, we discursively comment the effects of different risk attitudes by banks in evaluating consumption firms' probability of default. The example is useful to show that given the endogenous nature of private money, banks have significantly higher flexibility in extending credit than predicted by the loanable fund approach still employed in the vast majority of DSGE models. Changes in the risk attitude of banks can greatly affect the amount of credit lend to the economy, even when banks are subject to the same institutional constraints.

Figs. 2.6 and 2.7 show that higher values of risk aversion are associated with higher real output (higher real consumption and moderately lower real investment), lower unemployment, and higher inflation (as reflected by the dynamics of nominal GDP).

The analysis of the dynamics generating these properties is particularly insightful: a more prudent attitude by banks prevents consumption firms from going into excessive debt (Fig. 2.7, right) during expansionary phases, lessening in a significant way the amplitude and duration of the recession in the transition. In the three experiments in which the risk aversion parameter is the highest, the economy completely avoids the recession phase experienced in the baseline and low-risk-aversion scenarios.

In these cases the model displays a smooth transition toward the quasi-steady-state and tends to converge more rapidly than in low-risk-aversion cases.

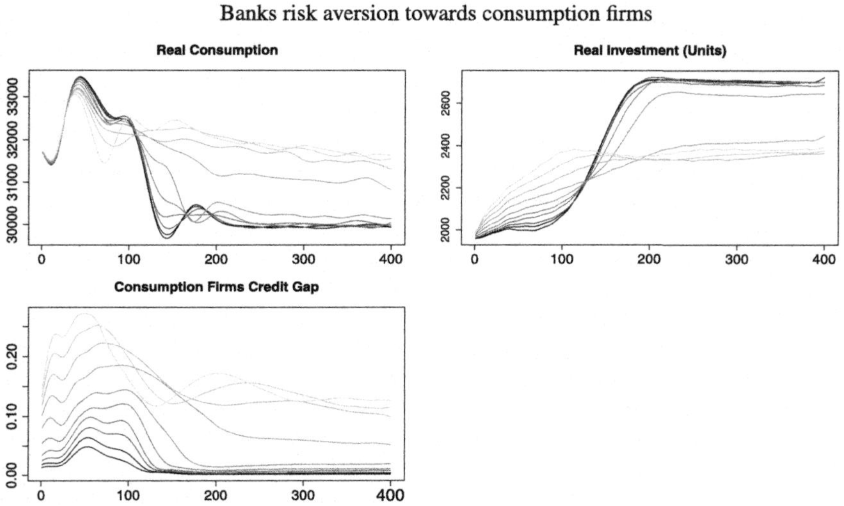

Banks risk aversion towards consumption firms

FIGURE 2.7   Consumption units, investment units, and share of unsatisfied credit (trends). Lighter gray lines correspond to higher values of the parameter.

The prevention of the recession, in turn, enables the system to attain a balanced growth of prices, wages, profits, investment, GDP, and credit, avoiding the emergence of excessive imbalances in financial flows between different sectors. The economy ends up having more real output and lower unemployment, but also more credit and more inflation than in the baseline, in spite of the fact that firms are individually subjected to stricter credit constraints.

These dynamics highlighted are in line with the main results of the overwhelming stream of literature that, since [77], has stressed the central role of financial factors and financial institutions in shaping business cycles. In particular, the marked recession experienced in the transition under the more risky scenarios and the slower convergence to the quasi-ss are in line with the recent findings of [64], showing that more credit-intensive expansions tend to be followed by deeper recessions and slower recoveries. In line with the recent empirical literature (see [103,104]) against the currently prevalent financial intermediation theory of banking, our experiments also highlight that banks, given the endogenous nature of money creation through credit, are far more flexible in their credit creation capability than they would be if they acted as simple intermediaries, collecting deposits and then lending them out.

2.2.12   An Application to Study Inequality and Economic Growth

In [17], no policy analysis is performed since the main focus was on the methodology and validation of the model. However, the model was later amended

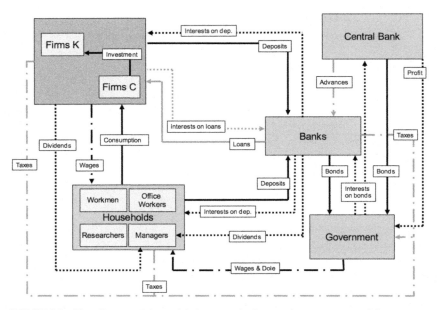

FIGURE 2.8 Flow diagram of the model. Arrows point from paying sectors to receiving sectors.

and augmented with some new functional blocks to investigate the relationship between income and wealth inequality on the one hand and innovation and economic development on the other. The results of this exercise are presented in [18]. This paper aims to assess the impact of different distributive regimes on innovation dynamics and economic development. The augmented model has a similar structure of that presented in [17], as depicted in Fig. 2.8.

However, to address our research question, three major modifications to the original model have been made:

1. We consider different classes of agents such as top managers, office workers, researchers and low-tier workers organized in different layers of firms' hierarchical structure, inspired by [23] (as shown in Fig. 2.8). Whereas top managers receive dividends out of firms' profits in addition to their wage, other workers' gross income coincides with wages plus interests on deposits. This feature, which mimics the actual behavior of the stock markets in which only a minority benefits from capital incomes, affects the evolution of inequality and then macroeconomic dynamics. In addition, wages of workers employed in different tiers endogenously emerge as the result of the workers' competition process on segmented labor markets, one for each type of workers.

2. To assess the impact of income and wealth distribution on consumption patterns, we abandon the common households' consumption function employed

in the previous paper, and we refer to empirical data in determining the average propensities to consume and save out of income for each income group, these values reflecting the well-known empirical fact that richer people tend to save a higher portion of their income with respect to poorer people, as originally argued by Keynes.

3. Whereas, in the original version of the model, we abstract from technological change, in the new one, we introduce innovation dynamics in an evolutionary flavor affecting the evolution of labor productivity through product innovation in the capital sector (i.e., different vintages characterized by different productivity levels) and process innovation in the consumption good sector arising from firms' investment in increasingly productive machineries. More precisely, we assume that capital good producers hire researchers (as shown in Fig. 2.8) to perform R&D, thereby possibly coming to produce more productive capital good vintages.[14]

The validation procedure yields very similar qualitative and quantitative results compared to the original model, suggesting that also the augmented version provided a good approximation of the properties displayed by real-world data and matched a huge variety of micro- and macroeconomic stylized facts.

The new version also provides realistic outcomes for both income and wealth distribution, as measured by the Lorenz curve and the Gini index. Furthermore, though income and wealth were initially distributed in the same way, wealth inequality ends up being significantly more marked than income inequality in all simulations performed, as observed in reality.

In addition, in the baseline configuration with a flat tax rate, both income and wealth inequality are characterized by a slightly increasing pattern. After having analyzed the dynamics of the model under the baseline scenario, we then conduct two policy experiments:

1. In the first one, we switched from the flat-tax rate regime characterizing the baseline scenario to increasingly redistributive tax regimes. To isolate the effect of redistribution, we checked that the overall tax load was the same across scenarios analyzed for given (aggregate) values of income and wealth and given distributions of income and wealth. In other words, the passage from each tax regime to the (more redistributive) next one could be interpreted as a "tax shift" from poorer to richer people.

2. The second experiment was conducted on the parameter representing threshold number of periods after which unemployed workers decreased their reservation wage: higher values of the parameter increased the downward

---

14. Since the seminal work of [78,79], the evolutionary literature has provided well-established mechanisms to model innovation and imitation in a Schumpeterian Mark II flavor, which have been progressively refined through the ages (see, e.g., [42,39–41] and its later versions).

rigidity of wages (while making upward revisions more likely), thus proxying the effects of labor market policies aiming at enhancing the bargaining power of workers (i.e., collective bargaining, minimum wage, etc.). Two experiments were conducted, one in which the parameter sweep affected all classes of workers and one in which it only affected low and middle tier workers, thus excluding top managers.

Our results showed that both increasing the redistributive character of the tax system and enhancing low and middle income workers' wages downward rigidity are effective in improving the economic system dynamics (i.e., the dynamics of real GDP, labor productivity, unemployment, and other macroeconomic aggregates) and tackling inequality.

However, both the long-term efficacy and the magnitude of this reduction can be significantly enhanced when income inequality is tackled directly on the labor market through policies aiming at sustaining wages of middle- and low-wage workers, rather than through an ex-post redistribution of income.[15]

Therefore, simulation results under labor market tough competition provided some ground for the thesis according to which labor market reforms aiming at increasing wages flexibility, and the progressive demise of collective bargaining have played a crucial role in causing the long-lasting polarization of income and wealth since the beginning of the 1980s.

The details of the model and a thorough analysis of results can be found in [18].

As a matter of example, Figs. 2.9 and 2.10 display the evolution of the system under the four scenarios analyzed: Experiment 1, the darkest line in the plots of Fig. 2.9, represents the scenario with more flexible wages, whereas Experiment 4 is the scenario with greater wages downward rigidity.[16] The plots show that in the first scenario the economy remains trapped in a depression with low income and productivity dynamics and high unemployment, whereas increasing wages downward rigidity significantly improves the situation. As far as inequality is concerned, more flexible scenarios are characterized by higher and increasing inequality, whereas enhancing wages downward rigidity significantly reduces inequality and dampens the increasing pattern throughout the simulation time span, as it is clear by looking at Fig. 2.10.

Apart from the conclusions of our simulation experiments, this "augmented" model also serves to highlight the great adaptivity of the original benchmark model, which makes it suitable for different applications and open to several possible integrations. Furthermore, the task of adding the new blocks presented

---

15. On the contrary, the labor market experiment in which wages rigidity was modified for all types of workers, including top managers, did not yield any significant result.
16. Experiment 2, the second darkest line, coincides with the baseline scenario.

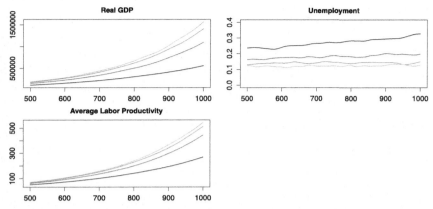

FIGURE 2.9 Labor Market Experiment—Low-Middle Tiers Workers Only. Lighter gray lines correspond to scenarios with greater wages downward rigidity. Left: Real GDP. Center: Unemployment. Right: Average Labor Productivity (weighted for consumption firms' output shares).

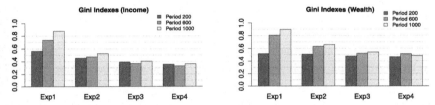

FIGURE 2.10 Labor Market Experiment—Low-Middle Tiers Workers Only. Left: Gini indexes (Income) at different simulation time steps. Right: Gini indexes (Wealth) at different simulation time steps.

above on the top of the original model was facilitated by the modularity of our JMAB platform discussed in Section 2.2.3, which allowed us to keep most of the classes developed for the benchmark model unaltered and to focus just on the development of classes defining new types of agents (e.g., firms with a hierarchical structure) and behaviors (e.g., R&D strategies by capital firms and capital vintages ranking strategies by consumption firms). Furthermore, rather than starting from zero, most of these new classes where created as subclasses of existent ones, exploiting the advantages brought by classes "inheritance." For example, firms now having a hierarchical structure were created as subclasses of the classes representing consumption and capital firms in the original model, thereby inheriting all their attributes and methods.

Other integrations of the "modellaccio" are ongoing. In particular, a new version [93] including the interbank market and a more realistic representation of the Central Bank functions is forthcoming. The model explorations, addressed to analyze the impact of monetary policy interest rate changes by the Central Bank and how the microlevel transmission mechanism affect their efficacy, suggest that the strength of the monetary transmission mechanism is highly dependent on the balance-sheet compositions of the Central Bank, commercial banks, firms, and households, indicating that the mechanism is not as clear cut as conventional theory would suggest.

2.3 CONCLUSIONS AND CHALLENGES AHEAD

In the present chapter, after a brief overview of the AB macromodeling literature, we turned our attention to the research conducted in Ancona under the supervision of Prof. Mauro Gallegati, often carried out in collaboration with the research group led by Prof. Domenico Delli Gatti at the Catholic University of Milan. Starting from the fundamental idea that agents' decentralized interaction could play a crucial role in explaining business fluctuations and the emergence of financial fragility, which is at the core of [33] seminal contribution, an organic research line arose, which unfolded trough different generations of models: [33] naturally evolved in [34], where the analysis of financially driven business cycles was enriched with an endogenously evolving network of commercial and credit relationships. The "matching protocols" proposed to mimic the evolution of the network were then refined in [86,87], who embedded them into the framework of the first "closed" decentralized macroeconomic model. The structure of these models was then further developed in the "modellaccio" [17,18], the first fully fledged AB-SFC model of the family, which provided a more accurate description of the real sector (e.g., with capital accumulation and technological change) and the financial sector (e.g., credit rationing on quantity and multiperiod loans with multiple banks).

The refinement of the models has gone hand in hand with the refinement of the technical tools adopted to simulate them. In this respect, we have argued that the features of our Java Macro-Agent-Based Simulation Platform can greatly help AB-SFC practitioners in pushing ahead the realism of their models while simplifying the coding part of the model building process. Nonetheless, we are aware that JMAB still requires further development to enhance its user friendliness and flexibility in order to ease its diffusion among scholars.

Similarly, despite the encouraging achievements of the recent AB macroeconomic literature, several theoretical and empirical challenges remain to be addressed.

On the empirical level, a first issue is related to the empirical foundation of the behavioral assumptions made in AB models. This is related both to the choice of the functional forms and to the setting of parameters values. One of the main reasons at the base of this criticism is that such an empirical foundation is tricky because data are often lacking or even not observable.[17]

The empirical foundation problem is also deeply connected to a second unresolved methodological issue, originating from the freedom from analytical constraints, which characterizes the AB approach, compared to analytical methods looking for closed-form solutions. As recently pointed out by [53], one of the major supporters of the diffusion of AB models in macroeconomics [51], even in the simplest applications, the number of plausible AB representations of a system is bewilderingly large and hard to discipline. Since the implications of ABM models can depend sensitively on these specific assumptions, the incredible variety of possible plausible specifications weakens the credibility of any particular model, thereby hampering the diffusion of these models not only in the academia, but also among international institutions and policy makers. Apart from the robustness issue, which can be somehow alleviated, though not completely solved, by the employment of sensitivity analysis techniques based on Monte Carlo simulation methods,[18] a third criticality concurs to make this argument even more cogent: a further byproduct of the incredible flexibility offered by the AB methodology has been to stimulate a continuous quest for more "sophistication," sometimes hiding or culminating in a theoretical blind spot. This lack of theoretical foundation in turn often makes the implications of these models difficult to interpret or, in the worst cases, redundant and logically incoherent.

In [17], we extensively argued that ensuring the Stock-Flow Consistency of AB macroeconomic models should be a primary concern for all macro-AB practitioners in order to address this "theoretical coherence" issue. A coherent representation of agents' balance sheets, financial flows, and asset-liability relationships, reflected in the accounting identities holding at the macroeconomic level, should be interpreted as a necessary, though insufficient, condition for internal logical coherence. A violation of these accounting rules informs about the presence of financial flows originating from or going into a black hole or about financial assets (liabilities) that do not find a liability (asset) counterpart, thereby embedding a theoretical leakage in the model dynamics. This in turn can eventually amplify throughout the simulation, thereby compromising the logical coherence and reliability of results.

---

17. However, even though the availability of data still remains a critical issue, many private and public datasets now provide statistics and data that can be of great help in overcoming this limitation.
18. For example, a very efficient method to reduce the computational burden of sensitivity methods has been recently proposed in [92], based on a combination of a very parsimonious sampling on the parameters space—based on Nearly Orthogonal Latin Hypercube (NOLH) sampling—and an innovative meta-modeling method called "kriging."

However, our work is not exempt from the criticisms discussed above. While helping to discipline ourselves and to set minimal logical consistency requirements, the Stock-Flow Consistency alone does not provide a final solution to the problem of the bewildering freedom of AB models.

In some measures, these drawbacks can still be ascribed to the fact that the diffusion of ABMs in the scientific community is still relatively recent, in particular, in the field of macroeconomics. However, it is also clear that much of the possibilities of AB macromodels to set themselves as a credible alternative to analytical and general equilibrium models, as advocated by [51] and [31], will depend on the efforts devoted to solve these issues. Whereas the scope of these problems should not be denied or neglected, we do believe that far more harmful for macroeconomics would be to react to them by discarding the AB methodology once and for all, taking refuge in the old general equilibrium models with representative agents, which, since their very foundation, have proven to be far more unresponsive to criticisms than they were immune from.

REFERENCES

[1] I. Arslan, E. Caverzasi, M. Gallegati, A. Duman, Long term impacts of bank behavior on financial stability. An agent based modeling approach, Journal of Artificial Societies and Social Simulation 19 (2016).

[2] T. Assenza, D. Delli Gatti, E Pluribus Unum: macroeconomic modelling for multi-agent economies, Journal of Economic Dynamics and Control 37 (8) (2013).

[3] T. Assenza, D. Delli Gatti, J. Grazzini, Emergent dynamics of a macroeconomic agent based model with capital and credit, Journal of Economic Dynamics and Control 50 (C) (2015) 5–28.

[4] E. Baroni, M. Richiardi, Orcutt's vision, 50 years on, in: LABORatorio R. Revelli Working Papers Series 65, Center for Employment Studies, 2007.

[5] R. Barwell, O. Burrows, Growing Fragilities? Balance Sheets in the Great Moderation, Financial Stability Paper 10, Bank of England, April 2011.

[6] R. Bennett, B. Bergmann, A Microsimulated Transactions Model of the United States Economy, John Hopkins University Press, Baltimore, 1986.

[7] B. Bergmann, A microsimulation of the macroeconomy with explicitly represented money flows, Annals of Economic and Social Measurement (1974) 475–489.

[8] B. Bernanke, M. Gertler, Agency costs, net worth and business fluctuations, The American Economic Review 79 (1989) 14–31.

[9] B. Bernanke, M. Gertler, Financial fragility and economic performance, The Quarterly Journal of Economics 105 (1990) 87–114.

[10] B. Bernanke, M. Gertler, S. Gilchrist, The financial accelerator in a quantitative business cycle framework, in: Handbook of Macroeconomics, vol. 1, North-Holland, Amsterdam, 1999, pp. 1341–1393.

[11] D. Bezemer, The economy as a complex system: the balance sheet dimension, Advances in Complex Systems 15 (2012) 22.

[12] D.J. Bezemer, No One Saw This Coming. Understanding Financial Crisis through Accounting Models, SOM Research Reports, 09002, University of Groningen, SOM Research School, Groningen, 2009.

[13] M. Bils, The cyclical behavior of marginal cost and price, Economic Review 77 (5) (1987) 838–855.

[14] M. Bils, J. Kahn, What inventory behavior tells us about business cycles, The American Economic Review 90 (3) (2000) 458–481.

[15] W.C. Brainard, J. Tobin, Pitfalls in financial model building, The American Economic Review 58 (2) (May 1968) 99–122.

[16] S. Burgess, O. Burrows, A. Godin, S. Kinsella, S. Millard, A dynamic model of financial balances for the United Kingdom, Bank of England Working Paper Series 614 (2016) 37.

[17] A. Caiani, A. Godin, E. Caverzasi, M. Gallegati, S. Kinsella, J.E. Stiglitz, Agent Based-Stock Flow Consistent macroeconomics: towards a benchmark model, Journal of Economic Dynamics & Control 69 (2016) 375–408.

[18] A. Caiani, A. Russo, M. Gallegati, Does inequality hamper innovation and growth?, SSRN eLibrary (2016) 39.

[19] A. Caiani, A. Russo, A. Palestrini, M. Gallegati, Economics with Heterogeneous Interacting Agents: A Practical Guide to Agent-Based Modeling, Springer, 2016.

[20] E. Catullo, M. Gallegati, Multi-country Decentralized Agent Based Model: Macroeconomic Dynamics and Vulnerability in a Simplified Currency Union, Finmap-working papers, Collaborative EU Project FinMaP – Financial Distortions and Macroeconomic Performance: Expectations, Constraints and Interaction of Agents, 2015.

[21] E. Catullo, M. Gallegati, A. Palestrini, Towards a credit network based early warning indicator for crises, Journal of Economic Dynamics & Control 50 (2015) 78–97.

[22] E. Caverzasi, A. Godin, Post-Keynesian stock-flow consistent modeling: a survey, Cambridge Journal of Economics 39 (1) (2015) 157–187.

[23] T. Ciarli, A. Lorentz, M. Savona, M. Valente, The effect of consumption and production structure growth and distribution. A micro to macro model, Metroeconomica 61 (1) (2010) 180–218.

[24] S. Cincotti, M. Raberto, A. Teglio, Credit money and macroeconomic instability in the agent-based model and simulator Eurace, Economics – The Open-Access, Open-Assessment E-Journal 4 (26) (2010).

[25] D. Colander, M. Goldberg, A. Haas, K. Juselius, A. Kirman, T. Lux, B. Sloth, The financial crisis and the systemic failure of the economics profession, Critical Review 21 (2–3) (2009) 249–267.

[26] M.A. Copeland, Social accounting for moneyflows, The Accounting Review 24 (3) (1949) 254–264.

[27] H. Dawid, S. Gemkow, P. Harting, S. Van der Hoog, M. Neugart, The Eurace@ Unibi Model: An Agent-Based Macroeconomic Model for Economic Policy Analysis, Bielefeld Working Papers in Economics and Management No. 05-2012, 2012.

[28] H. Dawid, P. Harting, M. Neugart, Economic convergence: policy implications from a heterogeneous agent model, Journal of Economic Dynamics & Control 44 (2014) 54–80.

[29] G. de Masi, M. Gallegati, Bank–firms topology in Italy, Empirical Economics 43 (2) (2007) 851–866.

[30] C. Deissenberg, S. Van Der Hoog, H. Dawid, Eurace: a massively parallel agent-based model of the European economy, Applied Mathematics and Computation 204 (2) (2008) 541–552.

[31] D. Delli Gatti, S. Desiderio, E. Gaffeo, P. Cirillo, M. Gallegati, Macroeconomics from the Bottom-up, Springer, 2011.

[32] D. Delli Gatti, C. Di Guilmi, E. Gaffeo, G. Giulioni, M. Gallegati, A. Palestrini, Business cycle fluctuations and firms' size distribution dynamics, Advances in Complex Systems (ACS) 7 (2) (2004) 223–240.

[33] D. Delli Gatti, C. Di Guilmi, E. Gaffeo, G. Giulioni, M. Gallegati, A. Palestrini, A new approach to business fluctuations: heterogeneous interacting agents, scaling laws and financial fragility, Journal of Economic Behavior & Organization 56 (2005) 489–512.

[34] D. Delli Gatti, E. Gaffeo, M. Gallegati, Complex agent-based macroeconomics: a manifesto for a new paradigm, Journal of Economic Interaction and Coordination 5 (2) (2010) 111–135.

[35] D. Delli Gatti, M. Gallegati, B. Greenwald, A. Russo, J. Stiglitz, Business fluctuations in a credit-network economy, Physica A 370 (2006) 68–74.

[36] D. Delli Gatti, M. Gallegati, B.C. Greenwald, A. Russo, J.E. Stiglitz, The financial accelerator in an evolving credit network, Journal of Economic Dynamics & Control 34 (2010) 1627–1650.

[37] D. Delli Gatti, M. Gallegati, A. Russo, B. Greenwald, J. Stiglitz, Business fluctuations and bankruptcy avalanches in an evolving network economy, Journal of Economic Interaction and Coordination 4 (2) (2009) 195–212.

[38] C.H. Dos Santos, Keynesian theorizing during hard times: stock-flow consistent models as an unexplored frontier of Keynesian macroeconomics, Cambridge Journal of Economics 30 (4) (2006) 541–565.

[39] G. Dosi, G. Fagiolo, M. Napoletano, A. Roventini, Wage formation, investment behavior and growth regimes: an agent-based analysis, Revue de L'OFCE 0 (5) (2012) 235–261.

[40] G. Dosi, G. Fagiolo, M. Napoletano, A. Roventini, Income distribution, credit and fiscal policies in an agent-based Keynesian model, Journal of Economic Dynamics and Control 37 (8) (2013) 1598–1625.

[41] G. Dosi, G. Fagiolo, M. Napoletano, A. Roventini, T. Treibich, Fiscal and monetary policies in complex evolving economies, Journal of Economic Dynamics and Control (2015).

[42] G. Dosi, G. Fagiolo, A. Roventini, Schumpeter meeting Keynes: a policy-friendly model of endogenous growth and business cycles, Journal of Economic Dynamics and Control 34 (9) (2010) 1748–1767.

[43] J. Duca, J. Muellbauer, Tobin lives: integrating evolving credit market architecture into flow of funds based macro-model, ECB Working Paper Series 1581 (2013) 33.

[44] G. Eliasson, Business Economic Planning: Theory, Practice and Comparison, Wiley, London, 1976.

[45] G. Eliasson, Modeling the experimentally organized economy: complex dynamics in an empirical micro-macro model of endogenous economic growth, Journal of Economic Behavior & Organization 16 (1991) 153–182.

[46] J. Epstein, R. Axtell, Growing Artificial Societies: Social Science from the Bottom-Up, MIT Press and Brooking Press, Washington, DC, 1996.

[47] J.M. Epstein, Agent-based computational models and generative social science, Complexity 4 (5) (1999) 41–57.

[48] J. Esptein, Remarks on the foundations of agent-based generative social science, in: L. Tesfatsion, K. Judd (Eds.), Handbook of Computational Economics, vol. 2, North-Holland, Amsterdam, 2006, pp. 1585–1602.

[49] G. Fagiolo, A. Moneta, P. Windrum, A critical guide to empirical validation of agent-based models in economics: methodologies, procedures, and open problems, Computational Economics 30 (2007) 195–226.

[50] G. Fagiolo, M. Napoletano, A. Roventini, Are output growth-rate distribution fat-tailed? Some evidence from OECD countries, Journal of Applied Econometrics 23 (2008) 639–669.

[51] J. Farmer, D. Foley, The economy needs agent-based modelling, Nature 460 (7256) (2009) 685–686.

[52] M. Flannery, K. Rangan, Partial adjustment toward target capital structures, Journal of Financial Economics 79 (3) (2006) 469–506.

[53] D. Foley, Crisis and theoretical methods: equilibrium and disequilibrium once again, in: Conference Paper Presented at the International Conference on Economics, Economic Policies and Sustainable Growth in the Wake of the Crisis, Ancona, 2016.

[54] M. Fowler, Inversion of control containers and the dependency injection pattern, http://martinfowler.com/articles/injection.html, 2004.

[55] N. Gilbert, Simulation for the Social Scientist, McGraw-Hill, 2008.

[56] W. Godley, Macroeconomics without Equilibrium or Disequilibrium, Working Paper Series 205, The Levy Economic Institute of Bard College, 1997.

[57] W. Godley, Seven Unsustainable Processes, Special Report Series, Levy Economics Institute, 1999, p. 16.

[58] W. Godley, F. Cripps, Macroeconomics, Oxford University Press, 1983.

[59] W. Godley, M. Lavoie, Monetary Economics: An Integrated Approach to Credit, Money, Income, Production and Wealth, Palgrave MacMillan, New York, 2007.

[60] W. Godley, L.R. Wray, Can Goldilocks Survive?, Tech. rep., The Levy Economic Institute of Bard College, 1999.

[61] W. Godley, G. Zezza, Debt and Lending: A cri de coeur, Tech. rep., Levy Institute at Bard College, 2006.

[62] A. Graziani, The Monetary Theory of Production, Cambridge University Press, Cambridge, 2003.

[63] R. Grilli, G. Tedeschi, M. Gallegati, Bank interlinkages and macroeconomic stability, International Review of Economics & Finance 34 (C) (2014) 72–88.

[64] O. Jorda, M. Schularick, A. Taylor, When credit bites back: leverage, business cycles, and crises, Federal Reserve Bank of San Francisco Working Paper Series 2011 (27) (2012) 42.

[65] S. Kinsella, Words to the wise: stock flow consistent modeling of financial instability, available at SSRN 1955613, 2011.

[66] S. Kinsella, M. Greiff, E.J. Nell, Income distribution in a stock-flow consistent model with education and technological change, Eastern Economic Journal 37 (2011) 134–149.

[67] A. Kirman, Whom or what does the representative individual represent?, The Journal of Economic Perspectives 6 (2) (1992) 117–136.

[68] P. Klenow, O. Kryvtsov, State-dependent or time-dependent pricing: does it matter for recent US inflation?, NBER Working Paper Series 11043 (2005) 54.

[69] P. Klimek, S. Poledna, J. Farmer, S. Thurner, To bail-out or to bail-in? Answers from an agent-based model, Journal of Economic Dynamics and Control 50 (2015) 144–154.

[70] M. Lavoie, Foundations of Post-Keynesian Economic Analysis, Edward Elgar, Aldershot, 1992.

[71] M. Leary, Bank loan supply, lender choice, and corporate capital structure, The Journal of Finance 64 (3) (2009).

[72] B. LeBaron, L. Tesfatsion, Modeling macroeconomies as open-ended dynamic systems of interacting agents, The American Economic Review: Papers and Proceedings 98 (2) (2008) 246–250.

[73] M. Lengnick, Agent-based macroeconomics: a baseline model, Journal of Economic Behavior & Organization 86 (2013) 102–120.

[74] C. Lown, D. Morgan, The credit cycle and the business cycle: new findings using the loan officer opinion survey, Journal of Money, Credit, and Banking 38 (6) (2006).

[75] S. Meyers, Capital structure puzzle, The Journal of Finance 39 (3) (1984) 575–592.

[76] N. Minar, R. Burkhart, C. Langton, M. Askenazi, The Swarm Simulation System: A Toolkit for Building Multi-Agent Simulations, Santa Fe Institute Working Paper Series 96-06-042, 1996.

[77] H.P. Minsky, Stabilizing an Unstable Economy, Yale University Press, New Haven, 1986.

[78] R. Nelson, S. Winter, Simulation of Schumpeterian competition, The American Economic Review 67 (1) (1977) 271–276.

[79] R. Nelson, S.G. Winter, An Evolutionary Theory of Economic Change, Harvard University Press, Cambridge, MA, 1982.

[80] G. Nuño, C. Thomas, Bank leverage cycles, ECB Working Paper Series 1524 (2013).

[81] G. Orcutt, A new type of socio economic system, Review of Economics and Statistics 58 (1957) 773–797.

[82] S. Phelps, Applying dependency injection to agent-based modeling: the JABM toolkit, CCFEA Working Paper 56 (12) (2012) 33.

[83] S. Phelps, K. Musial-Gabrys, Network motifs for microeconomic analysis, CCFEA Working Paper 63 (2012) 8.

[84] M. Raberto, A. Teglio, S. Cincotti, Debt, deleveraging and business cycles: an agent-based perspective, Economics – The Open-Access, Open-Assessment E-Journal 27 (2012) 50.

[85] L. Riccetti, A. Russo, M. Gallegati, Leveraged network-based financial accelerator, Journal of Economic Dynamics and Control 37 (8) (2013) 1626–1640.

[86] L. Riccetti, A. Russo, M. Gallegati, Unemployment benefits and financial factors in an agent based macroeconomic model, Economics – The Open-Access, Open-Assessment E-Journal 2013 (42) (2013).

[87] L. Riccetti, A. Russo, M. Gallegati, An agent-based decentralized matching macroeconomic model, Journal of Economic Interaction and Coordination 10 (2) (2015) 305–332.

[88] L. Riccetti, A. Russo, M. Gallegati, Financialisation and crisis in an agent based macroeconomic model, Economic Modelling 52 (PA) (2016) 162–172.

[89] L. Riccetti, A. Russo, M. Gallegati, Stock market dynamics, leveraged network-based financial accelerator and monetary policy, International Review of Economics & Finance 43 (C) (2016) 509–524.

[90] J. Rotemberg, M. Woodford, The cyclical behavior of prices and costs, NBER Working Paper Series 6909 (1999).

[91] A. Russo, L. Riccetti, M. Gallegati, Increasing inequality, consumer credit and financial fragility in an agent based macroeconomic model, Journal of Evolutionary Economics 26 (1) (March 2016) 25–47.

[92] I. Salle, M. Yildizoglu, Efficient sampling and meta-modeling for computational economic models, Computational Economics 44 (4) (2014) 507–536.

[93] J. Schasfoort, A. Godin, D. Bezemer, A. Caiani, S. Kinsella, Monetary Policy Transmission in a Macroeconomic Agent-Based Model, SOM Research Reports, Vol. 17010-GEM, University of Groningen, SOM Research School, Groningen, 2017.

[94] T. Schelling, Models of segregation, The American Economic Review: Papers and Proceedings 59 (2) (1969) 488–493.

[95] T.C. Schelling, Micromotives and Macrobehaviours, Norton, 1978.

[96] P. Seppecher, Monnaie endogène et agents hétérogènes dans un modèle stock-flux cohérent, in: Political Economy and the Outlook for Capitalism, Paris, France, 2012.

[97] J. Steindl, Maturity and Stagnation in American Capitalism, Blackwell, 1952.

[98] L. Tesfatsion, K. Judd, Handbook of Computational Economics, Agent-Based Computational Economics, vol. 2, North-Holland, Amsterdam, 2006.

[99] J. Tobin, Money and finance in the macroeconomic process, Journal of Money, Credit, and Banking 14 (2) (1982) 171–204.

[100] J.C. Trichet, Reflections on the nature of monetary policy non-standard measures and finance theory, Frankfurt, Opening address at the ECB Central Banking Conference, http://www. ecb.europa.eu/press/key/date/2010/html/sp101118.en.html, 18 November 2010.

[101] S. Van der Hoog, H. Dawid, Bubbles, Crashes and the Financial Cycle: Insights from a Stock-Flow Consistent Agent-Based Macroeconomic Model, Working Papers in Economics and Management, 1-2015, University of Bielefeld, 2015, p. 58.

[102] J. von Neuman, Theory of Self-Reproducing Automata, University of Illinois Press, 1966.

[103] R. Werner, Can banks individually create money out of nothing? – the theories and the empirical evidence, International Review of Financial Analysis 36 (2014) 1–19.

[104] R. Werner, A lost century in economics: three theories of banking and the conclusive evidence, International Review of Financial Analysis 46 (2015) 361–379.

[105] J. Yellen, Macroeconomic research after the crisis: a speech at "The Elusive 'Great' Recovery: Causes and Implications for Future Business Cycle Dynamics", in: 60th Annual Economic Conference Sponsored by the Federal Reserve Bank of Boston, October 14, 2016.

Chapter 3

AD-AS Representation of Macroeconomic Emergent Properties

Luca Riccetti*, Alberto Russo†, and Mauro Gallegati†
*University of Macerata, Macerata, Italy
†Marche Polytechnic University, Ancona, Italy

3.1 INTRODUCTION

Based on the simulation of the agent-based decentralized matching macroeconomic model proposed by [9,10], in this chapter, we show how to build the aggregate demand and supply curves from the bottom up. In particular, we perform a computational exercise through which we calculate the *notional* quantity of individual demands and supplies corresponding to a set of different good prices introduced as a shock to the price emerging from the model simulation. By summing up the notional quantity at individual level we obtain both the aggregate demand and supply. In this way, we provide a simple visualization of complex macroeconomic dynamics, similar to that proposed in the mainstream approach. Therefore, we can study the similarities and differences between the mainstream and the agent-based frameworks, trying to understand the role of heterogeneity and interaction in shaping aggregate curves and macroeconomic equilibria.

The chapter is organized as follows. Section 3.2 briefly reviews the standard textbook approach to the AD-AS equilibrium. Section 3.3 describes the agent-based macroeconomic model. Sections 3.4 and 3.5 illustrate the methodology used to build the aggregate demand and the aggregate supply curves, respectively. Section 3.6 concludes by discussing the difference between the mainstream equilibrium and the agent-based disequilibrium approach.

3.2 THE STANDARD AD-AS MODEL

The AD-AS model is a standard tool in macroeconomic analysis. AD represents the aggregate demand, whereas AS stays for aggregate supply. This is

Introduction to Agent-Based Economics. http://dx.doi.org/10.1016/B978-0-12-803834-5.00005-9

explained to students when the macroeconomic theory is introduced, often preceded by the IS-LM model (with fixed prices). Indeed, in an introductory course on macroeconomics, when organized starting from the analysis of the short-run to proceed with the medium- and then the long-run analysis of economic growth, one firstly is taught the IS-LM model, and then the AD curve can be constructed on this basis, corresponding to an IS-LM model with flexible prices. Based on the Phillips curve, which is on the inverse relationship between (wage) inflation and unemployment, typically assuming a constant mark-up, the AS curve is introduced, and the AD-AS model can be used for the macroeconomic analysis of the medium run.

In its simplest form, the AD-AS model is represented as the interaction between two linear curves, though nonlinear relationships are quite commonly employed. In general, however, we have a downward sloping AD and an upward sloping AS.[1] Depending on expectations, policy makers can (or cannot) exploit the trade-off between unemployment and inflation because of the different time intervals implied by the adjustment toward the equilibrium. In the extreme (but included in the textbook AD-AS model) case of "rational expectations," when the agents know the model and are able to anticipate the decisions of policy makers, the AS is vertical at the potential level of output (as if the adjustment was instantaneous), and the AD only determines the price level. The unemployment rate that corresponds to the equilibrium output is the NAIRU (Non-Accelerating Inflation Rate of Unemployment). According to this model, only movements of the AS influence the macroeconomic equilibrium in the long run, whereas a monetary or a fiscal expansion just leads to more inflation, thus suggesting that "structural reforms" are needed to reduce unemployment (i.e., the NAIRU), whereas the Keynesian tools of macroeconomic policy are ineffective (or can have an impact that is limited to the short run). As for stabilization, in such a "natural" equilibrium setting, monetary policy is considered as the primary tool to promote macroeconomic stability and, in general, a growth-enhancing environment [1]. However, neither monetary policy nor fiscal policy aimed at managing the aggregate demand is taught to be useful in affecting the "natural" macroeconomic equilibrium, for example, the NAIRU.

However, it is unlikely that rational expectations are a good approximation of real agents' behavior; thus an upward sloping AS curve seems to be a better representation of the macroeconomic reality, and the sustain of aggregate demand through fiscal or monetary policy can be effective, at least along the adjustment process (thus depending on how long the system takes to go back to the equilibrium). In other words, people are able to adapt, at least partially,

---

1. Limit cases can be studied, for instance, when the AD is vertical (e.g., private investment is insensitive to variations of the interest rate) or even upward sloping under debt deflation.

to policy changes, but not instantaneously. Adaptive expectations of some sort should be assumed to describe a relatively slow and possibly incomplete adjustment.

Moreover, in many cases, macroeconomic analysis does not involve distributive issues. In fact, considering the distribution of income (and of wealth) can lead to significant results. For instance, even in the AD-AS model, if we assume that agents are characterized by heterogeneous propensities to consume and in particular that the propensity to consume out of income (and wealth) is decreasing with the income (wealth) level, then we simply obtain a Keynesian multiplier that depends on the functional distribution between wages and profits through the mark-up, say z. A simple case is that of an AD-AS model with two social classes, workers and capitalists, in which capitalists have a relatively low propensity to consume, say c_K, whereas workers have a relatively high propensity to consume, say c_W. In the simplifying case $c_K = 0$, that is, with unitary propensity to save for capitalists, the multiplier depends positively on c_W and negatively on z, that is, a redistribution from wages to profits reduces the equilibrium output. Accordingly, an increase of inequality can result in lesser consumption and then a decrease of the aggregate demand and of the equilibrium level of output (but for a vertical AS). However, this slight modification seems to have far reaching consequences and a Post-Keynesian flavor, which is not in line with the conventional view neither at the level of textbook macroeconomics or at that of the New Keynesian Dynamic Stochastic General Equilibrium (NK-DSGE) model and its last extensions aimed at including a variety of financial frictions.[2]

Another factor, which is often left out by introductory macroeconomic analysis, is finance, for instance, the role of the "risk premium" and the mechanisms of the "financial accelerator" ([2], which is instead a well-known piece of advanced macroeconomics),[3] at least before the new edition of the classical book of [3]. Indeed, [3] has introduced an additional financial channel in the IS curve, where the investment is influenced by the real interest rate (e.g., the nominal interest rate minus expected inflation) plus a risk premium and by income: in particular, an increase of the "risk premium," for instance due to a negative financial shock, depresses investment, thus leading to a fall in aggregate demand (the IS curve moves leftward) and a decrease of aggregate income. However, finance can play an important role also in affecting the supply side since the availability of bank credit and other forms of financing allow firms

2. A notable exception is the DSGE model proposed by [7], where it is assumed that a subset of households does not only smoothly consume but also exhibits a "love for money" in the utility function.
3. Such a mechanism can be amplified by the complex structure of financial interlinkages as shown, for instance, by [4] and [8].

to finance production. In particular, firms can be rationed on the credit market due to the lack of collateral, and this effect can depend on different financial conditions faced by heterogeneous firms. This is not considered by the textbook AD-AS model, in which the aggregate supply is based on the labor market and the trade-off between inflation and unemployment (depending on the type of expectations). Credit rationing and, in general, the deterioration of financial conditions, instead, can have an impact on production since a "credit crunch" may reduce the financing of firms' production with a subsequent increase of unemployment and a fall of aggregate income.

In what follows, we explain how an agent-based model is able to highlight the role of heterogeneity and interaction in macroeconomic dynamics by reconstructing both the AD and AS curves from the bottom-up, that is, by simulating how each agent reacts to variations of the demand and supply conditions and what it emerges at the aggregate level.

3.3 AN AGENT-BASED MACRO MODEL

In this section, we describe the structure of the agent-based macroeconomic model we then employ to simulate and build the aggregate AD and AS curves. The economy evolves over a time span $t = 1, 2, \ldots, T$ and is composed by households ($h = 1, 2, \ldots, H$), firms ($f = 1, 2, \ldots, F$), banks ($b = 1, 2, \ldots, B$), the central bank, and the government. Agents are boundedly rational and live in an incomplete and asymmetric information context, and thus they follow simple rules of behavior and use adaptive expectations.

Firms follow a dynamic target leverage according to the Dynamic Trade-off Theory (see, e.g., [5,6]) to define the capital structure, determining a procyclical leverage.

Agents interact in four markets:

- credit market, in which firms are the demand side and banks are the supply side;
- labor market, in which firms and the government are the demand side and households are the supply side;
- goods market, in which households are the demand side and firms are the supply side;
- deposit market, in which banks are the demand side and households are the supply side.

The interaction between the demand and supply sides of the four markets follows a fully decentralized matching mechanism, which is common to all markets and represents a best partner choice in a context of imperfect information.

3.3.1   Timing and Interaction Mechanisms

In each period, firms and banks first interact in the credit market. Firms ask for credit to banks given the demand deriving from their net worth and leverage target; the leverage level changes according to expected profits and inventories. Banks set their credit supply depending on their net worth, deposits, and the quantity of money provided by the central bank. As said above, they must comply with some regulatory constraints. Then, government, firms, and households interact in the labor market. The government hires public workers. Afterwards, firms hire workers: labor demand depends on available funds, that is, net worth and bank credit. Subsequently, households and firms interact in the goods market. Firms produce consumption goods on the basis of hired workers. They put in the goods market their current period production and previous period inventories. Households decide their desired consumption on the basis of their disposable income and wealth. Finally, households determine their savings to be deposited in banks: banks and households interact in the deposit market.

The interaction between the demand and the supply side of the four markets is set by the following decentralized matching protocol. In general, each agent in the demand side observes a list of potential counterparts in the supply side and chooses the most suitable partner according to some market-specific criteria. At the beginning, a random list of agents in the demand side—firms in the credit market, firms in the labor market, households in the goods market, and banks in the deposit market—is set. Then, the first agent in the list observes a random subset of potential partners; this subset represents a fraction $0 < \chi \leq 1$ (which proxies the degree of imperfect information) of the whole set of potential partners; thus, the agent chooses the cheapest one. For example, in the labor market, the first firm on the list, say firm f_1, observes the asked wage of a subsample of workers and chooses the agent asking for the lowest one, say worker h_1. After that, the second agent on the list performs the same activity on a new random subset of the updated potential partner list. In the case of the labor market, the new list of potential workers to be hired no longer contains the worker h_1. The process iterates until the end of the demand side list (in our example, all the firms enter the matching process and have the possibility to employ one worker). Then, a new random list of agents in the demand side is set, and the whole matching mechanism goes on until either one side of the market (demand or supply) is empty or no further matchings are feasible because the highest *bid* (for example, the money till available to the richest firm) is lower than the lowest *ask* (for example, the lowest wage asked by till unemployed workers).

As for the entry–exit process, new entrants replace bankrupted agents according to a one-to-one replacement. New agents enter the system with initial conditions we will define further. Moreover, the money needed to finance entrants is subtracted from households' wealth.[4]

In what follows, we describe in more detail the working of different markets.

3.3.2 Credit Market

Firms may need credit to finance production, and banks can provide loans to this end. Firm's f credit demand at time t depends on its net worth A_{ft} and the leverage target l_{ft}. Therefore, the credit demand is

$$B^d_{ft} = A_{ft} \cdot l_{ft}. \tag{3.1}$$

The leverage target evolves according to the following rule:

$$l_{ft} = \begin{cases} l_{ft-1} \cdot (1 + \alpha \cdot U(0,1)) & \text{if } \pi_{ft-1}/(A_{ft-1} + B_{ft-1}) > i_{ft-1} \\ & \text{and } \hat{y}_{ft-1} < \psi \cdot y_{ft-1}, \\ l_{ft-1} & \text{if } \pi_{ft-1}/(A_{ft-1} + B_{ft-1}) = i_{ft-1} \\ & \text{and } \hat{y}_{ft-1} < \psi \cdot y_{ft-1}, \\ l_{ft-1} \cdot (1 - \alpha \cdot U(0,1)) & \text{if } \pi_{ft-1}/(A_{ft-1} + B_{ft-1}) < i_{ft-1} \\ & \text{or } \hat{y}_{ft-1} \geq \psi \cdot y_{ft-1}, \end{cases} \tag{3.2}$$

where $\alpha > 0$ is a parameter that represents the maximum percentage change of the target leverage, $U(0,1)$ is a uniformly distributed random number in the interval $(0,1)$, π_{ft-1} is the past period gross profit, B_{ft-1} is the previous period debt level, $\pi_{ft-1}/(A_{ft-1} + B_{ft-1})$ is the return on assets, that is, the profit rate, i_{ft-1} is the nominal interest rate on debts,[5] $\hat{y}_{ft-1}$ represents inventories (that is, unsold goods), $0 \leq \psi \leq 1$ is a parameter representing a threshold for inventories based on the previous period production y_{ft-1}. Eq. (3.2) means that the leverage target increases (decreases) if the profit rate is higher (lower) than the average interest rate and there is a low (high) amount of inventories.

As for the supply side, bank b offers the total amount of money B^d_{bt} depending on the net worth A_{bt}, the deposits D_{bt}, the central bank credit m_{bt}, and some legal constraints (proxied by the parameters $\gamma_1 > 0$ and $0 \leq \gamma_2 \leq 1$ that represent the maximum admissible leverage and maximum percentage of equity to be invested in lending activities, respectively):

$$B^d_{bt} = \min(\hat{k}_{bt}, \bar{k}_{bt}), \tag{3.3}$$

---

4. In the extreme case in which private wealth is not enough, the government intervenes. However, we can anticipate that it never happens in our simulations.

5. The interest rate is calculated as the weighted average of interests paid to the lending banks.

where $\hat{k} = \gamma_1 \cdot A_{bt}$ and $\bar{k} = \gamma_2 \cdot A_{bt} + D_{bt-1} + m_{bt}$. To reduce risk concentration, banks can lend up to a maximum fraction β of the total amount of the credit B_{bt}^d to a single counterpart.

Bank b charges an interest rate on the firm f at time t as follows:

$$i_{bft} = i_{CBt} + \hat{i}_{bt} + \bar{i}_{ft}, \tag{3.4}$$

where i_{CBt} is the nominal interest rate set by the central bank at time t, $\hat{i}_{bt}$ is a bank-specific component, and $\bar{i}_{ft} = \rho^{l_{ft}}/100$ is a firm-specific component, that is, a risk premium on firm target leverage (with $\rho > 0$).

The bank-specific component evolves as follows:

$$\hat{i}_{bt} = \begin{cases} \hat{i}_{bt-1} \cdot (1 - \alpha \cdot U(0,1)) & \text{if } \hat{B}_{bt-1} > 0, \\ \hat{i}_{bt-1} \cdot (1 + \alpha \cdot U(0,1)) & \text{if } \hat{B}_{bt-1} = 0, \end{cases} \tag{3.5}$$

where $\hat{B}_{bt-1}$ is the amount of money that the bank did not manage to lend to firms in the previous period.

Based on firm–bank matchings, each firm ends up with a credit $B_{ft} \le B_{ft}^d$, and each bank lends to firms an amount $B_{bt} \le B_{bt}^d$. The difference between desired and effective credit is equal to $B_{ft}^d - B_{ft} = \hat{B}_{ft}$ and $B_{bt}^d - B_{bt} = \hat{B}_{bt}$ for firms and banks, respectively. Moreover, we assume that banks ask for an investment in government securities equal to $\Gamma_{bt}^d = \bar{k}_{bt} - B_{bt}$. If the sum of desired government bonds exceeds the amount of outstanding public debt, then the effective investment Γ_{bt} is rescaled according to the factor $\Gamma_{bt}^d / \sum \Gamma_{bt}^d$. Instead, if the public debt exceeds the banks' desired demand, then the central bank buys outstanding public securities.

3.3.3   Labor Market

The government hires a fraction g of households. The remaining part is available for working in the firms. Firm's f labor demand depends on the total capital available, $A_{ft} + B_{ft}$. Each worker posts a wage w_{ht}, which is updated as follows:

$$w_{ht} = \begin{cases} w_{ht-1} \cdot (1 + \alpha \cdot U(0,1)) & \text{if } h \text{ employed at time } t - 1, \\ w_{ht-1} \cdot (1 - \alpha \cdot U(0,1)) & \text{if } h \text{ unemployed at time } t - 1. \end{cases} \tag{3.6}$$

The required wage has a minimum equal to $\theta \hat{p}_{t-1}(1 + \tau)$, where θ is a positive parameter, $\hat{p}$ is the maximum price of a single good, and τ is the tax rate on labor income. This means that a worker asks at least a wage net of taxes able to buy a multiple θ of a good.

As a result of the decentralized matching between labor supply and demand, each firm ends up with a number of workers n_{ft} and a residual cash (insufficient to hire an additional worker). Obviously, a fraction of households may remain unemployed. In the baseline model, the wage of the unemployed is set equal to zero.

3.3.4   Goods Market

In the goods market, households and firms interact. The households' desired consumption is set according to the following rule:

$$c_{ht}^d = c_1 \cdot w_{ht} + c_2 \cdot A_{ht}, \tag{3.7}$$

where $0 < c_1 \leq 1$ is the propensity to consume current income, and $0 \leq c_2 \leq 1$ is the propensity to consume wealth A_{ht}. If the amount c_{ht}^d is smaller than the average price of one good $\bar{p}$, then $c_{ht}^d = \min(\bar{p}, w_{ht} + A_{ht})$.

Firm f's production is

$$y_{ft} = \phi \cdot n_{ft}, \tag{3.8}$$

where $\phi \geq 1$ is a productivity parameter, and n_{ft} is the number of workers employed by firm f at time t.

Firms want to sell this produced output plus the inventories $\hat{y}_{ft-1}$. The selling price is set as follows:

$$p_{ft} = \begin{cases} p_{ft-1} \cdot (1 + \alpha \cdot U(0,1)) & \text{if } \hat{y}_{ft-1} = 0 \text{ and } y_{ft-1} > 0, \\ p_{ft-1} \cdot (1 - \alpha \cdot U(0,1)) & \text{if } \hat{y}_{ft-1} > 0 \text{ or } y_{ft-1} = 0. \end{cases} \tag{3.9}$$

Therefore, a firm rises the price if there are no inventories (and it produced some goods in the previous period) and vice versa. The minimum price at which firms want to sell their output is set such that it is at least equal to the average cost of production, that is, the ex ante profits are at worst equal to zero.

Based on household–firm interactions, each household may end up with a residual cash, that is, not enough money to buy an additional good and that will be deposited in a bank; by the same token, firms sell an amount $0 \leq \bar{y}_{ft} \leq y_{ft}$, and they may remain with unsold goods; as a consequence, in the next period the firm will try to sell the inventories $\hat{y}_{ft} = y_{ft} - \bar{y}_{ft}$.

3.3.5   Deposit Market

In this market, banks represent the demand side (given that they need capital to extend credit), and households are on the supply side. Banks offer an interest rate on deposits according to their funds requirement:

$$i_{bt}^D = \begin{cases} i_{bt-1}^D \cdot (1 - \alpha \cdot U(0,1)) & \text{if } \bar{k}_{bt} - B_{bt} - \Gamma_{bt} > 0, \\ \min\{i_{bt-1}^D \cdot (1 + \alpha \cdot U(0,1)), i_{CBt}\} & \text{if } \bar{k}_{bt} - B_{bt} - \Gamma_{bt} = 0, \end{cases} \quad (3.10)$$

where Γ_{bt} is the amount of public debt bought by bank b at time t. Therefore, if a bank exhausts the credit supply by lending to private firms or government, then it decides to increase the interest rate paid on deposits, so to attract new depositors, and vice versa. However, the interest rate on deposits can increase till a maximum given by the policy rate i_{CBt}, which is both the rate at which banks could refinance from the central bank and the rate paid by the public sector on public securities.

Households set the minimum interest rate they want to obtain on bank deposits as follows:

$$i_{ht}^D = \begin{cases} i_{ht-1}^D \cdot (1 - \alpha \cdot U(0,1)) & \text{if } D_{ht-1} = 0, \\ i_{ht-1}^D \cdot (1 + \alpha \cdot U(0,1)) & \text{if } D_{ht-1} > 0, \end{cases} \quad (3.11)$$

where D_{ht-1} is the household's h deposit in the previous period. This means that a household that found a bank paying an interest rate higher or equal to the desired one decides to ask for a higher remuneration. In the opposite case, the household keeps her money in cash and asks for a lower rate. We assume that a household deposits all the available money in a single bank that offers an adequate interest rate.

3.3.6 Wealth Dynamics

3.3.6.1 Firms

Firm's f profit is equal to

$$\pi_{ft} = p_{ft} \cdot \bar{y}_{ft} - W_{ft} - I_{ft}, \quad (3.12)$$

where W_{ft} is the firm's f wage bill, that is, the sum of wages paid to employed workers, and I_{ft} is the sum of interests paid on bank loans. Firms pay a proportional tax τ on positive profits; negative profits are subtracted in the computation of the taxes that should be paid on the next positive profits. We indicate net profits with $\bar{\pi}_{ft}$. Finally, firms distribute a percentage δ_{ft} of (positive) net profits. The fraction $0 \le \delta_{ft} \le 1$ evolves according to the following rule:

$$\delta_{ft} = \begin{cases} \delta_{ft-1} \cdot (1 - \alpha \cdot U(0,1)) & \text{if } \hat{y}_{ft} = 0 \text{ and } y_{ft} > 0, \\ \delta_{ft-1} \cdot (1 + \alpha \cdot U(0,1)) & \text{if } \hat{y}_{ft} > 0 \text{ or } y_{ft} = 0. \end{cases} \quad (3.13)$$

This implies that firms distribute less dividends when they need self-financing to expand production (that is, they do not have inventories) and vice versa. The profit net of both taxes and dividends is indicated by $\hat{\pi}_{ft}$. In case of negative profits, $\hat{\pi}_{ft} = \pi_{ft}$.

Consequently, the evolution of firm's f net worth is given by

$$A_{ft} = (1 - \tau') \cdot [A_{ft-1} + \hat{\pi}_{ft}], \tag{3.14}$$

where τ' is the tax rate on wealth.[6]

If the net worth turns to be null or negative, that is, $A_{ft} \leq 0$, then the firm goes bankrupt, and a new entrant enters the market. The initial net worth of the new entrant is a multiple of the average goods price, whereas the leverage is one. Moreover, the initial price is equal to the mean price of survival firms. Banks linked to defaulted firms lose a fraction of their loans (the loss given default rate is calculated as $1 - (A_{ft} + B_{ft})/B_{ft}$).

3.3.6.2 Banks

Bank's b profit is equal to

$$\pi_{bt} = int_{bt} + i_t^{\Gamma} \cdot \Gamma_{bt} - i_{bt-1}^{D} \cdot D_{bt-1} - i_{CB}^{t} \cdot m_{bt} - bad_{bt}, \tag{3.15}$$

where int_{bt} is the interest on lending to nondefaulted firms, i_t^{Γ} is the interest rate on government securities (Γ_{bt}), and bad_{bt} represents the nonperforming loans due to firm defaults. The last variable is the loss given default of the total loan, that is, the fraction $1 - (A_{ft} + B_{ft})/B_{ft}$ of the loan to defaulted firm f connected with bank b.

Banks pay a proportional tax τ on positive profits; negative profits will be used to reduce taxes paid on the next positive profits. We indicate net profits with $\bar{\pi}_{bt}$.

Finally, banks pay a percentage δ_{bt} as dividends on positive net profits. The fraction $0 \leq \delta_{bt} \leq 1$ evolves according to the following rule:

$$\delta_{bt} = \begin{cases} \delta_{bt-1} \cdot (1 - \alpha \cdot U(0, 1)) & \text{if } B_{bt} > 0 \text{ and } \hat{B}_{bt} = 0, \\ \delta_{bt-1} \cdot (1 + \alpha \cdot U(0, 1)) & \text{if } B_{bt} = 0 \text{ or } \hat{B}_{bt} > 0. \end{cases} \tag{3.16}$$

Therefore, if the bank does not manage to lend the desired supply of credit, then it decides to distribute more dividends (because it does not need high reinvested profits), and vice versa.

---

6. This tax is applied only on wealth exceeding a threshold $\bar{\tau}' \cdot \bar{p}$, that is, a multiple of the average goods price.

The profit net of taxes and dividends is indicated by $\hat{\pi}_{bt}$. In case of negative profits, $\hat{\pi}_{bt} = \pi_{bt}$.

Hence, the bank's b net worth evolves as follows:

$$A_{bt} = (1 - \tau') \cdot [A_{bt-1} + \hat{\pi}_{bt}], \tag{3.17}$$

where τ' is the tax rate on wealth.[7]

If the net worth is null or negative, that is, $A_{bt} \leq 0$, then the bank defaults, and a new entrant takes its place, with an initial net worth equal to a random number around a multiple of the cost of the average price of a good (and the money is taken from households proportionally to their wealth). Households linked to defaulted banks lose a fraction of their deposits (the loss given default rate is calculated as $(A_{bt} + D_{bt})/D_{bt}$). The initial net worth of the new entrant is a multiple of the average goods price. Moreover, the initial bank-specific component of the interest rate $(\hat{i}_{bt})$ is equal to the mean value across banks.

3.3.6.3 Households

Household's h wealth evolves as follows:

$$A_{ht} = (1 - \tau') \cdot \left[A_{ht-1} + (1 - \tau) \cdot w_{ht} + div_{ht} + int_{ht}^D - c_{ht}\right], \tag{3.18}$$

where τ' is the tax rate on wealth,[8] τ is the tax rate on income, w_{ht} is the wage gained by employed workers, div_{ht} is the fraction (proportional to the household h's wealth compared to overall households' wealth) of dividends distributed by firms and banks net of the amount of resources needed to finance new entrants (hence, this value may be negative), int_{ht}^D represents interests on deposits, and $c_{ht} \leq c_{ht}^d$ is actual consumption. Households linked to defaulted banks lose a fraction of their deposits as explained above.

3.3.7 Government and Central Bank

Government's current expenditure is given by the wages paid to public workers (G_t) and the interest paid on public debt to banks.[9] As for revenues, government collects taxes on incomes and wealth and receives the interest gained by the central bank. The difference between expenditures and revenues is the public deficit Ψ_t. Consequently, public debt is $\Gamma_t = \Gamma_{t-1} + \Psi_t$. The central bank

---

7. This tax is applied only on wealth exceeding a threshold $\bar{\tau}' \cdot \bar{p}$, that is, a multiple of the average goods price.
8. This tax is applied only on wealth exceeding a threshold $\bar{\tau}' \cdot \bar{p}$, that is, a multiple of the average goods price.
9. In the extreme case in which the government has to intervene to finance new entrants, when private wealth is not enough, also this amount Ω_t has to be considered as public spending.

sets the policy rate i_{CBt} and then the quantity of money to inject into the economic system in accordance with the interest rate. Moreover, the central bank is committed to buy outstanding government bonds.

3.3.8   Simulation Results

For a complete description of the simulation results produced by this model, see [10]. In a nutshell, our agent-based macroeconomic model generates endogenous business cycles as a consequence of the interaction between real and financial factors: when firms' profits are improving, firms aim at expanding production, and if banks extend the required credit, then this results in more employment; the decrease of the unemployment rate leads to the rise of wages, which, on the one hand, increases the aggregate demand and, on the other hand, reduces firms' profits, and this may cause the inversion of the business cycle. As for the specific role of financial factors, there is a nonlinear relationship between bank's leverage (firm's leverage is more stable) and the unemployment rate (that is, the main macroeconomic variable of our modeling framework): for low levels of banks' leverage, its increase allows more firms to finance their desired production due to the larger availability of banks' credit, thus reducing the unemployment rate; this positive relationship, however, faces a limit when the level of banks' leverage becomes "excessive," and it can even reverse for higher leverage levels. In other words, the expansion of finance can have beneficial effects on the economy by providing credit to the corporate sector, but an excess of finance may be dangerous due to the increase of financial instability that makes the system more crisis-prone. Model simulations highlight that even extended crises can endogenously emerge when a large fall of the real wage happens: it causes a lack of aggregate demand that, in turn, induces firms to decrease production, so enlarging the unemployment rate in a vicious circle. In these cases, the system may remain trapped in an underunemployment situation for a long time without the possibility of spontaneously recovering, unless an exogenous intervention occurs.

The model has been extended in different directions to analyze a variety of macroeconomic phenomena, from financialization [11] to inequality [13] and financial regulation [12].

3.4   AGGREGATE DEMAND

We make a "simulation within the simulation," showing how to reconstruct the AD and AS curves even in a disequilibrium model. In particular, we start a simulation of the model till a certain time t (chosen within a stable macroeconomic phase; more on that below), and we simulate the two aggregate curves by shocking the price of goods. The shock is applied to the simulation only at period t.

Therefore, we run the model for $T = 300$ periods but deleting the first 100 periods that are used to initialize the simulation. Then, we compute the average unemployment rate in the remaining 200 periods, finding a value of 8.67%. To perform the computational exercise aimed at building the aggregate demand and supply curves, we choose a period t that is both representative of the average statistical equilibrium of the model and characterized by low instability. In this way the construction of the two curves is not biased by the choice of peculiar situations (such as too high or too low unemployment). In practice, we detect the period t that minimizes the following function:

$$|u(t+1) - \hat{u}| + |u(t) - \hat{u}| + |u(t-1) - \hat{u}|, \qquad (3.19)$$

where $\hat{u}$ is the mean unemployment rate (8.67%). By this minimization we choose a period in which the unemployment rate is at 8.80%, preceded by a period with $u = 8.40\%$ and followed by a period with again $u = 8.80\%$. Now, we can perform the simulation perturbation to the price of goods in order to describe the "out of equilibrium" demand (and supply, in the next section) function.

3.4.1 Microfounded AD

We compute the aggregate demand function in two ways. Both methods consider the individual demands for the consumption of goods and introduce a shock of the same magnitude to the individual prices of the goods produced by each firm. However, the two methods are different because:

- the first method preserves the interaction through the matching mechanism, but it cannot represent a true demand function if constrained by the total supply of goods;
- the second method allows for agents' interaction to obtain a mean price from the simulation, and then it builds the AD based on the computed mean price; in this way the AD is not constrained by the aggregate supply.

As already said, both methods introduce a shock of the same magnitude to the individual prices of the goods produced by each firm. For instance, assuming a shock of +10% of the prices, a firm that sets a price equal to 1 in the baseline simulation and asks for a price of 1.10 in the shocked scenario, whereas a firm that asks for a price equal to 1.2 in the baseline simulation sets a price of 1.32 in the shocked one.

We build the AD curve through 21 points each representing a simulation with a shock that ranges from +10% to −10% with step 1%.

The first method lets the model run in the standard way, and the emerging AD curve is the one that joins the points drawn with circles in Fig. 3.1. It is evident

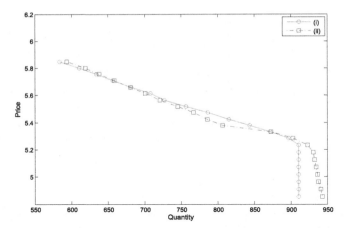

FIGURE 3.1   AD curves that consider the individual demands for goods. They are built joining 21 simulation outputs, obtained with a price shock from +10% to −10% (step 1%).

that the curve is constrained by the overall supply of goods (equal to the actual production, 873 units, plus the past inventories, 38 units, for an overall amount of 911): for lower prices, consumers would buy a larger amount of goods, but the matching is unfeasible for the lack of supply.

As for the second method, we compute the mean price of the realized exchanges for each simulation. Then, we calculate the number of purchased goods for each household, as the amount that the households want to spend divided by the mean price previously computed. In this case, there is no supply constraint. The emerging AD curve in Fig. 3.1 is the dotted line that joins the points drawn with squares. We can observe that the use of the average simulation price can slightly distort the curve compared to the previous one. However, the demand can be also observed when it is above the total supply of 911 goods.

In our view the second method is theoretically preferable if a supply constraint applies, whereas the first method should be chosen if the supply side constraint is not binding because the average price can distort the aggregate demanded amount of goods. Given that in the supply unconstrained part, where the first method is theoretically preferable, the difference between the two curves is not too relevant, whereas in the supply constrained part, where the second method is theoretically better, the difference is wider, we consider the second method as the best one to build our AD curve.

We can exactly show how the AD curve is built from the microlevel. To do this, we compute the amount of goods bought by each household and report the values in Table 3.1. This table highlights that the AD curve emerges from the bottom-up aggregating households' choices when they change their desired consumption at different levels of the price. Each household changes the level

TABLE 3.1 Number of Households that Demand 0 or 1 or 2 Goods for a Given Price Shocks From +10% to −10% With Step 1% and the Total Number of Demanded Goods, That Is, the AD Curve Computed With the Second Method

Shock	0	1	2	AD
+10	44	318	138	594
+9	44	293	163	619
+8	44	274	182	638
+7	44	253	203	659
+6	44	231	225	681
+5	44	211	245	701
+4	44	191	265	721
+3	44	166	290	746
+2	44	145	311	767
+1	44	126	330	786
0	44	105	351	807
−1	1	125	374	873
−2	1	95	404	903
−3	1	75	424	923
−4	0	69	431	931
−5	0	67	433	933
−6	0	65	435	935
−7	0	63	437	937
−8	0	62	438	938
−9	0	59	441	941
−10	0	57	443	943

of consumption once in this price range, but the AD is always downward sloping because households are heterogeneous. Moreover, we can see that the curve is not linear because the number of household that passes from a desired level of consumption to another is different for every step of the price shock. For instance, a price reduction of 1% from the baseline level makes a very large number of households (43) that were unable to buy a good, to buy one good after the price shock; at the same time, 23 households that asked for only one good in the baseline simulation after the shock ask for two goods with an overall increase of the aggregate demand of 66 units. Instead, a price reduction above 3% increases the aggregate demand only by a few amount because: (i) the number of households that do not ask for any good goes to zero, (ii) the number of households that passes from one to two demanded goods decreases given that the vast majority of household already asks for two goods and the households

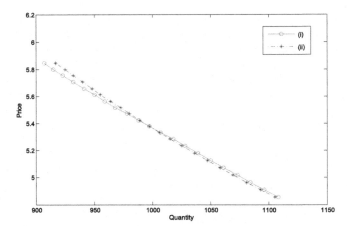

FIGURE 3.2 AD curves built on aggregate consumption. They are built joining 21 simulation outputs, obtained with a price shock from +10% to −10% (step 1%).

that ask for one good are usually very poor (for instance, they ask zero goods in the baseline scenario), (iii) no household is rich enough to ask for three goods. Therefore, the AD curve radically changes its slope in the part with a price shock between −4% to −10%.

3.4.2 AD Curve and Aggregation Effects

To build the previous two kinds of AD curves, we consider the individual demands and then aggregate them. In this way the macrolevel can be different from the microlevel. Moreover, the macrolevel is really microfounded. Now, we want to highlight the importance of the aggregation mechanisms. In order to do that, we build two other AD curves starting from aggregate consumption, computed as the sum of the money that all households in the whole want to spend. Then, we divide the aggregate consumption by:

- the mean price emerging from the baseline model multiplied by a factor ranging from 1.1 to 0.9 with step 1%;
- the mean price emerging from the model when shocks (that still ranges from +10% to −10% with step 1%) of the same magnitude are set at the individual level, as in the method used to build the AD curve chosen in the previous section.

Fig. 3.2 shows that the two curves are different: the first curve, which joins the points drawn with circles, is slightly different from the second represented by the dotted line, which joins the points drawn with stars. This result confirms the importance of considering the microlevel and agents' interaction.

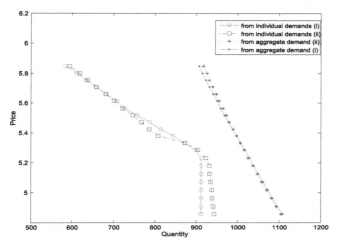

FIGURE 3.3 AD curves: the difference between the ones that start from the individual demands (bottom-up approach) and the ones that start from the aggregate demand (top-down approach).

However, the most relevant differences are those between these two curves and the two curves obtained in the previous section, highlighting both the relevance of heterogeneity and of the aggregation procedure. First of all, the two last methods significantly overestimate the aggregate demand because the aggregate balance constraint is less binding than a balance constraint for each household. For instance, if two households want to spend the money to buy 2.5 goods, then aggregating first the consumption, we obtain an aggregate demand of 5 goods, whereas, in the "reality of simulation," they can buy only 4 goods (two for each one). Fig. 3.3 shows this difference between an AD curve built from the bottom up and an AD curve obtained with a top-down aggregation method.

Another important difference regards the shape of the curves: aggregating first the consumption, the curves are almost linear, whereas if we first consider individual consumptions, then summing up households' consumption choices, strong nonlinearities can emerge.

However, we have to remark that assuming that households can buy fractions of the consumption goods, the differences between the two aggregation procedures (and consequently between the two sets of AD curves) should reduce.

3.5 AGGREGATE SUPPLY

Similarly to the AD curve case, we simulate the model till a certain period t and then perform the simulation perturbation to the price of goods. Differently from the previous case, to have a change in the goods production, we have to change the expectations at time $t - 1$ about the price of goods at time t. Indeed, firms' production is related to their capital that is used to employ workers. Firms' capital for financing production is equal to the sum of equity and debt. Given the equity accumulated by a firm in a given period, changing the level of debt is the only way to modify overall production. Debt is related to the firm's desired leverage, which, in turn, is a function of the expected price (and of the inventories, that is, previous period unsold goods), which determines the expected profit: if the expected profit is above the interest rate paid on the debt, then the firm asks for more debt to banks in order to expand the production, and vice versa. Therefore, we introduce a shock by multiplying the expected price by a factor ranging from 1.1 (+10%) to 0.9 (−10%) with step 1%. The shock modifies the expected profit, and it can modify the desired debt and, finally, the production. Model simulation shows that a nonlinear AS curve emerges and that it is less sloping than the AD. However, this is not a too strong result: in the mainstream framework, the AS curve is often represented as vertical because the supply side is tied to structural features of the economy.

Let us explain the features that can create a nonlinear AS curve in more detail. Firstly, as already said, in this simple model the shock does not affect firm's equity (which is endogenously determined as accumulated retained profits) but only its debt. Moreover, the target leverage changes only by one step upward or downward: just to make an example, if in the baseline simulation the desired leverage of firm i is decreasing and needs a shock of +5% of expected prices to pass from reduction to increase, then a shock of +4% is ineffective, and a shock of +10% is exactly equal to the shock of +5%. However, in this respect the mechanism is very similar to the one that concerns household in the AD construction. Secondly, the target leverage change cannot modify the firm's supply if the additional money is not enough to hire at least one more worker. This feature can also be affected by the matching in the labor market. Thirdly, the supply of goods changes by steps equal to workers' productivity, which is supposed to be a constant parameter in the model. In other words, in our baseline setting with a fixed workers' productivity equal to three, hiring a new worker implies an increase of three units of produced goods. Fourthly, the distributed credit can decrease (increase) when the target leverage increases (decreases). This peculiar feature can be caused by the matching mechanism. If one or more smaller firms increase their leverage and ask credit to a large and liquid bank first, and receive the required debt, then they can reduce the supply of the bank's credit to bigger firms. Therefore, a bigger firm can be forced to go to other small banks that can lend only a small amount in order to comply to the regulatory rules (in particular, in the model a maximum for the amount lent to a single counterpart is set), and the large firm can be credit rationed, decreasing the overall lent

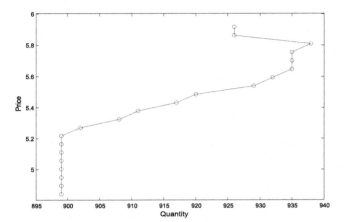

FIGURE 3.4 AS curve.

credit in the economic system. This feature can even generate a nonmonotonic AS curve.

Lastly, there is a fixed number of households, and the total supply cannot go beyond the production related to the full employment. However, this feature is realistic and is also present in the short/medium-run AS curve of the mainstream framework.

In the light of all the enumerated features that can create nonlinearities, the nonmonotonic AS curve emerging at the selected time t is not surprising (see Fig. 3.4).

3.6 AD-AS (DIS)EQUILIBRIUM

In the mainstream framework the economy is located at the intersection between the AD and AS curves, that is, at the equilibrium point. Now, we show that the economy is usually out of the equilibrium point in a continuous dynamic process of fluctuation, which often makes the economy tunes around a quasi-steady-state (but it can also make the economy to radically diverge from this kind of equilibrium).

Fig. 3.5 shows the AD and AS curves in the same graph. The AD curves resulting from both methods that consider the individual demands for goods consumption are represented.

The figure highlights some features. Firstly, the AS curve is less sloping than the AD. As already observed in the previous section, even if this characteristic is due to some debatable model assumptions, then it is a plausible characteristic common to our framework and the mainstream one: indeed, the supply side is tied to structural features of the economy that cannot be modified rapidly; there-

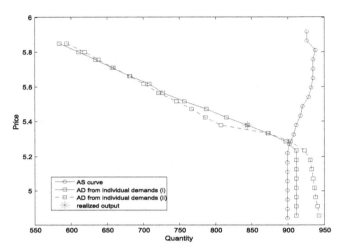

FIGURE 3.5 AD and AS curves.

fore, the AS is often represented as a vertical or almost vertical curve. Secondly, the realized level of goods exchange on the market, represented as a red (gray in print version) star, is located on the AD continuous line by definition because it is built by joining the squares that represent the simulation output. A potential demand excess cannot be seen by looking at this line. Instead, the dotted AD is a proxy of the other line with the advantage of not being constrained by the total supply (as already explained), but with the possibility that the realized number of trades can be slightly different (even on the right of the curve, as in this case). Thirdly, the realized price level corresponds to a point on the AS curve, that is, the level at which the AD depicted as a continuous line is constrained by the total supply.

At the selected time t (as it happens very frequently), there is an excess supply (with the consequent presence of inventories). This is the main feature: the actual realization, that is, the couple of price and quantity, which emerges from the model simulation, is not on the intersection between the two curves. The economic system is in a dynamic disequilibrium that continuously fluctuates. However, the gap between demand and supply, which causes the excess supply, is smaller if we consider the output production instead of the supply, as shown by Fig. 3.6. Indeed, goods production and supply are two parallel lines, where the supply is simply the production plus the previous period inventories. In this context, we can consider a sort of disequilibrium around an implicit null value of inventories (that is, the intersection of the AD and AS curves) or a sort of disequilibrium around a quite stable but positive number of inventories, which implies a coherent value of production and demand.

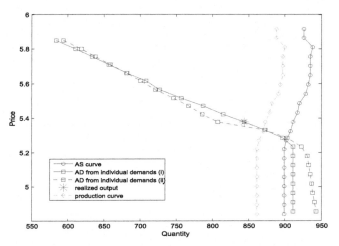

FIGURE 3.6 AD-AS curves and the line representing the goods production (dotted line, with rhombuses).

In conclusion, the AD-AS representation we have described highlights that the economic system is almost always out of equilibrium, without the need of an external shock, along a continuous process of dynamic fluctuation.

REFERENCES

[1] C. Allsopp, D. Vines, The assessment: macroeconomic policy, Oxford Review of Economic Policy 16 (4) (2000) 1–32.

[2] B. Bernanke, M. Gertler, S. Gilchrist, The financial accelerator in a quantitative business cycle framework, in: J. Taylor, M. Woodford (Eds.), Handbook of Macroeconomics, vol. 1, North Holland, Amsterdam, 1999.

[3] O. Blanchard, Macroeconomics, 7th edition, Pearson, 2017.

[4] D. Delli Gatti, M. Gallegati, B. Greenwald, A. Russo, J. Stiglitz, The financial accelerator in an evolving credit network, Journal of Economic Dynamics and Control 34 (9) (2010) 1627–1650.

[5] M. Frank, V. Goyal, Tradeoff and pecking order theories of debt, in: B. Espen Eckbo (Ed.), The Handbook of Empirical Corporate Finance, North Holland, Amsterdam, 2008.

[6] M. Frank, V. Goyal, The profits-leverage puzzle revisited, Review of Finance (2014) 1–39.

[7] M. Kumhof, R. Ranciere, P. Winant, Inequality, leverage and crises, The American Economic Review (2015) 1217–1245.

[8] L. Riccetti, A. Russo, M. Gallegati, Leveraged network-based financial accelerator, Journal of Economic Dynamics and Control 37 (8) (2013) 1626–1640.

[9] L. Riccetti, A. Russo, M. Gallegati, Unemployment benefits and financial leverage in an agent based macroeconomic model, Economics: The Open-Access, Open-Assessment E-Journal 37 (8) (2013) 1626–1640.

[10] L. Riccetti, A. Russo, M. Gallegati, An agent-based decentralized matching macroeconomic model, Journal of Economic Interaction and Coordination 10 (2) (2015) 305–332.

[11] L. Riccetti, A. Russo, M. Gallegati, Financialisation and crisis in an agent based macroeconomic model, Economic Modelling 52 (PA) (2016) 162–172.

[12] L. Riccetti, A. Russo, M. Gallegati, Financial regulation and endogenous macroeconomic crises, Macroeconomic Dynamics (2017), forthcoming.

[13] A. Russo, L. Riccetti, M. Gallegati, Increasing inequality, consumer credit and financial fragility in an agent based macroeconomic model, Journal of Evolutionary Economics 26 (1) (2016) 25–47.

Chapter 4

Heterogeneity in Macroeconomics: DSGE and Agent-Based Model Approach

Federico Giri
Marche Polytechnic University, Ancona, Italy

4.1 INTRODUCTION

The analysis of heterogeneity is nowadays one of the cornerstones of modern economics. This was not always the case at the beginning of the economic discipline. Classical economists such as Adam Smith or David Ricardo were more interested in understanding aggregate relations at the macrolevel than developing a proper theory to explain the behavior of economic agents at the individual level. Only at the end of the 19th century, the so-called *marginal revolution* [43], shifted the attention of the discipline toward the microlevel aspects of economic decisions. Nevertheless, the newborn branch of economics discipline, called *Microeconomics*, turned its primary attention on the formalization of the behavior of an "average" representative agent that could synthesize the main features of the economic decisions of all the individuals. Heterogeneity among individuals sat on a bench for more than fifty years while Microeconomics and Macroeconomics went along their separate path. Macroeconomics continued to focus its interest on aggregate relation (Keynes's *General Theory*, [36], is the classical example) while, at the same time, Microeconomics developed a more sophisticated way to describe the individual behavior as the game theory [44].

The only notable exception was the contribution of Ramsey [46], who developed a (microfounded, as we call it today) model of saving where the decision of consumption and saving boiled down from the utility maximization of the representative consumer. At the end of the 1970s, it became the building block of the modern Dynamic Stochastic General Equilibrium model and of the modern macroeconomics.

During the 1960s, under the supervision of the *Cowles commission*, the economic profession tried to estimate the first aggregate structural macroeconometric models. As reported by Fair [21], the most notable example of a model

Introduction to Agent-Based Economics. http://dx.doi.org/10.1016/B978-0-12-803834-5.00006-0

inspired by the *Cowles commission* directives was the model proposed by Klein and Goldberger [38]. According to Vroey and Malgrange [54], the work of Klein and Goldberger was directed to produce an empirical and testable model based on Keynes *General Theory*. The further extension like Fromm and Klein [24] expanded the original model including more than 400 equations.

During the 1970s, the capacity of the old macroeconometric models based on the philosophy of the *Cowles commission* was questioned by their inability to explain some of the new stylized facts that emerged during the great inflation. One of the pillar of the Keynesian tradition was the existence of a trade-off relationship between inflation and unemployment. Under this framework, the government authorities were always capable of reducing the unemployment, using, for instance, the fiscal policy, at the cost of a higher inflation rate. The oil shocks of the 1970s shattered these beliefs and undermined all the policy conclusions obtained with the state-of-the-art macroeconomics model of the 1960s.

The strongest criticism to the *Cowles commission* modeling and estimation approach boiled down from a group of economists headed by Robert Lucas. The so-called *Lucas critique* severely undermined at the bases the fundamental principle of macroeconometric model built following the *Cowles commission* approach. In his paper *Understanding the business cycles*, Robert Lucas said:

> *Yet the ability of a model to imitate actual behavior in the way tested by the Adelmans (1959) has almost nothing to do with its ability to make accurate conditional forecasts, to answer questions of the form: how would behavior have differed had certain policies been different in specified ways? This ability requires invariance of the structure of the model under policy variations of the type being studied. Invariance of parameters in an economic model is not, of course, a property which can be assured in advance, but it seems reasonable to hope that neither tastes nor technology vary systematically with variations in countercyclical policies. In contrast, agents' decision rules will in general change with changes in the environment. An equilibrium model is, by definition, constructed so as to predict how agents with stable tastes and technology will choose to respond to a new situation. Any disequilibrium model, constructed by simply codifying the decision rules which agents have found it useful to use over some previous sample period, without explaining why these rules were used, will be of no use in predicting the consequences of nontrivial policy changes.*
>
> [42, p. 12]

The failure of aggregate macroeconomic model in explaining the great inflation of the 1970s fostered the birth of a new generation of models called *Real Business Cycles*. The starting point of this new research agenda was to pose great emphasis on defining a structure of preference for the agent populating the economy. The new macroeconomic models were developed following the strong conviction that the only way of producing solid results was to derive the aggregate behavior from the microbehavior of the single agents. In order to do that, the character of the *representative agents* became a key figure in the macroeconomic model.

Curiously, almost at the same time, technological progress and new dataset availability at individual level allowed us to highlight a very important feature of microdata: they were full of heterogeneity! The 2000 Nobel prize winner James Heckman was the pioneer of this new branch of microeconomics called *microeconometrics*. In his Nobel lecture, he emphasized the pervasive role of heterogeneity on defining economic relation:

> *Microeconometrics extended the Cowles theory by building richer economic models where heterogeneity of agents plays a fundamental role and where the equations being estimated are more closely linked to individual data and individual choice models. At its heart, economic theory is about individuals and their interactions in markets or other social settings. The data needed to test the micro theory are micro data. The econometric literature on the aggregation problem (Theil, 1954; see, e.g., Green, 1964, or Fisher, 1969 for surveys) demonstrated the fragility of aggregate data for inferring either the size or the sign of microrelationships.*
>
> [29, p. 5]

Nevertheless, for several years, the role of heterogeneity was forgotten by macroeconomists, especially when we had to deal with macroeconomic models. Only at the end of the 1980s, there was a first attempt to reintroduce heterogeneity into a Dynamic General Equilibrium framework [33].

The purpose of this chapter is to review the role of heterogeneity in macroeconomics and to present the more recent advances in this field of research. The chapter is organized as follows: Section 4.2 presents a standard RBC model with representative agent. Section 4.3 extends the RBC framework taking into account heterogeneity. Section 4.3.2 presents a practical shortcut to deal with heterogeneity in the context of representative agents with a special focus on financial markets. Section 4.4 introduces the Agent-Based model and its difference with respect to the optimizing agent framework. Section 4.5 concludes.

4.2 THE REPRESENTATIVE AGENT PARADIGM

Following [41], the problem of a representative agent can be formalized as follows:

$$\max_{c_t, l_t} E_t \left\{ \sum_{t=0}^{\infty} \beta^t U(c_t, 1 - l_t) \right\}. \tag{4.1}$$

The representative agent has to maximize his utility function over time. He enjoys consumption and dislikes to work preferring leisure. The weight β is assigned by the consumer to future utility, the so-called intertemporal discount factor. Moreover, he has to obey to the intertemporal budget constraint where the left-hand side of Eq. (4.2) represents the household expenditure, and the right-hand side represents the sources of income:

$$c_t + a_{t+1} = w_t l_t + (1 + r_t) a_t. \tag{4.2}$$

Solving the dynamic optimization problem allows us to obtain the *optimal* decision rules with respect to consumption and labor supply

$$U_t^c = \beta E_t \left\{ U_{t+1}^c (1 + r_{t+1}) \right\}, \tag{4.3}$$

$$w_t = \frac{U_t^l}{U_t^c}. \tag{4.4}$$

Eq. (4.3) is the so-called *Euler equation of consumption*. It gives us the optimal consumption path over time. Eq. (4.4) represents the household labor/leisure decision trade-off. The supply side of the economy is represented by a representative firm that maximizes its profits function

$$\Pi_t = F(K_t, L_t) - r_t K_t - w_t L_t. \tag{4.5}$$

From the maximization problem of the representative firm we obtain the demand function of labor and capital, which are equal their respective marginal returns

$$r_t = F_k(K_t, L_t), \tag{4.6}$$

$$w_t = F_L(K_t, L_t). \tag{4.7}$$

The model is closed with the following equilibrium condition, which says that the aggregate variables are equal to the one of the representative agent:

$$c_t = C_t, \tag{4.8}$$

$$a_t = K_t, \tag{4.9}$$

$$l_t = L_t, \tag{4.10}$$

$$C_t + I_t = Y_t. \tag{4.11}$$

Eq. (4.9) is a pretty standard in RBC setup. It says that the aggregate capital stock is equal to the savings of the representative household. As we will see, calculating the aggregate capital stock will be trickier in the context of hetero-geneous optimizing agents.

In general terms, the RBC problem can be written as

$$E_t \mathcal{F}(X_{t+1}, X_t, \epsilon_t, \theta) = 0, \tag{4.12}$$

which is a dynamic nonlinear system of difference equations; X is a vector of state variables, ϵ_t contains all the exogenous shocks of the model, and θ is a vector of "deep parameters." This system can be solved using several different techniques (see [2] for a complete review and comparison). However, the solu-tion of such a system can be formalized as

$$X_t = \mathcal{G}(X_{t-1}, \epsilon_t, \theta). \tag{4.13}$$

Eq. (4.13) represents the so-called *policy functions*, that is, the optimal behav-ioral rules of the representative agent. This structure will be a common ground to analyze both rational heterogeneous and Agent-Based models.

Despite the common consensus around the new neoclassical synthesis, the representative rational agent paradigm was criticized over the years under sev-eral aspects. Forni and Lippi [23] attacked the idea of the representative agents defining it as misleading when we want to tackle aggregate relation. For in-stance, microdata that show evidence of cointegration at microlevel cannot present the same features at macrolevel and vice versa making the exercise of inferring the macrobehavior from microfounded model fruitless. As a con-sequence, all the restrictions (both in SVAR and DSGE models) imposed to identify microrelation can result in completely wrong description at aggregate level.

Another source of criticism is the assumption of perfect rationality assumed in the RBC kind of model. The seminal contributions of Simon [51], Sar-gent [50], and Kahneman [34] in the field of experimental economics proofed that the hypothesis of rational expectation is hardly defensible at empirical/ex-perimental level underlined as the human behavior can be better described by some kind of *bounded rationality*.

4.3 MACROECONOMICS AND HETEROGENEITY

4.3.1 The Optimizing Heterogeneous Agents Framework

Despite the common belief, *mainstream* macroeconomics has recognized the importance of heterogeneity to describe several stylized facts of macroeco-nomics. The Aiyagari [1] model was one of the first attempts to introduce hetero-geneity into a neoclassical growth model within a standard rational expectation framework. In the Aiyagari [1] model the key innovation is the introduction of an infinite number of consumers: they are ex ante all equal but they are ex post different since they have a different (stochastic) labor endowment to employ every period in the labor market. As a consequence, the capacity of accumulate savings varies across the whole population living the economy. Following the notation of Guvenen [27], the problem can be formalized as follows:

$$\max_{c_t} E_0 \sum_{t=0}^{\infty} \beta^t U(c_t) \tag{4.14}$$

subject to the individual balance sheet constraint

$$c_t + a_{t+1} = w_t l_t + (1 + r_t) a_t. \tag{4.15}$$

Moreover, the individual consumer has to obey to a borrowing constraint limit

$$a_t \geq -B_{\min}. \tag{4.16}$$

The labor endowment l_t evolves according to a Markov chain process. The supply side is constituted by a standard representative firm that determines its labor and capital demand according to the marginal return of both production factor:

$$r_t = F_K(K_t, L_t), \tag{4.17}$$

$$w_t = F_L(K_t, L_t). \tag{4.18}$$

The aggregate capital stock is defined as

$$K = \sum_{\epsilon \in \{e,u\}} \int_{a_{\min}}^{\infty} a \Phi(a, \epsilon) da. \tag{4.19}$$

To forecast the future path of prices, individual agents have to know the aggregate capital stock of the economy. In a standard representative agent model, the problem can be solved in a trivial way since individual savings and aggregate capital stock coincide. The introduction of heterogeneity among agents introduces a further complication in the forecasting of future prices. In the heterogeneous agents setup the aggregate capital stock depends on the related distributions of savings across individual consumers. To forecast future prices, every single agent has to take into account into his decision rule not only his singular behavior but also the behavior of the all continuum of the other agents in the economy. The distribution of savings became a crucial element of the optimization problem with heterogeneous agents. The consumer's problem in recursive formulation can be described as

$$V(a, l, \Phi) = \max u(c) + \beta \sum_{h' \in H^t} \pi(l'|l) V(a', h', \Phi') \qquad (4.20)$$

subject to

$$c + a' = w(\Phi)l + (1 + r(\Phi))a, \qquad (4.21)$$

$$\Phi' = H(\Phi), \qquad (4.22)$$

where F is the law of motion of *wealth distribution*. The employment status evolves according to a first-order Markov chain

$$\pi(l'|l) = \begin{bmatrix} p_{uu} & p_{ue} \\ p_{eu} & p_{ee} \end{bmatrix}.$$

The solution of such an optimization problem poses several challenges in terms of computational issues. In general, the policy function of such a problem can be written as

$$c_t = g(a_t, l_t, \Phi_t(a_t, l_t)). \qquad (4.23)$$

The real issue is how to treat the distribution of wealth inside the policy function? By definition Φ_t is an infinite-dimensional object that depends on the number of state variables of the model. Over the years, several numerical algorithms have been developed to approximate Φ_t. A detailed exposition is beyond the scope is this survey, and the interested reader can refer to Den Haan [16] for a deeper description of the solution algorithm.

In general, the approximation of the distribution of wealth is made assuming that the agents are *bounded rational* and that they are not able to understand the entire distribution. For instance, [40] allows each individual to know only the first moment of the wealth distribution. The solution and the related decision rule can be written as

$$c_t = g(a_t, l_t, m'\{\Phi_t()\}), \qquad (4.24)$$

where m' is the first moment of the wealth distribution. More generally, the decision rules of a rationale expectation model with heterogeneous agents can be described as

$$X_t = \mathcal{G}(X_{t-1}, \epsilon_t, m'[\Phi_t(X, \epsilon_{t_1})], \theta), \qquad (4.25)$$

where X_t is a vector of endogenous states, ϵ_t is a vector of exogenous shocks, and θ is a vector of parameters. One of the main disadvantages of the heterogeneous agent rational expectation framework is the computational complexity of finding a solution of the problem even in approximate form. In fact, the cost of computing the approximation of distribution Φ increases together with the number of states variables contained in the model. A modern medium-scale DSGE model like [53] or [8] contained dozens of state variables making virtually impossible to introduce heterogeneity in such framework.

4.3.2 Dealing With Heterogeneity Within the Representative Agent Framework: The Case of Financial Markets

After the 2007 financial crisis, one of the major advancements in the DSGE model literature was the introduction of the financial markets inside the otherwise standard New Keynesian framework. As stated by Quadrini [45], heterogeneity is an essential feature to describe the borrower/lender relation. In fact, both Bernanke et al. [5] and Kiyotaki and Moore [37] frameworks are built upon a heterogeneous agent framework even if the two approaches are slightly different: The Kiyotaki and Moore [37] model assumes the existence of two different types of representative agents, borrowers, and savers, who have, for instance, different kinds of preferences. Alternatively, Bernanke et al. [5] assume that there is a continuum of agents, but the linearity of preference and technologies allow us to obtain a model with only workers and entrepreneurs [45, p. 215].

The financial accelerator framework is built upon a New Keynesian Model with price stickiness that allows the possibility of credit relations between the households and the entrepreneurs. In this context, households are net savers, and they transfer resources to the deficit operators, the entrepreneurs. The entrepreneurs use the acquired funds from the households to purchase physical capital used in the production of the intermediate goods. The intermediate goods are bought by the final goods producers and sold to the households. The key equation of the entire mechanism is

$$E_t[R_{t+1}^k] = s\left(\frac{N_{t+1}^j}{Q_t K_{t+1}^j}\right) R_t, \qquad (4.26)$$

where R_{t+1}^k is the cost of external funding for the entrepreneurs. It depends strongly on the N_{t+1}^j, which is the accumulated net worth. The higher is the entrepreneurs capacity of financing the purchase of capital with his own funds, the lowest is the burden of external finance premium. They justify the existence of an external premium embedding an agency cost problem, previously proposed by Carlstrom and Fuerst [6], into a fully microfounded NKM.

The other common approach to introduce a credit market friction into a dynamic model is the strategy followed by Kiyotaki and Moore [37]. Iacoviello

[32] extended the Kiyotachi model adding two new features to the old framework. First, the collateral used by entrepreneurs to obtain external funds is no longer land, but the possibilities of borrowing are tied to the house stock owned by the entrepreneurs. The basic model is made of patient households, intermediate entrepreneurs, final goods retailers, and the monetary authority. In every period, patient households choose consumption, the house endowment, the labor supply, and the quantity of real money to detain. Since they are net savers, they lend in real terms a quantity b_t to the intermediate firms, and they get back an amount of resources equal to $R_{t-1}b_{t-1}$, where R is the nominal interest rate on loans. The patient households have to maximize the following objective function:

$$\max E_0 \sum_{t=0}^{\infty} \beta^t \left(\ln c'_t + j \ln h'_t - \frac{(L'_t)^{\eta}}{\eta} + \chi \ln \left(\frac{M'_t}{P'_t} \right) \right) \tag{4.27}$$

subject to the budget constraint

$$c'_t + q_t \Delta h'_t + \frac{R_{t-1}b'_{t-1}}{\pi_t} = b'_t + w^i_t L'_t + F_t + T'_t - \Delta \frac{M'_t}{P_t}. \tag{4.28}$$

On the other hand, the entrepreneurs are net debtors, and they maximize the following objective function:

$$\max E_0 \sum_{t=0}^{\infty} \gamma^t \left(\ln C_t \right) \tag{4.29}$$

subject to a budget and borrowing constraints. The flow of funds could be represented by the following expression:

$$\frac{Y_t}{X_t} + b_t = c_t + q_t \Delta h_t + \frac{R_{t-1}b_{t-1}}{\pi_t} + w'_t L_t, \tag{4.30}$$

where Y_t is the classical Cobb–Douglas production function

$$Y_t = A \left(h_{t-1} \right)^{\upsilon} \left(L_t \right)^{1-\upsilon}. \tag{4.31}$$

The borrowing constraint is similar to that proposed by Kiyotaki and Moore [37]:

$$b_t \leq m E_t \left(\frac{q_{t+1} h_t \pi_{t+1}}{R_t} \right). \tag{4.32}$$

The meaning of the previous expression is straightforward. The intermediate firm could accumulate a debt, which must be less than or at least equal to the future (real) value of the owned houses. The presence of the borrowing constraint slightly modifies the usual form of the Euler equation for both consumption and houses demand. Savers and borrowers have a similar objective function, but they differ for their degree of impatience. Heterogeneity is introduced assuming a different intertemporal discount factor for savers and borrowers. Imposing $\beta^t > \gamma^t$ ensures that patient households are net savers. At the end of the story, heterogeneity is introduced ex ante imposing a different set of preferences for savers and borrowers.

A relatively recent stream of literature tried to introduce heterogeneity into the banking sector in the otherwise standard DSGE model with financial frictions (see, among others, [26,18,25,30,7]). The modeling philosophy is quite close to that used to describe the savers–borrowers relation into standard DSGE model. The starting assumption is a limited participation constraint (see [45]) that creates ex ante heterogeneous banks, namely surplus banks that gather liquidity from the savers and deficit banks that are net debtors on the interbank market and provide funds to the firms. In this sense, [17] is a prominent example of this modeling strategy. In particular, the authors built an RBC model in which they include a fully microfounded interbank market in which a deposit bank raises savings from the households and decides the amount of resource to allocate between the interbank market and the corporate investment market. The maximization program of the surplus bank is synthesized by the expression

$$
\max_{I_t^l, D_t^l, B_t^l, F_t^l, \pi_t^l} \sum_{s=0}^{\infty} E_t \left(\beta^s \left[\log(\pi_{t+s}) + d_{fl} \left[F_{t+s}^l - k \left(\overline{w}_{t+s} I_{t+s}^l + \tilde{w}_{t+s} B_{t+s}^l \right) \right] \right] \right)
$$

(4.33)

subject to a series of constraints

$$
F_t^l = (1 - \zeta_l) F_{t-1}^l + v_l \pi_t,
$$

(4.34)

$$
\pi_t^l = \delta_t I_{t-1}^l + \frac{D_t^l}{1 + r_t^l} - D_{t-1}^l - \frac{I_t^l}{1 + i_t} + \zeta_l (1 - \delta_{t-1}) I_{t-2}^l + (1 - \rho_t) B_t^l - B_t^l.
$$

(4.35)

The variable π represents the profit function for the deposits bank, whereas Eq. (4.34) describes the dynamics of the own funds possessed by the bank. The surplus bank receives an interest rate equal to i_t on its interbank loans I_t^l, and it has to pay an interest rate r_t on the deposits provided by the households; δ_t is the time-varying default rate on the interbank market loans; ζ and v are two parameters representing respectively the depreciation rate of the internal funds and the share of profits used to accumulate new capital in the next period.

The parameter k represents the coverage ratio of risky asset, and it fixes the minimum amount of own funds the bank have to possess. It is influenced by the two parameters $\overline{\omega}$ and $\tilde{\omega}$, which are the weight assign respectively to the loans to firms and the market books.

The merchant banks are net borrowers on the interbank market. They maximize a function that resembles to the previous one:

$$\max_{\delta_t, I_t^b, L_t^b, B_t^b, F_t^b, \pi_t^b} \sum_{s=0}^{\infty} E_t \left(\beta^s \left[\log(\pi_{t+s}) - d_b \left(1 - \delta_{t+s} \right) \right. \right.$$
$$\left. \left. + d_{fb} \left[F_{t+s}^b - k \left(\overline{w}_{t+s} I_{t+s}^b + \tilde{w}_{t+s} B_{t+s}^b \right) \right] \right] \right) \tag{4.36}$$

subject to a series of constraints

$$F_t^b = (1 - \zeta_b) F_{t-1}^b + v_b \pi_b, \tag{4.37}$$

$$\pi_t^b = \alpha_t L_{t-1}^b + \frac{I_t^b}{1 + i_t^l} - \delta_t I_{t-1}^l - \frac{\omega_b}{2} \left[(1 - \delta_{t-1}) I_{t-2}^b \right]^2 + \zeta_b (1 - \alpha_{t-1}) L_{t-2}^b$$
$$+ (1 - \rho_t) B_t^b - B_t^b. \tag{4.38}$$

The variable L_t^b represents the entrepreneurial loans provided by the merchant banks to the firms. Besides L_t^b, the other choice variables for the merchant banks are the amount of interbank loans I_t^b, their own funds F_t^b, the default rate on the interbank market borrowing δ_t^b, the associated disutility cost d_b in the objective function of the bank, and the share of defaulted credit from the firms α.

Gertler and Kiyotaki [25] refined this limited market participation linking the liquidity position of the banks to the arrival of new investment projects. They developed a model with financial frictions including an interbank market. In their framework the financial market is structured as follows. At the first stage, there is a retail market in which banks can gather deposits from the households. After that, investing opportunity arrives at the banks. Banks and nonfinancial firms live in two different islands. In every period, banks can exploit investments opportunity with probability π_t. Banks with new investment opportunity need gather liquidity becoming net debtors on the interbank market. Banks that receive an excess of investment project go into the interbank market and raise interbank funds at the wholesale level, whereas the banks on the other island became net lenders. The credit market closes when the debtor pays back the banks on the other islands. The model could be used to represent a situation in which banks are not willing to lend each other. To generate an endogenous constraint on the capability of raising funds both at retails and wholesale level, the author embeds a simple agency cost problem into the bankers maximization problem.

Bankers can divert part of the resources obtained from the market for their own purposes. This mechanism can generate a collapse of the interbank market with repercussions over the entire economy. Formally, the problem of the bankers can be represented as

$$V_t = \max E_t \sum_{t=0}^{\infty} (1 - \sigma) \sigma^{t-1} \Lambda_t \eta_t^h, \tag{4.39}$$

where Λ is the usual consumption-based intertemporal discount factor, and η is the net wealth of the banks defined as

$$\eta_t^h = \left[Z_t + (1 - \delta) Q_t^h \right] \psi_t s_{t-1} - R_{b,t} b_{t-1} - R_t d_{t-1}, \tag{4.40}$$

where Z_t are the dividends obtained from the loans, Q_t^h is the price of the financial claims, and s, b, and d are the assets, the interbank liabilities, and the deposits gather from the savers. Banks have to obey the following balance sheet constraint:

$$Q_t^h s_t = \eta_t^h + b_t^h + d_t. \tag{4.41}$$

Besides, banks have to satisfy the following incentive constraint:

$$V(s_t^h, b_t^h, d_t) \geq \theta (Q_t^h s_t^h - \omega b_t^h). \tag{4.42}$$

Eq. (4.42) is a key equation of the model; θ gives us the quantity of assets that bankers could divert in their own favor. We could also interpret $1 - \theta$ as the quantity of credit that lending bank could obtain back after the default of the debtors. The total amount of divertible assets is defined as $(Q_t^h s_t^h - \omega b_t^h)$. The parameter ω measures the degree of interbank market friction in the system, and it is bounded: $0 \leq \omega \leq 1$. When ω assumes the value 1, we are in the case frictionless interbank market. In this case the lending bank could recover all the loans, and, as a consequence, the deficit bank is not constraint on the interbank market. Setting up the Bellman equation, we obtain

$$
\begin{aligned}
&V_{t-1}(s_{t-1}^h, b_{t-1}^h, d_{t-1}) \\
&= E_{t-1} \Lambda_{t-1,t} \sum_{h=,i,n} \pi^h \left\{ (1 - \sigma) \eta_t^h + \sigma \max_{d_t} \left[\max_{s_t, b_t} V_t(s_t^h, b_t^h, d_t) \right] \right\},
\end{aligned}
\tag{4.43}
$$

where π represents the probability of new investment opportunities for the banks. As we said before, these are the financial intermediaries that have to go in the interbank market to find new resource to finance the investment project of the firms of their island. Consequently, $(1 - \pi)$ is the probability of not receiving any kind of investment request.

4.4 THE AGENT-BASED MODEL PROPOSAL

The agent-based methodology became very popular in the last few years, and this kind of framework is already used to analyze a macroeconomic scenario and to evaluate policies. For instance, Delli Gatti et al. [15] explore the role of monetary policy including agent's learning; Russo et al. [48] focus on fiscal policy and its effect on R&D dynamics; Haber [28] and Dosi et al. [20] investigate the effects of both fiscal and monetary policies; Cincotti et al. [9,10] investigate macroeconomic instability and the role of deleveraging; Babutsidze [4] analyzes the implications for monetary policy of price-setting; Cincotti et al. [11] analyze the role of banking regulation finding that both unregulated financial systems and overly restrictive regulations have destabilizing effects; Dosi et al. [19] consider the interplay between income distribution and economic policies; Salle et al. [49] focus on monetary policy and inflation targeting; da Silva and Lima [12] study the interplay between the monetary policy rate and financial regulation; Krug et al. [39] evaluate the impact of Basel III on financial instability; Ashraf et al. [3] analyze the impact of the trend rate of inflation on macroeconomic performance; Riccetti et al. [47] explore the effects of banking regulation on financial stability and endogenous macroeconomic crises. All in all, ABMs represent an alternative approach for studying a complex macroeconomy that may highlight relevant implications for economic policy design [13]. Given the blossoming of contributions in this field, a comparison between the standard DSGE setting became a natural experiment. However, given deep differences between the two approaches, this is not an easy task at all. In fact, in a recent paper, [31, p. 20] defined an Agent-based model "... the polar opposite to that of DSGE."

Chris Sims once referred to Bayesian statistics: "Bayesian inference is a way of thinking, not a basket of methods" [22, p. 8]. The same analogy can be applied to the Agent-Based model framework. The ABMs are more than a simple technique, and their economic theory background is deeply different from the standard neoclassical approach of DSGE models. In general, ABM modeling is based on two pillars:

- The representative agent hypothesis is removed.
- Optimizing rational agents leave place to simple behavior.

The two previous points together described a very different setup with respect to the dynamic general equilibrium model. Nevertheless, from a technical point of view, it can be interesting to compare the structure of an ABM with a DSGE model.

Following Dilaver et al. [55], the general form of a standard Agent-based model can be written as

$$X_t = \mathcal{G}(X_{t-1}, \epsilon_{t-1}, \theta), \tag{4.44}$$

which is very similar to Eq. (4.25). However, the process that allows us to obtain equations (4.25) and (4.44) is very different. The former is obtained from a maximization problem, whereas the latter are rule-of-thumbs behavioral rules. Differently from rational expectation model, the behavioral decision rules are more flexible than the optimal rules implied by the optimizing framework. For instance, assuming *myopic* allowing agents to behave accordingly to simple rules is a way to circumvent the problem of approximating the distribution of wealth. Under this assumption, it is unnecessary to include any elements of the distribution of wealth.

Despite the growing stream of literature in the field of Agent-based macroeconomics, very few contributions tried to compare the two frameworks and, more importantly, to include elements of one setup into the other. On the other hand, mainstream macroeconomics seems to look at Agent-Based model as a potential stimulus to introduce new elements into the otherwise standard optimizing framework. For instance, De Grauwe [14] tried to include both heterogeneity and bounded rationality in an otherwise standard New Keynesian model. Other scholars tried to reconcile optimizing agents with some degrees of "irrationality." Sims [52] introduced the concept of *irrational inattention*: agents are rational optimizing agents but they are bounded by the flow of information they can process to make their decision.

On the heterogeneity part of the story, Kaplan et al. [35] built a New Keynesian model with heterogeneous agents founding relevant difference with respect to the representative agent version. The representative agent story shows the predominant role of interest rates in the transmission mechanism of monetary policy through the consumption smoothing. The heterogeneous agent version emphasizes the role of general equilibrium mechanism through an indirect variation of labor demand as a consequence of a new monetary policy decision. Therefore, heterogeneity seems to be a potential key element to solve some of the macroeconomics puzzle we daily face as modelers.

4.5 CONCLUSION

In this chapter, we reviewed how macroeconomics discipline and heterogeneity interacts during the last thirty years. Despite the common knowledge, *mainstream* Macroeconomics tried to include heterogeneity into rational expectation models in several different ways. However, technical and computational difficulties limited the development of such framework for quite a long time. At the same time, Agent-Based methodology proved to be a valid alternative to deal with complexity and heterogeneity. The hope for future researches is that the interaction between these two different modeling approaches can help us to have a better model in order to have better policy analyses.

REFERENCES

[1] S.R. Aiyagari, Uninsured idiosyncratic risk and aggregate saving, The Quarterly Journal of Economics 109 (3) (August 1994) 659–684.

[2] S.B. Aruoba, J. Fernandez-Villaverde, J.F. Rubio-Ramirez, Comparing solution methods for dynamic equilibrium economies, Journal of Economic Dynamics and Control 30 (12) (December 2006) 2477–2508.

[3] Q. Ashraf, B. Gershman, P. Howitt, How inflation affects macroeconomic performance: an agent-based computational investigation, Macroeconomic Dynamics 20 (Special Issue 02) (2016) 558–581.

[4] Z. Babutsidze, Asymmetric (s, s) pricing: implications for monetary policy, Revue de L'OFCE 124 (2012) 177–204.

[5] B.S. Bernanke, M. Gertler, S. Gilchrist, The financial accelerator in a quantitative business cycle framework, in: J.B. Taylor, M. Woodford (Eds.), Handbook of Macroeconomics, vol. 1, June 1999, pp. 1341–1393, Ch. 21.

[6] C.T. Carlstrom, T.S. Fuerst, Agency costs, net worth, and business fluctuations: a computable general equilibrium analysis, The American Economic Review 87 (5) (December 1997) 893–910.

[7] C. Carrera, H. Vega, Interbank Market and Macroprudential Tools in a DSGE Model, Working Papers 2012-014, Banco Central de Reserva del Perú, June 2012, http://ideas.repec.org/p/rbp/wpaper/2012-014.html.

[8] L.J. Christiano, M. Eichenbaum, C.L. Evans, Nominal rigidities and the dynamic effects of a shock to monetary policy, Journal of Political Economy 113 (1) (February 2005) 1–45.

[9] S. Cincotti, M. Raberto, A. Teglio, Credit money and macroeconomic instability in the agent-based model and simulator EURACE, Economics – The Open-Access, Open-Assessment E-Journal 4 (26) (2010).

[10] S. Cincotti, M. Raberto, A. Teglio, Debt deleveraging and business cycles. An agent-based perspective, Economics – The Open-Access, Open-Assessment E-Journal 6 (27) (2012).

[11] S. Cincotti, M. Raberto, A. Teglio, Macroprudential policies in an agent-based artificial economy, Revue de L'OFCE 124 (2012) 205–234.

[12] M.A. da Silva, G.T. Lima, Combining Monetary Policy and Financial Regulation: An Agent-Based Modeling Approach, Working Paper 394, 2015.

[13] H. Dawid, M. Neugart, Agent-based models for economic policy design, Eastern Economic Journal 37 (1) (2011) 44–50.

[14] P. De Grauwe, Booms and busts in economic activity: a behavioral explanation, Journal of Economic Behavior & Organization 83 (3) (2012) 484–501.

[15] D. Delli Gatti, E. Gaffeo, M. Gallegati, The apprentice wizard: monetary policy, complexity and learning, New Mathematics and Natural Computation 1 (1) (2005) 109–128.

[16] W.J. Den Haan, Comparison of solutions to the incomplete markets model with aggregate uncertainty, Journal of Economic Dynamics and Control 34 (1) (January 2010) 4–27.

[17] G. De Walque, O. Pierrard, A. Rouabah, Financial (in)stability, supervision and liquidity injections: a dynamic general equilibrium approach, The Economic Journal 120 (549) (December 2010) 1234–1261.

[18] A. Dib, Banks, Credit Market Frictions, and Business Cycles, Working Papers 10-24, Bank of Canada, 2010.

[19] G. Dosi, G. Fagiolo, M. Napoletano, A. Roventini, Income distribution, credit and fiscal policies in an agent-based Keynesian model, Journal of Economic Dynamics and Control 37 (8) (2013) 1598–1625.

[20] G. Dosi, G. Fagiolo, M. Napoletano, A. Roventini, T. Treibich, Fiscal and monetary policies in complex evolving economies, Journal of Economic Dynamics and Control 52 (C) (2015) 166–189.

[21] R.C. Fair, The Cowles Commission Approach, Real Business Cycle Theories, and New Keynesian Economics, Working Paper 3990, National Bureau of Economic Research, February 1992.

[22] J. Fernández-Villaverde, The econometrics of DSGE models, SERIEs, Journal of the Spanish Economic Association 1 (1) (March 2010) 3–49.

[23] M. Forni, M. Lippi, Aggregation and the Microfoundations of Dynamic Macroeconomics, No. 9780198288008 in OUP Catalogue, Oxford University Press, May 1997.

[24] G. Fromm, L.R. Klein, The Brookings-s.s.r.c. quarterly econometric model of the United States: model properties, The American Economic Review 55 (1/2) (1965) 348–361.

[25] M. Gertler, N. Kiyotaki, Financial intermediation and credit policy in business cycle analysis, in: B.M. Friedman, M. Woodford (Eds.), Handbook of Monetary Economics, vol. 3, Elsevier, 2010, pp. 547–599, Ch. 11.

[26] C.A.E. Goodhart, C. Osorio, D.P. Tsomocos, Analysis of Monetary Policy and Financial Stability: A New Paradigm, Tech. rep., 2009.

[27] F. Guvenen, Macroeconomics with Heterogeneity: A Practical Guide, Working Paper 17622, National Bureau of Economic Research, November 2011.

[28] G. Haber, Monetary and fiscal policy analysis with an agent-based macroeconomic model, Jahrbucher fur Nationalokonomie und Statistik 228 (2–3) (2008) 276–295.

[29] J.J. Heckman, Micro data, heterogeneity and the evaluation of public policy: Part 1, The American Economist 48 (Fall 2004).

[30] B. Hilberg, J. Hollmayr, Asset Prices, Collateral and Unconventional Monetary Policy in a DSGE Model, Working Paper Series 1373, European Central Bank, August 2011, http://ideas.repec.org/p/ecb/ecbwps/20111373.html.

[31] P. Howitt, What have central bankers learned from modern macroeconomic theory?, Journal of Macroeconomics 34 (1) (2012) 11–22.

[32] M. Iacoviello, House prices, borrowing constraints, and monetary policy in the business cycle, The American Economic Review 95 (3) (June 2005) 739–764.

[33] A. Imrohoroğlu, Cost of business cycles with indivisibilities and liquidity constraints, Journal of Political Economy 97 (6) (1989) 1364–1383.

[34] D. Kahneman, Maps of bounded rationality: psychology for behavioral economics, The American Economic Review 93 (5) (December 2003) 1449–1475.

[35] G. Kaplan, B. Moll, G.L. Violante, Monetary Policy According to HANK, NBER Working Papers 21897, National Bureau of Economic Research, Inc., January 2016.

[36] J.M. Keynes, General Theory of Employment, Interest and Money, Cambridge University Press, 1936.

[37] N. Kiyotaki, J. Moore, Credit cycles, Journal of Political Economy 105 (2) (April 1997) 211–248.

[38] L.R. Klein, A.S. Goldberger, An Econometric Model for the United States, 1929–1952, North-Holland, Amsterdam, 1955.

[39] S. Krug, M. Lengnick, H.-W. Wohltmann, The impact of Basel III on financial (in)stability – an agent-based credit network approach, Quantitative Finance 15 (12) (2015) 1917–1932.

[40] P. Krusell, A.A. Smith Jr., Income and wealth heterogeneity in the macroeconomy, Journal of Political Economy 106 (5) (October 1998) 867–896.

[41] F.E. Kydland, E.C. Prescott, Time to build and aggregate fluctuations, Econometrica 50 (6) (November 1982) 1345–1370.

[42] R.E. Lucas, Understanding business cycles, Carnegie-Rochester Conference Series on Public Policy 5 (1) (January 1977) 7–29.

[43] A. Marshall, Principles of Economics, Macmillan and Co., London, 1920.

[44] J. Nash, The bargaining problem, Econometrica 18 (2) (April 1950) 155–162.

[45] V. Quadrini, Financial frictions in macroeconomic fluctuations, Economic Quarterly 3Q (2011) 209–254.

[46] F.P. Ramsey, A mathematical theory of saving, The Economic Journal 38 (152) (1928) 543–559.

[47] L. Riccetti, A. Russo, M. Gallegati, Financial regulation and endogenous macroeconomic crises, Macroeconomic Dynamics (2017), http://dx.doi.org/10.1017/S1365100516000444.

[48] A. Russo, M. Catalano, E. Gaffeo, M. Gallegati, M. Napoletano, Industrial dynamics, fiscal policy and R&D: evidence from a computational experiment, Journal of Economic Behavior & Organization 64 (3–4) (2007) 426–447.

[49] I. Salle, M. Yildizoglu, M.-A. Sénégas, Inflation targeting in a learning economy: an ABM perspective, Economic Modelling 34 (C) (2013) 114–128.

[50] T. Sargent, Bounded Rationality in Macroeconomics: The Arne Ryde Memorial Lectures, Oxford University Press, 1993.

[51] H.A. Simon, A behavioral model of rational choice, The Quarterly Journal of Economics 69 (1) (1955) 99–118.

[52] C.A. Sims, Rational inattention and monetary economics, in: B.M. Friedman, M. Woodford (Eds.), Handbook of Monetary Economics, vol. 3, Elsevier, 2010, pp. 155–181, Ch. 4.

[53] F. Smets, R. Wouters, Shocks and frictions in US business cycles: a Bayesian DSGE approach, The American Economic Review 97 (3) (June 2007) 586–606.

[54] M.D. Vroey, P. Malgrange, From The Keynesian Revolution to the Klein–Goldberger model: Klein and the dynamization of Keynesian theory, History of Economic Ideas 20 (2) (2012) 113–136.

[55] Ö. Dilaver, R. Jump, P. Levine, Agent-Based Macroeconomics and Dynamic Stochastic General Equilibrium Models: Where Do We Go from Here?, School of Economics Discussion Papers 0116, School of Economics, University of Surrey, January 2016.

Chapter 5

Early Warning Indicator for Crises in an Agent-Based Macromodel

Ermanno Catullo
Marche Polytechnic University, Ancona, Italy

5.1 INTRODUCTION

It is important to make the distinction between two questions: Can we do better at anticipating the crisis? Can we do better at responding to it? On the first question, I would insist that it is too much to expect economists or economic historians to accurately forecast complex contingent events like financial crises. In the 1990s, I did some work on currency crises, instances when exchange rates collapse, with Charles Wyplosz and Andrew Rose. We found that what works on historical data or, in other words, what works in sample does not also work out of sample. We were out-of-consensus skeptics about the usefulness of leading indicators of currency crises, and I think that a subsequent experience has borne out our view. Paul Samuelson made the comment that economists have predicted 13 out of the last seven crises. In other words, there are type 1 error and type 2 errors (the problem of false positives and false negatives).

[8]

The aim of this chapter is to give some insights into the role that agent-based macromodel may play in isolating early warning indicator for crises. Predicting complex events as economic crises is intrinsically problematic. Therefore, we do not try to forecast crises, but we aim at improving our understanding of the conditions that may foster their occurrence. Indeed, early warning indicators may be useful to detect the associations between macro- and meso-dynamics.

In agent-based macromodel, crises are generated endogenously as a consequence of the amplification and diffusion of local shocks to the whole economic systems [5,6,10]. In this chapter, we present a simple agent-based model built on the theoretical framework developed in the so-called "Modellone" [11] and "Modellaccio" [4]. The model describes a closed economy with labor as the

Introduction to Agent-Based Economics. http://dx.doi.org/10.1016/B978-0-12-803834-5.00007-7

unique production factor. Thus, households supply labor to firms that hire labor demand paying it with their net-worth and credit lent by banks, whereas government collects taxes and emits bonds in order to provide public expenditure in the form of money transfer to households. The main difference with respect to the models of [11] and [4] is that we use a "generative" approach for the initialization of the economy. At the beginning of the simulation, there are just households, government injects money in the economy distributing money transfers to households, and this money injection is covered through emitting bonds that are bought by the central bank. Households use part of the money they receive to fund the formation of firms and banks. In the following periods, firms employ workers and produce final goods, whereas banks provide credit to firms and buy bonds from the government.

We isolate early warning indicators of crises from simulated data using a signal methodology [9,2,3,7,1], which considers macro- and meso-variable variations as signals that may anticipate the occurrence of crises. The effectiveness of these signals is valued according to their capacity of reducing the trade-off between hits and false alarms: some signals may anticipate the occurrence of a particular event with high probability (hit probability), but usually they may produce false alarm too, and thus good signals are those that present a high hit probability without incurring in too many false alarms.

Simulated data show that during expansionary phases the seeds for future crises are sowed. Indeed, during expansions, credit growth leads to increasing firm leverage that augments the economic system vulnerability. Moreover, agent-based model dynamics are derived from the interaction of heterogeneous agents, and thus variations of distributional measure of agents' heterogeneity may be associated with business cycle fluctuations. Indeed, in simulated data, when the polarization of firm size distribution increases and thus when few firms assume a central role in the economy, the possibility that a negative shock that hits one of these firms has a significant impact to the banking system and, consequently, to the whole economy increases.

5.2 THE MODEL

The simulated economy is populated by a fixed number H of households, each of them endowed with a unit of labor. Households invest into the formation of firms and banks, and thus households own shares of firms and banks and receive dividends from them. Firms may borrow money from banks to employ workers. Therefore firms use their net-worth and credit to produce different varieties of the same final good. Government public expenditure is made of transfers to families, and it is funded through tax collection and bonds emission. Bonds are bought by banks and by the central bank.

TABLE 5.1 Simulation Parameters

	$\phi_{t=0}$	1.0	
H	200	δ	0.04
l^S	1.0	χ	0.05
r_d	0.0	ζ	0.01
τ	0.4	μ	10.0
c_y	0.8	r_{re}	0.0
c_D	0.2	re_c	0.01
λ_1	0.4	$\bar{r}$	0.005
F	1.0	ξ	0.2
ξ^{IN}	2	$\overline{IN}$	0.0075
ψ	10	β	1.0
A^m	10.0	υ	4.0
χ_B	0.005		

The following subsections describe agents' behaviors: households, firm, banks, government, and central bank. The last subsection illustrates interaction mechanisms. The list of the parameters of the baseline simulation is shown in Table 5.1.

5.2.1 Agents

5.2.1.1 Households

Each household supplies a given quantity of labor (l^S). They may be employed in different firms (l_{hit} with $l_{ht} = \sum_i^n l_{hit}$), thus receiving different wages from each firm (w_{hit}). However, the effective labor employed (l_{ht}) may be lower than the quantity supplied (l^S). Workers do not accept jobs at wages that are lower than their reserve wage (w^R).

The reserve wage (w_{ht}^R) changes according to the difference between labor supply (l^S) and labor effectively employed in the previous period ($l_{h,t-1}$) and the probability of increasing the reserve wage depends on the unemployment rate $Pr(u_t) = 1 - u_{t-1}^{\upsilon}$:

$$w_{ht} = \begin{cases} w_{h,t-1}(1 + U[0,\delta]) & \text{if } l_{h,t-1}^S - l_{h,t-1} = 0 \text{ with } Pr(u_t), \\ w_{h,t-1}(1 - U[0,\delta]) & \text{if } l_{h,t-1}^S - l_{h,t-1} < 0. \end{cases} \tag{5.1}$$

Moreover, households receive income from interest (r_d) payed by banks on deposits (D_{ht}), government transfers (TF_t), and dividends from firms and banks shares (Div_{ht}).

Thus, the family income (y_{ht}) and disposable income (y_{ht}^D) after taxation are:

$$y_{ht} = \sum_i^n w_{hit} l_{hit} + r_d D_{ht} + Div_{ht}, \tag{5.2}$$

$$y_{ht}^D = (1 - \tau) y_{ht} + TF_t, \tag{5.3}$$

where τ is the income tax rate.

The consumption desired (C_{it}^D) and, thus, savings desired (S_{ht}^D) are a constant proportion of disposable income (y_{ht}^D) and of the wealth accumulated by households in the form of deposits ($c_D D_{ht}$):

$$C_{ht}^D = c_y y_{ht}^D + c_D D_{ht}, \tag{5.4}$$

$$S_{ht}^D = y_{ht}^D - C_{it}^D, \tag{5.5}$$

with $0 < c_y < 1$.

The desired savings are distributed according to a given constant between deposits (D_{ht}^D) and firm participations (A_{ht}^D) trough the preference for liquidity lp_{ht}:

$$D_{ht}^D = lp_{ht} S_{ht}^D, \tag{5.6}$$

$$A_{ht}^D = (1 - lp_{ht}) S_{ht}^D, \tag{5.7}$$

where lp_{it} changes according to the consumer dividends:

$$\begin{cases} lp_{h,t} = \lambda_1 e^{-\lambda_2 \left(\frac{Div_{h,t-1}}{A_{h,t-1}} - r_d \right)} & \text{if } \frac{Div_{h,t-1}}{A_{h,t-1}} \geq r_d, \\ lp_{h,t} = \lambda_1 & \text{if } \frac{Div_{h,t-1}}{A_{h,t-1}} < r_d, \end{cases} \tag{5.8}$$

with $0 < \lambda_1 < 1$ and $\lambda_2 > 0$ (in our case $\lambda_2 = 1$).

Thus, if the shares owned are lower than those desired ($A_{h,t-1} < A_{ht}^D$), then consumer h will try to invest in the creation of a new firm, which will be funded jointly with other households.

According to a circular Hotelling's locational specification of preferences, we assume that good varieties produced by firms and consumer variety preferences are randomly located on a circle with unitarian diameter, a radian value associated to each firm (ω_i) and consumer (ω_h). The lower the price p_{it} with respect to the average level of prices (P_{it}) and the smaller the distance between a firm and a consumer (d_{hi}), the higher the utility (u_{hit}) that the consumer extracts from that good:

$$u_{hit} = \frac{P_t}{(1 + d_{hi})^\beta p_{it}} \tag{5.9}$$

with β as the weighting preference for variety and, thus, the degree of homogeneity of the perception of good consumption.

Each period, households deposit savings in randomly chosen banks from which they receive interests at a given interest rate (r_d), which is the same for all the banks.

5.2.1.2 Firms

Firms produce different varieties of a final good with labor as the unique production factor:

$$q_{it} = \phi l_{it}. \tag{5.10}$$

The desired production (q_{it}^D) derives from the previous sales ($\hat{q}_{i,t-1}$) and previous effective production ($\bar{q}_{i,t-1}$).

If the sales ($\hat{q}_{i,t-1}$) are lower than production ($\bar{q}_{i,t-1}$), the desired production ($q_{i,t}^D$) declines otherwise it augments according to a random value extracted from a uniform distribution between 0 and the adjustment parameter δ:

$$q_{it}^D = \begin{cases} q_{i,t-1}^D(1 + U[0, \delta]) & \text{if } \bar{q}_{i,t-1} - \hat{q}_{i,t-1} = 0, \\ q_{i,t-1}^D(1 - U[0, \delta]) & \text{if } \bar{q}_{i,t-1} - \hat{q}_{i,t-1} > 0. \end{cases} \tag{5.11}$$

Similarly, selling price (p_{it}) changes according to previous period sales:

$$p_{it} = \begin{cases} p_{i,t-1}(1 + U[0, \delta]) & \text{if } \bar{q}_{i,t-1} - \hat{q}_{i,t-1} = 0, \\ p_{i,t-1}(1 - U[0, \delta]) & \text{if } \bar{q}_{i,t-1} - \hat{q}_{i,t-1} > 0. \end{cases} \tag{5.12}$$

Thus, labor demand is given by

$$l_{it}^D = \frac{q_{it}^D}{\phi}. \tag{5.13}$$

The effective quantity of labor employed (l_{it}) may be lower than the demanded one (l_{it}^D).

The wage offered changes according to the difference between labor demanded ($l_{i,t-1}^D$) and labor effectively employed in the previous period ($l_{i,t-1}$), and the probability of reducing the wage offered depends on the unemployment rate $Pr(u_t) = 1 - u_t^v$:

$$w_{it} = \begin{cases} w_{i,t-1}(1 + U[0, \delta]) & \text{if } l_{i,t-1}^D - l_{i,t-1} = 0, \\ w_{i,t-1}(1 - U[0, \delta]) & \text{if } l_{i,t-1}^D - l_{i,t-1} > 0 \text{ with } Pr(u_t). \end{cases} \tag{5.14}$$

The firm labor demand is financed through firm net-worth (A_{it}) and loans (L_{it}). The loan demand is given by the desired labor expenditure that is not covered by internal resources:

$$L_{it}^D = \begin{cases} w_{it}l_{it}^D - A_{it} & \text{if } w_{it}l_{it}^D > A_{it}, \\ 0 & \text{if } w_{it}l_{it}^D \leq A_{it}. \end{cases} \tag{5.15}$$

Firms may not receive all the loan demanded, and thus the loan effectively received (L_{it}) is lower than or equal to the one demanded ($L_{it} \leq L_{it}^D$).

Thus, profits depend on sales ($p_{it}q_{it}$), labor expenditure ($w_{it}l_{it}$), interest rate on loans ($r_{it}L_{it}$), and deposits ($r_d D_{it}$):

$$\pi_{it} = p_{it}q_{it} - w_{it}l_{it} - r_{it}L_{it}. \tag{5.16}$$

When profits are positive ($\pi_{it} > 0$), firms pay taxes (T_{it}^π) on profit and distribute dividends (Div_{it}^π):

$$T_{it}^\pi = \begin{cases} \tau\pi_{it} & \text{if } \pi_{it} > 0, \\ 0 & \text{if } \pi_{it} \leq 0, \end{cases} \tag{5.17}$$

$$Div_{it}^\pi = \begin{cases} (1-\delta)(\pi_{it} - T_{it}^\pi) & \text{if } \pi_{it} > 0, \\ 0 & \text{if } \pi_{it} \leq 0. \end{cases} \tag{5.18}$$

The dividends are distributed to consumers according to the share of the firm they own. Therefore, firm net-worth evolves according to

$$A_{i,t+1} = A_{it} + \pi_{it} - T_{it}^\pi - Div_{it}^\pi. \tag{5.19}$$

5.2.1.3 Banks

Banks collect deposits from consumers, paying a given interest on deposits (r_d). At the same time, banks provide loans to firms. The probability of receiving credit (p_{it}^L) and the interest rate charged on loans (r_{it}) depends on firm target leverage (L_{it}^D/A_{it}), computed as the ratio between desired loans (L_{it}^D) and firm's net-worth (A_{it}):

$$p_{it}^L = 1 - L_{it}^D/A_{it}, \tag{5.20}$$

$$r_{it} = \chi L_{it}^D/A_{it} + r_t, \tag{5.21}$$

where r_t is the discount rate fixed by the central bank.

The desired supply of loans depends on bank net-worth ($L_{zt}^{DS} = \mu A_{zt}$). The maximum amount that a bank may provide to each single firm is a maximum share of its supply (ζL_{zt}^{DS}).

Banks have to deposit in the central bank a minimum amount of reserves (R_{zt}^M) as a proportion of deposits:

$$R_{zt}^M = re_c D_{zt}. \qquad (5.22)$$

The remaining amount of bank liquidity is used for acquiring public bonds (B_{zt}^D).

If a bank has low reserves, it will ask for loans to the central bank (L_{zCt}). Therefore the bank profit (π_{zt}) is equal to:

$$\pi_{zt} = \sum_i^n r_{it} L_{izt} + r_{bt} B_{zt} + r_{re} R_{zt} - BD_{izt} - r_d D_{zt} - r_t L_{zCBt}, \qquad (5.23)$$

where interests r_{bt} and r_{re} are respectively the interest rates on bonds and on reserves. Bad debts (BD_{izt}) are those loans that are not entirely payed back because of firm failures.

When profits are positive ($\pi_{zt} > 0$), banks pay taxes (T_{it}^π) on profit and distribute dividends (Div_{zt}^π with $\rho = 1 - \delta$):

$$T_{zt}^\pi = \begin{cases} \tau \pi_{zt} & \text{if } \pi_{zt} > 0, \\ 0 & \text{if } \pi_{zt} \leq 0, \end{cases} \qquad (5.24)$$

$$Div_{zt}^\pi = \begin{cases} (\rho)(\pi_{zt} - T_{zt}^\pi) & \text{if } \pi_{zt} > 0, \\ 0 & \text{if } \pi_{zt} \leq 0, \end{cases} \qquad (5.25)$$

$$A_{z,t+1} = A_{zt} + \pi_{zt} - T_{zt}^\pi - Div_{zt}^\pi. \qquad (5.26)$$

5.2.1.4 Central Bank

Central banks collect reserves (R_{Ct}) and offer loans to cover the liquidity necessity of banks (L_{Ct}). Moreover, central banks buy bonds emitted by government (B_t) that are not absorbed by banks. Central banks profit (π_{Ct}) is derived from interests on bonds and loans minus interests on compulsory reserves:

$$\pi_{CBt} = r_{bt} B_{CBt} + r_t L_{CBt} - r_{re} R_{CBt}. \qquad (5.27)$$

The discount interest rate is fixed following the Taylor rule on average levels of inflation:

$$r_t = \bar{r}(1 - \xi) + \xi * r_{t-1} + (1 - \xi) * \xi^{IN}(IN_{t-1} - \overline{IN}), \qquad (5.28)$$

where ξ is an adjustment parameter, $\bar{r}$ is the long-run interest rate, ξ^{IN} is the inflation sensibility, IN_{t-1} is the level of inflation, and $\overline{IN}$ is the inflation target level.

5.2.1.5 Government

Government collects income taxes from households (h), firms (i), and banks (z) when respectively household income (y_{ht}), firm profit (π_{it}), and bank profit (π_{zt}) are positive. Indeed, the total amount of taxes collected (T_t) is

$$T_t = \sum_{h}^{H} \tau y_{ht} + \sum_{i,\pi>0}^{I} \tau \pi_{it} + \sum_{z,\pi>0}^{Z} \tau \pi_{zt}. \tag{5.29}$$

The government public primary expenditure G_t is shared equally among households as transfers (TF_t).

Public expenditure (G_t) and tax rate (τ_t) are gradually adjusted according to the expenditure desired ($G_t^d = P_t \Phi_t G$) under the public deficit constraint (d^M) with $d_{it} = DEF_t/Y_t$:

- if $d_t \geq d^M$:

$$G_{t+1} = G_t(1 - U[0, \delta]), \tag{5.30}$$
$$\tau_{t+1} = \tau_t(1 + U[0, \delta]); \tag{5.31}$$

- if $d_t < d^M$ and $G_t^d \leq G_t$:

$$G_{t+1} = G_t(1 - U[0, \delta]), \tag{5.32}$$
$$\tau_{t+1} = \tau_t(1 - U[0, \delta]); \tag{5.33}$$

- if $d_t < d^M$ and $G_t^d > G_t$:

$$G_{t+1} = G_t(1 + U[0, \delta]), \tag{5.34}$$
$$\tau_{t+1} = \tau_t, \tag{5.35}$$

where A_t is the public government eventual advance from the previous period in case expenditures are lower than taxes ($A_t = T_{t-1} - G_{t-1} - r_{b,t-1}B_{t-1}$ with $T_{t-1} > G_{t-1} + r_{b,t-1}B_{t-1}$).

Moreover, government has to repay bonds and interest of bonds on the previous period. The bond interest depends on the level of debt over output (B_t/Y_t) and on the central bank discount rate (r_t):

$$r_{bt} = \chi_B B_t/Y_t + r_t. \tag{5.36}$$

Besides, government has to cover deposits in case of bank failures. In this case, government issues bonds to give back the money of the lost deposits to consumers and firms. These bonds are bought by the central bank.

In effect, if taxes are not enough to cover primary expenditure (G_t) and the service of the public debt, then new bonds are issued, whereas in the case of budget surplus, surplus (SU_t) is used to fund public expenditure in the following periods. Thus country public deficit (PD_t) and debt (DE_t) are respectively

$$PD_t = T_t - G_t + r_{b,t-1}DE_{t-1} - SU_{t-1}, \tag{5.37}$$

$$DE_t = DE_{t-1} + PD_t. \tag{5.38}$$

5.2.2 Interaction Structure

5.2.2.1 Asset Ownership

In part, household savings provide funds for the formation of new firms. In each country, when an amount of savings of at least A_t^m is disposable, a new firm or bank is created, and the households that provide these funds become shareholders, and thus the initial firm or bank net-worth is $A_{it} = A_t^m$, where A_t^m is equal to the average net-worth level.

We try to preserve a constant proportion of firms and banks. Thus if the number of banks is lower than a certain percent (η) of that of firms, then there is a given probability that a new bank enters (the probability has for simplicity the same value η). Moreover, when a firm enters the market, it tries to fund its production asking for an amount of credit equal to its net-worth, and thus, at the beginning, the firm target leverage is equal to one.

Firms and banks with a net-worth level lower than $F_t = W_t F$ exit from the market, with $F = 1$ firms that are not able to employ at least a worker exit from the market.

5.2.2.2 Good Market

In a random order, each consumer expresses its preferences considering a maximum number (ψ) of goods offered. Each consumer orders the selected goods according to their preferences. If the quantity disposable of the first best good is not enough to cover the desired consumption expenditure (Section 5.2.1.1), then the consumer buys the second best, and so on, until the resources allocated to consumption are exhausted or until there are no more goods left to buy on the market after another consumer expresses his demand. The matching process ends when no more matching possibilities are left.

5.2.2.3 Labor Market

Labor is the only production factor in the economy (Section 5.2.1.2). Each period t, each firm i demands a certain amount of labor (l_{it}^D) at a determined level of wage (w_{it}). Household express a given supply of work (l_h), and they may work at the same time in more than one firm. Each period, households look for job; because of limited information and search costs, they may compare the job demand of a given number of firms (ψ).

5.2.2.4   Credit Market

Banks collect deposits and provide loans to demanding firm. Firms may receive loans from different banks. Loans are lent with a certain probability and with a given interest rate that depends on firm target leverage. Banks have to respect capital and liquidity requirements.

5.2.2.5   Bond Market

Government collects taxes and issues bonds (Section 5.2.1.4) that are bought by demanding banks. When the government is not able to allocate all the bonds to banks, the central bank will buy the remaining bonds.

5.3   SIMULATION RESULTS

5.3.1   Macroeconomic Dynamics

As shown in Fig. 5.1, at the beginning, output is equal to zero. During simulations, nominal output increases due to price growth: inflation is usually positive and fluctuates around the 0.01 per cent growth, whereas in the absence of productivity growth, the real growth rate on average is equal to zero and reflects employment variations.

As expected (Fig. 5.2), macroeconomic variables dynamics are strictly correlated. Considering cross-correlations of the cyclical components, credit lent by banks to firms is positively correlated to output and anticipates output growth. Even firm net-worth anticipates output variations. Indeed, both credit and net-worth increase the productive capacities of firms allowing them to employ more workers and, thus, leading to higher good demand. Moreover, leverage is positively correlated with output, whereas public expenditure is anticyclical.

Indeed, as shown in Fig. 5.3, a higher firm net-worth increases the productive capacity of the economy, thus, leading to real output growth. Conversely, higher real output sustains firm net-worth accumulation. Moreover, expansionary phases are also associated with both public and private debt growth, in the form respectively of credit lent by banks to firm and public debt. In effect, whereas credit fosters economic growth from the supply side, public debt sustains the economy increasing the aggregate demand through transfers to households.

5.3.2   Early Warning Indicator for Crisis

We define a crisis as a huge decrease in firm net-worth: a reduction is lower than -0.05%. We choose this indicator of crisis because the firm net-worth plays a crucial role in the model. It represents the first financing source of firms and thus impacts consistently on firm productive capacity. At the same time, net-worth is

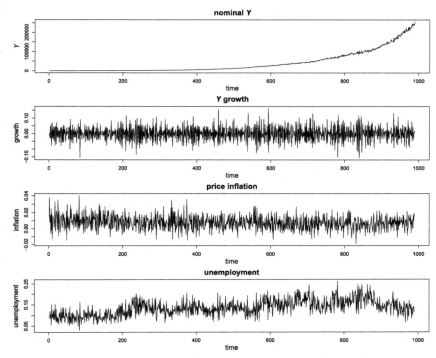

FIGURE 5.1 Simulation macro variables. Nominal income (Y), real income growth rate, price inflation and unemployment.

the collaterally associated with credit; in fact, the probability of receiving loans and the interest rate depends on firms' target leverage that is the ratio between loan demand and firm net-worth. Moreover, the firm net-worth is one of the forms in which households detain their wealth.

We tested several variables as possible early warning measures of the crisis. Following [12], we made Panel Logit regressions with lags of the possible predictors and as dependent variable a dichotomic variable that represents the occurrence or not of a crisis. Predictors may be compared considering coefficients' significance, the value of the pseudo-R^2, the AIC, and the AUROC. The AUROC is the value of the area below the curve that represents the trade-off between false alarm and hit of each early warning indicator (Fig. 5.5): in synthesis, the higher the AUROC, the better the indicator as early warning measure. In Table 5.2, we present the result of four early warning measures: the variation of private credit (credit), variation of real income (y), variation of public debt (debt), and a relative size distribution measure (rel. size: the ratio between the

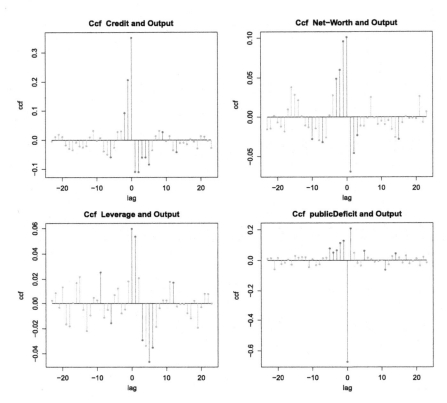

FIGURE 5.2 Cross correlations between macro variables.

average of firm size in the last decile of the distribution and the whole average firm size).

Credit and real income lagged variations are positively correlated with crisis' probability, so credit growth and real growth increase the probability of huge firms' net-worth slowdowns. In effect, during expansionary phases, credit augments more than firm net-worth; thus firms' leverage rises, and, consequently, the vulnerability of the system may increase. Public debt leg variations are negatively correlated with crisis' probability because public debt growth sustains aggregate demand, thus, reducing the impact of negative shocks on the economic system. Moreover, distributional variables may be effective as early warning measures. Indeed, when the relative dimension of larger firms increases, a negative shock that hits one of the largest firms may be easily diffused and amplified by banks: when one of the largest firm fails, the volume of credit that is not payed back can be relatively huge, and thus some banks may fail, or, more generally, they have to reduce their credit supply in order to respect capital re-

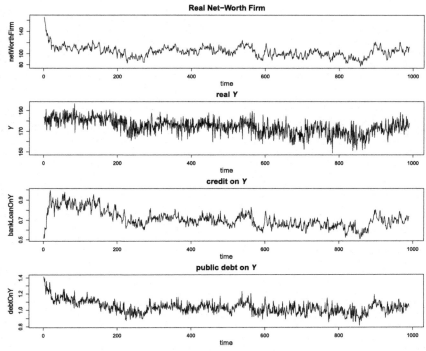

FIGURE 5.3 Simulation macro variables. Real net-worth of firms, real income, firms' credit on income and public debt on income.

quirements. Fig. 5.4 shows the average variations of the relative size of the last decile of the firm size population before and after a crisis; we see that crises, at time $t = 0$, are anticipated by an average increase of the largest firm that, thus, augments the vulnerability of the system.

Moreover, we tested combinations of the previously selected indicators. As expected, combining more indicators increases the effectiveness of the early warning measure as shown by Pseudo-R^2, AIC, and AUROC (Fig. 5.5 and Table 5.3). All the four indicators maintain their significance. In particular, considering firm size polarization, Table 5.2 and Fig. 5.5 show that size concentration indicators may be effective early warning measures. Indeed, when firms are relatively larger than the average emerge, the probability of crisis occurrence increases, and some firms become "too big to fail."

5.3.3 Varying Credit Supply

In the model, banks' credit supply is limited by a capital requirement constraints (Basilea's agreements), and we report the effect of variation of this fundamental

TABLE 5.2 EWI, Different Early Warning Measures. As Dependent Variable, Crisis Probability. As Independent Variables, Variation Lags of Firms' Credit, Real Income, Real Debt, and Relative Average Size of the Last Decile of Firms Over the Whole Average Firm Size. Significance, **: 5%, *: 10%

Coefficient	Credit	y	Debt	Relative size
$L1 \Delta \log(x)$	11.144 **	28.126 **	−47.487 **	44.934 **
	(1.16)	(1.606)	(2.767)	(3.26)
$L2 \Delta \log(x)$	11.832 **	26.501 **	−9.627 **	22.611 **
	(1.189)	(1.951)	(2.47)	(3.143)
$L3 \Delta \log(x)$	9.883 **	14.242 **	8.023 **	16.328 **
	(1.168)	(1.969)	(2.497)	(3.11)
$L4 \Delta \log(x)$	4.586 **	7.923 **	2.338	1.878
	(1.123)	(1.804)	(2.573)	(3.021)
$L5 \Delta \log(x)$	4.067 **	2.185	4.8 *	9.87 **
	(1.097)	(1.368)	(2.553)	(3.026)
Pseudo R^2	0.071	0.136	0.13	0.089
AIC	3020.428	2812.097	2832.938	2962.956
AUROC	0.685	0.758	0.747	0.71
	(0.012)	(0.011)	(0.011)	(0.012)
n. run	10	10	10	10

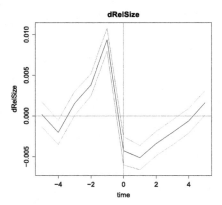

FIGURE 5.4 Crises and relative size.

variable governing the vulnerability of the economic system in order to show the robustness of simulation results. In the baseline specification of the model, the capital requirement is fixed to 10 ($\mu = 10$), so banks can offer credit for an amount that is ten times their net-worth. We run simulations halving the capital requirement ($\mu = 5$), thus restricting credit to firms and also doubling

TABLE 5.3 EWI, Combined Variable Regressions. Significance, **: 5%, *: 10%

	credit	y	debt	relSize	all
L1 Δ log(credit)	11.144 **	7.318 **	31.748 **	8.437 **	26.531 **
	(1.16)	(1.316)	(1.81)	(1.33)	(2.528)
L2 Δ log(credit)	11.832 **	5.05 **	27.324 **	9.551 **	17.886 **
	(1.189)	(1.367)	(1.901)	(1.371)	(2.782)
L3 Δ log(credit)	9.883 **	7.001 **	20.197 **	5.86 **	14.063 **
	(1.168)	(1.367)	(1.834)	(1.345)	(2.721)
L4 Δ log(credit)	4.586 **	1.402	9.394 **	1.943	4.622 *
	(1.123)	(1.324)	(1.618)	(1.309)	(2.557)
L5 Δ log(credit)	4.067 **	3.406 **	5.633 **	0.344	1.01
	(1.097)	(1.31)	(1.276)	(1.234)	(2.118)
L1 Δ log(y)		24.45 **			6.846 **
		(1.691)			(2.575)
L2 Δ log(y)		24.295 **			13.228 **
		(2.172)			(2.97)
L3 Δ log(y)		12.284 **			6.335 **
		(2.247)			(3.054)
L4 Δ log(y)		8.155 **			4.618
		(2.11)			(2.97)
L5 Δ log(y)		1.404			0.586
		(1.623)			(2.364)
L1 Δ log(debt)			−66.881 **		−61.626 **
			(3.373)		(4.902)
L2 Δ log(debt)			−55.392 **		−35.889 **
			(3.649)		(5.241)
L3 Δ log(debt)			−35.912 **		−28.054 **
			(3.757)		(5.412)
L4 Δ log(debt)			−29.01 **		−21.148 **
			(3.778)		(5.428)
L5 Δ log(debt)			−11.458 **		−10.896 **
			(3.493)		(5.051)
L1 Δ log(relSize)				35.473 **	24.279 **
				(3.548)	(4.597)
L2 Δ log(relSize)				18.63 **	19.873 **
				(3.609)	(4.732)
L3 Δ log(relSize)				19.495 **	14.799 **
				(3.637)	(4.566)
L4 Δ log(relSize)				8.162 **	11.59 **
				(3.533)	(4.388)
L5 Δ log(relSize)				14.857 **	18.638 **
				(3.49)	(4.203)
Pseudo R^2	0.071	0.154	0.268	0.114	0.29
AIC	3020.4	2763.9	2397.7	2893.1	2345.5
AUROC	0.685	0.775	0.855	0.736	0.866
	(0.012)	(0.011)	(0.008)	(0.012)	(0.011)
run	10	10	10	10	10

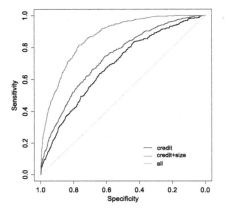

FIGURE 5.5 AUROC representation.

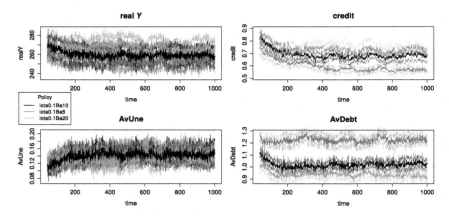

FIGURE 5.6 Macrovariables varying credit supply capital requirement μ.

capital requirement ($\mu = 20$). As expected (Fig. 5.6), when credit is restricted ($\mu = 5$), the volume of credit allocated is lower, and, thus, the real output is on average lower than the baseline specification, but, at the same time, public deficit increases. Therefore, public debt tends to compensate the reduction of credit. The opposite happens when the credit constraints is reduced ($\mu = 20$).

Considering the effectiveness of the early warning measures, regressions do not show any qualitative difference with respect to the baseline scenario (Tables 5.4 and 5.5), whereas public debt variations assume a stronger role in predicting crisis when credit is more constrained ($\mu = 5$). Indeed, in this last case the level of pubic debt increases sharply, and, thus, it assumes greater importance in affecting the vulnerability of the system.

TABLE 5.4 EWI, Combined Variable Regressions, $\mu = 5$. Significance, **: 5%, *: 10%

	credit	y	debt	relSize	all
L1Δ log(credit)	10.165 **	4.83 **	43.593 **	4.626 **	33.146 **
	(1.979)	(2.282)	(3.145)	(2.252)	(4.405)
L2Δ log(credit)	14.157 **	4.063 *	37.831 **	12.344 **	32.093 **
	(2.033)	(2.33)	(3.339)	(2.298)	(4.792)
L3Δ log(credit)	11.243 **	4.905 **	24.211 **	9.328 **	20.669 **
	(1.995)	(2.307)	(3.186)	(2.262)	(4.852)
L4Δ log(credit)	9.572 **	8.592 **	16.893 **	6.33 **	16.527 **
	(1.946)	(2.323)	(2.882)	(2.231)	(4.474)
L5Δ log(credit)	3.295 *	2.189	6.648 **	−2.57	−0.902
	(1.854)	(2.178)	(2.267)	(2.117)	(3.648)
L1Δ log(y)		31.727 **			14.051 **
		(2.394)			(3.355)
L2Δ log(y)		30.05 **			11.927 **
		(3.03)			(3.85)
L3Δ log(y)		14.77 **			7.357 *
		(3.174)			(4.149)
L4Δ log(y)		2.07			2.501
		(2.946)			(3.995)
L5Δ log(y)		3.25			4.625
		(2.256)			(3.227)
L1Δ log(debt)			−100.456 **		−80.855 **
			(5.874)		(7.634)
L2Δ log(debt)			−78.349 **		−64.816 **
			(5.955)		(8.329)
L3Δ log(debt)			−49.047 **		−42.913 **
			(6.136)		(9.003)
L4Δ log(debt)			−24.231 **		−25.624 **
			(6.25)		(8.973)
L5Δ log(debt)			−25.6 **		−19.436 **
			(5.8)		(8.378)
L1Δ log(relSize)				42.057 **	21.27 **
				(5.479)	(7.579)
L2Δ log(relSize)				11.935 **	5.805
				(5.53)	(7.559)
L3Δ log(relSize)				9.827 *	8.005
				(5.59)	(7.619)
L4Δ log(relSize)				20.652 **	9.547
				(5.497)	(7.221)
L5Δ log(relSize)				22.077 **	27.945 **
				(5.559)	(6.945)
Pseudo R^2	0.056	0.174	0.303	0.097	0.322
AIC	1937.9	1709	1447.4	1865.2	1428.9
AUROC	0.674	0.81	0.887	0.739	0.897
	(0.017)	(0.014)	(0.009)	(0.015)	(0.014)
run	10	10	10	10	10

TABLE 5.5 EWI, Combined Variable Regressions, $\mu = 20$. Significance, **: 5%, *: 10%

	credit	y	debt	relSize	all
L1Δ log(credit)	11.509 **	7.63 **	25.213 **	7.727 **	20.338 **
	(0.95)	(1.06)	(1.388)	(1.16)	(2.036)
L2Δ log(credit)	11.472 **	7.15 **	19.764 **	8.308 **	13.424 **
	(0.937)	(1.049)	(1.356)	(1.132)	(2.023)
L3Δ log(credit)	7.192 **	4.883 **	11.758 **	2.977 **	6.649 **
	(0.883)	(1.011)	(1.252)	(1.077)	(1.883)
L4Δ log(credit)	5.593 **	3.544 **	7.975 **	2.353 **	4.311 **
	(0.865)	(1.014)	(1.135)	(1.07)	(1.799)
L5Δ log(credit)	3.521 **	2.597 **	3.709 **	0.804	2.328
	(0.822)	(0.971)	(0.939)	(0.998)	(1.581)
L1Δ log(y)		23.909 **			6.901 **
		(1.656)			(2.402)
L2Δ log(y)		20.748 **			7.9 **
		(2.021)			(2.697)
L3Δ log(y)		12.587 **			5.385 *
		(2.111)			(2.782)
L4Δ log(y)		7.594 **			4.853 *
		(1.983)			(2.717)
L5Δ log(y)		2.255			−1.848
		(1.543)			(2.207)
L1Δ log(debt)			−61.954 **		−54.864 **
			(3.067)		(4.218)
L2Δ log(debt)			−41.038 **		−31.443 **
			(3.047)		(4.371)
L3Δ log(debt)			−27.605 **		−19.671 **
			(3.091)		(4.32)
L4Δ log(debt)			−19.402 **		−11.56 **
			(3.116)		(4.283)
L5Δ log(debt)			−10.804 **		−14.913 **
			(2.975)		(4.23)
L1Δ log(relSize)				31.283 **	17.962 **
				(3.308)	(4.324)
L2Δ log(relSize)				19.809 **	17.523 **
				(3.432)	(4.409)
L3Δ log(relSize)				18.12 **	13.029 **
				(3.379)	(4.212)
L4Δ log(relSize)				11.005 **	6.83 *
				(3.357)	(4.09)
L5Δ log(relSize)				9.213 **	8.333 **
				(3.288)	(3.906)
Pseudo R^2	0.091	0.16	0.273	0.126	0.285
AIC	3244.1	3009.1	2610.7	3131.5	2588.2
AUROC	0.704	0.777	0.86	0.739	0.865
	(0.012)	(0.01)	(0.007)	(0.011)	(0.01)
run	10	10	10	10	10

5.4 CONCLUSIONS

Following the "Modellone" and "Modellaccio" theoretical framework [11,4], we modeled a simple closed economy that evolves thanks to the decentralized interactions of heterogeneous agents. Thus, agents' interactions determine the macroeconomic dynamics and, in particular, the occurrence of crises.

The analysis of simulated data shows that it is possible to isolate effective early warning measures of crises. As expected, the credit and income are predictors of crises: during expansions, credit augments, increasing the average level of leverage and thus raising the vulnerability of the system to local shocks, whereas public debt variations seem to reduce the probability of crises: public debt sustains aggregate demand, thus, softening the amplitude of income and net-worth contractions. Moreover, simulations underline the importance of agents' heterogeneity in determining aggregate results. Indeed, when agents' net-worth distribution is more polarized, with bigger firms representing a higher share of the total firm net-worth, a local shock that hits one of these big firms may have a significant impact on the credit system, thus, affecting the whole economy: some firms become "too big to fail."

Therefore, agent-based macro economic models thanks to the reproduction of emerging heterogeneity among agents can offer some insights into the analysis of the conditions that may lead to systemic crises, thus helping to define theoretical basis for isolating early warning indicators for crises.

Moreover, agent-based models can be implemented for making policy experiments on macroprudential policies, for instance, focusing on the consequences of varying banks' capital requirements, or they can be used to test micropolicies applied to particular agents as the more interconnected or the bigger ones.

REFERENCES

[1] L. Alessi, A. Antunes, J. Babecky, S. Baltussen, M. Behn, D. Bonfim, O. Bush, C. Detken, J. Frost, R. Guimaraes, T. Havranek, M. Joy, K. Kauko, Comparing Different Early Warning Systems: Results from a Horse Race Competition among Members of the Macro-Prudential Research Network, MPRA Paper 62194, University Library of Munich, Germany, February 2015.

[2] G. Babecky, T. Havranek, J. Matiju, M. Rusnak, K. Smidkova, B. Vasieek, Early Warning Indicators of Crisis Incidence: Evidence from a Panel of 40 Developed Countries, Working Papers IES 2011/36, Charles University Prague, Faculty of Social Sciences, Institute of Economic Studies, November 2011.

[3] F. Betz, S. Oprică, T.A. Peltonen, P. Sarlin, Predicting distress in European banks, Journal of Banking & Finance 45 (C) (2014) 225–241.

[4] A. Caiani, A. Godin, E. Caverzasi, M. Gallegati, S. Kinsella, J. Stiglitz, Agent based-stock flow consistent macroeconomics: towards a benchmark model, Journal of Economic Dynamics and Control 69 (C) (2016) 375–408.

[5] D. Delli Gatti, C. Di Guilmi, E. Gaffeo, G. Giulioni, M. Gallegati, A. Palestrini, A new approach to business fluctuations: heterogeneous interacting agents, scaling laws and financial fragility, Journal of Economic Behavior & Organization 56 (4) (April 2005) 489–512.

[6] D. Delli Gatti, M. Gallegati, B. Greenwald, A. Russo, J.E. Stiglitz, The financial accelerator in an evolving credit network, Journal of Economic Dynamics and Control 34 (2010).

[7] M. Drehmann, M. Juselius, Evaluating early warning indicators of banking crises: satisfying policy requirements, International Journal of Forecasting 30 (3) (2014) 759–780.

[8] B. Eichengreen, Economic history, the Great Depression, and the recent financial crisis, Interview with Barry Eichengreen, Federal Reserve Bank of Cleveland, June 2013.

[9] G. Kaminsky, C. Reinhart, The twin crises: the causes of banking and balance-of-payments problems, The American Economic Review 89 (1999) 473–500.

[10] L. Riccetti, A. Russo, M. Gallegati, Leveraged network-based financial accelerator, Journal of Economic Dynamics and Control 37 (8) (2013) 1626–1640.

[11] L. Riccetti, A. Russo, M. Gallegati, An agent based decentralized matching macroeconomic model, Journal of Economic Interaction and Control 10 (2) (March 2014) 305–332.

[12] M. Schularick, A.M. Taylor, Credit booms gone bust: monetary policy, leverage cycles, and financial crises, 1870–2008, The American Economic Review 102 (2) (April 2012) 1029–1061.

Part III

Macroeconomic ABM: Perspectives and Implications

Chapter 6

Expectation Models in Agent-Based Computational Economics

Antonio Palestrini

Marche Polytechnic University, Ancona, Italy

6.1 INTRODUCTION

In the history of macroeconomics, the role of agents' expectations was considered important from the very beginning. In this chapter, we interpret the evolution of these expectations from the 1970s, trying to explain them as a logical evolution of the choice made in macroeconomics after the publication of the existence theorems for a utility function representing given preferences [4].

Before becoming familiar with such powerful theorems, the behavioral approach in macroeconomics was, in a sense, naive; based on reasonable rules like the Keynesian consumption function modeling the relationship between consumption and income or the relation between savings and interest rate. Of course, many scholars in microeconomics, in order to derive optimal behavioral rules, used utility functions long before the 1970s. But in macroeconomics, they were not common until the 1970s. The period between 1950 and 1980 saw a mathematical economic revolution in our discipline. A number of powerful minds discovered theorems linking preferences to scalar functions allowing one to map representation of preferences to the real line. This gives our discipline a way to derive behavioral rules without assuming them.

Then, at least this is the interpretation suggested here, in the macroeconomic discipline, from the 1960s but above all from the 1970s, we start to build models as in the following approach:

1. Assume that agents' preferences are given.
2. Given agent's preferences, under regularity conditions, there exists a utility function representing such preferences from which, in principle, optimal behavioral rules can be derived.

Introduction to Agent-Based Economics. http://dx.doi.org/10.1016/B978-0-12-803834-5.00009-6

3. The economist/modeler knows a functional form for the utility function that can approximate the correct utility function. In other words, it is possible to represent preferences within appropriate function families.

Point 1 can be justified, and it was, saying that the role of the economist is not to discuss agents' preferences, but to produce positive and normative analysis given people attitudes. Point 2 uses the discovered existence theorems. Finally, point 3 is the most difficult to justify and in our interpretation is the key point to understand what happens in macroeconomics from the 1970s: The rational expectation revolution.

Our reading of the history is as follows: *if we, as a modeler, assume to know (at least the functional form) of agents' utility function, agents themselves MUST know their utility function. Otherwise, the economist is something similar to a divinity knowing people's brain better than the people themselves.*

If they know the objective function, then the logical consequence is to choose, as a behavioral rule, the "arg max" of the utility function. This is because the underlying assumption of Adam Smith, wildly accepted in economics, is the self-interest behavior of human beings. If they know the expected objective function, then doing "the best they can" is in fact their maximum.

With this interpretation in mind, the reason for using rational expectations relies on its ability of producing "robust" behavioral rules. Rules that can face the Lucas critique [12] implying that, in evaluating the effect of economic policies, we have to incorporate such policies in agents' behavior. In other words, the behavior of well informed optimizing agents changes when economic policies change.

Summarizing, we read what happens in the recent macroeconomic literature claiming that points 1, 2, and 3 imply behavioral rules of agents derived by solving the following problem:

$$\arg\max_{x} E_t V(x),$$

where $V(x)$ is the agent's utility or payoff function and E_t is the expectation operator condition on all the relevant information available at time t.

Regarding agent-based models, it is still true that economic actions need to forecast the future. This means that we have to understand the value of our action, that is, what we gain in the future by performing the action. In economics, we say that agents want to know the *value function of a given action*. This means that agents need a certain knowledge of the economic system they are interacting with. For example, firms set selling price according to their individual expected demand, which, as a result, depends on the choices of other firms. As an other example, consumers may decide their reserve price according to expectations on average prices but also imitating the style of consumption of other agents.

The final goal of an agent's decision process is to understand the more he/she can about the *properties of the value function of rules or actions*.

In agent-based models, agents are rational in the sense that they realize the complexity of the environment in which they have to make decisions. Consequently, agent-based models usually describe the economic environment resulting from the interaction of heterogeneous agents as a *complex adaptive system* in which agents have bounded rationality and follow heterogeneous behaviors and expectations in order to improve their situation.

According to Gigerenzer et al. [10], it is possible to describe agent behaviors as the result of heuristics based on a given informational set. Agents may try different rules/strategies and, observing realized payoffs, choose the one that gives better results.

In ABM the key assumption is a partial knowledge of agents' heterogeneous objective functions. In other words, the agent-based methodology tries to work without using point 3 but instead replacing it with something like:

3'. Agents search, during simulations, the best rule within a space of possible strategies arising from data, logical reasoning, and recently also from experimental economics.

The approach is that the modeler (and, consequently, the agents) can have only a partial knowledge of the objective function or the utility function representing agents' choices. This is because of the complexity of the system generated by the interaction with other agents.[1] As a consequence, the modeling strategy is to use directly behavioral switching rules. Agents can change their mind in learning the value function of the action. This raises the problem: is the space generated by the set of rules a good representation of actual behaviors? In this case, we can produce good agent-based models. What we gain, removing assumption 3, is a tool to analyze complex economic environments without solving the aggregation problem with unrealistic assumptions.[2]

6.2 RULES COME FROM EXPECTATIONS, AND RULES IS WHAT YOU REALLY WANT

In the introduction, we discuss the trivial fact that even the rational expectation assumption is a way to produce behavioral rules. For researchers analyzing a

---

1. There is a famous example in game theory to understand the ABM approach. It is the 1980 Axelrod tournament described by Axelrod [3], *the evolution of cooperation*. He asked many scholars to send him strategies to play the repeated prisoner dilemma. He found that the strategy that won more often was the *TIT-FOR-TAT* (first move cooperate and then repeat the previous opponent's move). The lesson he took from this tournament is the nonexistence of a "best strategy" but that only some strategies perform better than others and that good strategies adapt to the circumstances.
2. See Chapter 1 of [6] for a richer discussion.

particular economic problem, those rules are what you want and what you need at the end. This expectation process, under the assumption of a perfect knowledge of the environment by the agents—and thus a perfect knowledge of their respective objective functions—generates optimal rules. To illustrate this point, think about a simple representation of a first-order condition derived by optimizing agents in microfounded economic model

$$x_{it} = E_t g(x_{it+1}, z_{it}, \varepsilon_{it})$$

about the choice of an economic variable x_{it} made by agent i. The variable depends on the conditional expectation at time t of a function g of its future values, a vector of exogenous or predetermined variables z_{it} at time t, and idiosyncratic shocks ε_{it}.

The solution of the above equation is another function, say h, that is,

$$x_{it}^* = h(z_{it}).$$

Two things are worth noting: (1) The function h is a rule in the sense of an action given an information set [6]; (2) The symbol "*" refers to the fact that the rule h is optimal under the assumption that agents know perfectly the objective function and the probability distribution of the economic model. If we remove the assumptions under which the model is built, then the function h loses its optimality and returns being just a rule; a rule among others.

For this reason, having removed in ABMs the perfect knowledge assumption of the agents' objective functions, the problem becomes the switching among a set of rules or searching in the space generated combining the rules in a given set. In this way, agents learn the properties of the value function of actions.

To make an example, suppose we want to analyze an aggregate variable, say x_t. One possibility is to relay on the empirical literature, which says that at the microlevel, for example, this relation is approximately linear with respect to another variable y_{it} with coefficient k_{it} at time t, that is,

$$x_{it} = k_{it} y_{it}.$$

Heterogeneous agents, in an ABM, may try different specifications of the linear relation. Agents' choices can switch over time according to a feedback mechanism such as the *reinforcement learning* suggested in [16] using a payoff function at time t. Essentially, it is a *fitness function* reinforcing strategies with a good past record. Agents may use this fitness function to update how good a given strategy is compared to the others.

The computational evolution of the agent-based model produces a joint distribution of k_{it} and y_{it}, from which we can derive the aggregate variable x_t:

$$x_t = \sum_i k_{it} y_{it}.$$

How does this methodology relate to the standard macroeconomic approach using rational expectations?

A simple comparison may be done using the well-known *optimal growth model* derived by solving the aggregate maximization problem

$$\max_{C_t} E_0 \sum_{t=0}^{\infty} \beta^t U(C_t), \tag{6.1}$$

$$K_{t+1} = Y_t + (1 - \delta)K_t - C_t, \tag{6.2}$$

with the firm's production function defined by the equation[3]

$$Y_t = F(K_t, z_t), \tag{6.3}$$

where, again, z_t follows an exogenous autoregressive process. In this problem the information set is $\Omega_t = \{x_t, e_t\}$, where $x_t = (K_t, z_{t-1})$, and e_t is the information that markets are perfectly competitive.

FOC with respect to C_t and K_{t+1} give the Euler equation

$$U'(C_t) = \beta E_t U'(C_{t+1})\big(F_k(K_{t+1}, z_{t+1}) + 1 - \delta\big).$$

To solve the model, assume the Cobb–Douglas production function

$$Y_t = F(K_t, z_t) = z_t K_t^{\alpha}, \tag{6.4}$$

$\delta = 1$, and the condition for perfect aggregation of consumer decisions (homothetic preferences)

$$U(C_t) = \ln(C_t).$$

The solution of the problem is the consumption rule

$$C_t = (1 - \alpha\beta)Y_t. \tag{6.5}$$

We can calibrate this rule with numbers given from empirical studies. For example, α is around 1/3, and β is in the range $(0.8, 1)$, say $\beta = 0.9$. This gives the linear optimal rule

$$C_t = 0.7Y_t, \tag{6.6}$$

---

3. Note that, to simplify the analysis, we assume a constant level of labor.

which can be expressed in per-capita terms (with N agents), $y_t = Y_t/N$ and $c_t = C_t/N$:

$$c_t = 0.7y_t, \tag{6.7}$$

that is, the model may be presented as if the aggregate consumption is the result of identical agents using the above rule.

But the same aggregate consumption may be generated by heterogeneous agents with a mean propensity to consume equal to 0.7.[4]

A more subtle problem with this result is that this rule is optimal only under the simple environment specified and the assumptions made. Otherwise, it is just a rule, i.e., it loses the optimality property. Nevertheless, in principle, the two approaches may give the same result. In other words, even though the two methodologies are different, it is possible that an agent-based model with switching rules generates an aggregate consumption

$$C_t = \sum_i c_{it} y_{it} = 0.7Y_t,$$

similar to that obtained with the standard approach. In other words, when the joint distribution of agents converges to a stable one, then the aggregate result may or may not be equal to the standard solution.

In the particular case of similar solutions, we can conclude that agents and firms' heterogeneity, direct interaction in consumption, and production choices (e.g., herding behaviors) are not important in explaining aggregate dynamics. This result is intuitive given the simplicity of the above economic model.

As we said, in ABM, those behavioral rules are not fixed. Agents can switch between different expectation rules or different strategies. Let us analyze the two approaches starting with the case of switching rules.

6.3 THE SWITCHING OF RULES

The discussion regarding the switching of rules approach will be developed here following the literature that analyzes price expectation in a situation in which agents do not have enough information to compute the rational expected price [6].

The approach is described by Brock and Hommes [5] and Anufriev and Hommes [1], showing that it is possible to replicate experimental data on asset prices through simulation allowing agents to formulate their expectation on prices according to different heuristics, which consider both the expectation and the effective realization of prices.

---

4. Simplifying a lot the aggregation problem. See [6].

The approach can be described assuming that agents need forecast an economic variable, say x_t, exploiting a set of switching rules:

1. Simple adaptive rule:

$$x_{t+1}^e = x_t^e + \lambda_A (x_{t-1} - x_t^e); \tag{6.8}$$

in case $\lambda_A = 1$, we have the so-called "naive" expectations $p_{t+1}^e = p_{t-1}$, and agent expectations are equal to the previous realization.

2. Trend-following rule:

$$x_{t+1}^e = x_{t-1} + \lambda_T (x_{t-1} - x_{t-2}) \tag{6.9}$$

with $\lambda_T > 1$. The higher λ_T, the stronger the impact on trends on expectations.

3. Anchoring and adjustment rule:

$$x_{t+1}^e = 0.5(x_f + x_{t-1}) + (x_{t-1} - x_{t-2}), \tag{6.10}$$

where x^f is, say, a fundamental level of the price that may be used as an anchor; for instance, x^f may be the average of the past realizations, $x^f = (1/t)\sum_{j=0}^{t-1} x_j$.

Note that the set is really simple, but its mix, the space of rules generated, may be rich enough to explain experimental data.

As said before, each agent learns in the complex environment measuring the performance $(V_{h,t})$ of all the h rules, that is, a way of learning the value function, in predicting the variable realization x_t:

$$V_{h,t} = -(x_t - x_{h,t}^e)^2 + \eta V_{h,t-1}, \tag{6.11}$$

where η is a measure of the value given on past performance of the heuristics. Using the measured performance, agents can compute the probability of choosing an heuristic or rule, say $p_{h,t}$:

$$p_{h,t} = \delta p_{h,t-1} + (1-\delta)\frac{\exp(\beta V_{h,t-1})}{Z_{t-1}}, \tag{6.12}$$

where Z_{t-1} is a normalizing factor $(Z_{t-1} = \sum_{h=0}^{H} \exp(\beta V_{h,t-1}))$, and $0 \leq \delta \leq 1$ determines the persistence of the impact of each rule in the agent's choice among different heuristics.

Note that when $\beta = 0$ the probability converges to 1 over the number of rules. In other words, in this case agents have no information to disentangle the value function of different rules. When $\beta > 0$ agents do the best they can to learn the value function, and the associated probabilities to play the rules, given the available information set. In doing so, agents learn something about the properties of the "best" rule, changing their mind during the simulation. As said before, this implies that the actual rule they use is a combination[5] of the set of rule/heuristics they have.

In the following section, we describe the other approach, the switching of strategies, following the same line of reasoning of the switching of the heuristics. In principle, they are so similar that can be represented within the same framework. The separation is done merely for the sake of didactic purposes.

6.4 THE SWITCHING OF STRATEGIES

The first step of the approach is the discretization of the agent's action support. Agents choose an action/strategy, say (a), among a finite set (H). This is a very common and important step in every computational analysis [6]. The agent's choice is a simple generalization of the Tesfatsion and Judd [16] reinforcement learning algorithm. In every period, agents decide one strategy in a given set with a probability distribution described further. At the end of the period, agents observe the result of their choices, i.e., the payoff (π) received. In other words, the payoff is used to value effectiveness of a strategy, say the value function

$$V_t(a) = (1 - \chi)V_{t-1}(a) + \pi_t. \tag{6.13}$$

The probability of choosing a particular strategy (a) from the strategy set H_a is given by $p(a)$:

$$X_a = \left(\frac{V_t(a)}{c}\right)^v, \tag{6.14}$$

$$p(a) = \frac{e^{X_a}}{\sum_{Ha} e^{X_a}}. \tag{6.15}$$

The effectiveness/value of a strategy $V_t(a)$ is reduced by a small percentage (χ) each period. Moreover, to allow a continuous exploration of the action space, there is also a small probability (μ) that choices do not depend on past experience but are taken randomly among the possible actions (similar to *mutation operator* in *genetic algorithms*).

However, in this basic learning mechanism, agents do not take into consideration the volatility of profits associated with different strategies, that is, the choice mechanism does not consider the risk level associated with every choice.

---

5. In the sense that the set of rules generates a space of rules. The task of the modeler is using data, logic, and experimental economics to start with a set of rules rich enough to generate a reasonable space of rules.

For this reason, Catullo et al. [7] generalize the Tesfatsion and Judd [16] framework assuming that agents compute also the riskiness of a strategy, say $v_t(a)$, using the variability of profits (σ_π) to correct their action decisions. The profit standard deviation (σ_π) is computed for the last k values of profit[6] for each action a.

The value of an action $V_t(a)$ is updated using the profit level, and $v_t(a)$ is updated using the profit volatility:

$$v_t(a) = (1 - \chi)v_{t-1}(a) + \sigma_{\pi_{t-1}}. \tag{6.16}$$

We are now able to compute the probability of choosing a particular strategy (a) among the possibility set (Ha), considering also profit variability. Such a probability is denoted by $p_\sigma(a)$, that is,

$$X_a = \left(\frac{V_t(a)}{c + \psi v_t(a)} \right)^\nu, \tag{6.17}$$

$$p_\sigma(a) = \frac{e^{X_a}}{\sum_{Ha} e^{X_a}}, \tag{6.18}$$

where the parameter ψ is the sensitivity to risk.

This way of modeling agent's learning behavior is powerful, but it may produce not perfectly rational dynamics. This means that expectations may be (1) biased and (2) with non minimal error variance with respect to the relevant information set. Let us analyze the two points: Regarding point 1, the aggregate expectation is really relevant, not the individual one. If the bias distribution of agents has zero mean, then, on average, agents in the market have a correct forecast of the economic variable. This is not an unlikely result if expectations are heterogeneous and not correlated too much.[7]

Regarding point 2, we may, again, exploit the heterogeneity of expectations and not too strong correlation. Even though individual expectations may have a huge one-step ahead error standard deviation, once we aggregate them, computing the average expectation, the error standard deviation may shrink. In the simple case with uncorrelated expectations between N agents, the error standard deviation decreases with velocity $\sqrt{N}$, that is, exactly the Galton case in 1906.

This last point is important since it implies that, in ABM, the case of perfect rationality is not only impossible to compute, but also not necessary.

---

6. Catullo et al. [7] use $k = 20$.
7. This result was first shown in 1906 by the statistician Francis Galton. He discovered—during a competition to guess the weight of an ox—that people are capable (collectively) at guessing averages of unknown quantities [15]. In fact, the average guess was extremely close to the actual weight of the ox.

To illustrate this last point with an example, in the following section, we discuss an ABM simple enough to compute the perfectly rational solution and compare it with the bias and one-step-ahead error variance produced by adaptive agents.

The model is built so that *by construction* adaptive agents have an expectation bias when variables are nonstationary. As stressed by Palestrini and Gallegati [13], the simple, and fixed, adaptive expectation rule

$$x^e_{t+1} = x^e_t + \lambda(x_t - x^e_t) = \lambda x_t + (1 - \lambda)x^e_t, \tag{6.19}$$

in which the expectation is revised according to the error made in the previous period multiplied by a correction parameter λ between zero and one, has a bias exactly equal to the drift of the forecast variable

$$x^e_{t+1} - x_{t+1} = E[\Delta x_{t+1}]. \tag{6.20}$$

When the trend is smooth, the bias can be simply corrected estimating the drift.

6.5 A SIMPLE ABM COMPARING BIASED AND UNBIASED ADAPTIVE AGENTS WITH THE PERFECTLY RATIONAL SOLUTION

In this section, we analyze individual and aggregate bias generated by an agent-based model of a closed economy populated by households and N_F heterogeneous firms. Firm i produces output Y_i using only labor N_i supplied by households. Households are not explicitly modeled here. They supply labor inelastically and absorb production using their wages. The production function is

$$Q_{it} = A_t N_{it}^{\frac{1}{\delta}} \tag{6.21}$$

with $\delta > 1$.

The optimal production is computed maximizing the expected profit

$$\Pi^{e_i}_{it+1} = P^{e_i}_{t+1} Q_{it} - P_t w_t N_{it}, \tag{6.22}$$

where P^{e_i} is the expected market price of agent i. The individual market price may be affected by idiosyncratic components as in [14], that is, the individual firm's price is $P_{it+1} = u_{it+1} P_{t+1}$ with a random variable u_{it+1} with mean equal to 1.

Substituting Q_{it} and applying FOC

$$\frac{1}{\delta} P^{e_i}_{t+1} A_t N_{it}^{\frac{1}{\delta}-1} - P_t w_t = 0,$$

we obtain the optimal amount of labor, $N_{it}^*(P^{ei}) = \left(\frac{P_{t+1}^{ei} A_t}{\delta w_t P_t}\right)^{\frac{\delta}{\delta-1}}$, and the output

$$Q_{it}^*(P_{t+1}^{ei}) = A_t \left(\frac{P_{t+1}^{ei} A_t}{\delta w_t P_t}\right)^{\frac{1}{\delta-1}} = A_t^{\frac{2\delta-1}{\delta-1}} \left(\frac{P_{t+1}^{ei}}{\delta w_t P_t}\right)^{\frac{1}{\delta-1}}.$$

Agents forecast the $(t+1)$th market price using heterogeneous adaptive expectations:

$$P_{t+1}^{ei} = \lambda_i P_t + (1 - \lambda_i) P_t^{ei} + \gamma \zeta_t. \tag{6.23}$$

The parameters λ_i are drawn from a uniform distribution between 0.4 and 1 meaning that there are heterogeneous adaptive expectations. The term ζ_t is the bias correction term (BCT) estimated with mean of the market price differentials $\zeta_t = 4^{-1} \sum_{i=1}^{4} \Delta P_{t-i}$.

The variable γ is an indicator function equal to 0 if we want to implement standard adaptive expectations and equal to 1 when we want to investigate the bias correction discussed by Palestrini and Gallegati [13].

The market price is assumed to evolve according to the stochastic tâtonnement equation

$$P_{t+1} = P_t \exp\left(\gamma_p (w_t N_t - Q_t)\right) \exp(\varepsilon_{P,t+1}), \tag{6.24}$$

where $Q_t = \sum_{i=1}^{K} Q_{it}(P_{t+1}^{ei})$ is the aggregate production, $N_t = \sum_{i=1}^{K} N_{it}(P_{t+1}^{ei})$ is the aggregate labor demand, γ_p is a parameter governing reaction of market price to total net demand, and $\varepsilon_{P,t+1}$ is an independent shock-affecting price dynamics, so that

$$P_{t+1} = P_t \exp\left(\gamma_p \left(w_t \sum_{i=1}^{K} N_{it}(P_{t+1}^{ei}) - \sum_{i=1}^{K} Q_{it}(P_{t+1}^{ei})\right)\right) \exp(\varepsilon_{P,t+1}). \tag{6.25}$$

In simulations, $K = 200$ and $\gamma_p = 0.01$.

Wage evolves according to a unit root with a positive drift d:

$$w_t = \rho_w w_{t-1} + d + \sigma_\varepsilon \varepsilon_t$$

with $\rho_w \in [0, 1)$.

In the following, with this simple model, we will be able to evaluate the following important aspects in the ABM methodology:

1. Analyze the ABM one-step-ahead error forecast versus the one-step-ahead error forecast of the perfectly rational solution (RE) solution.

2. Analyze agents' choices, with and without the BCT, compared to the choice of the representative agent RE solution

$$N = \left(\frac{1 + E_t \pi_{it+1}}{\delta w_t} \right)^{\frac{\delta}{\delta-1}}. \tag{6.26}$$

The RE solution, say N^{RE}, may be computed assuming that, in the market, there are identical rational agents knowing the expected value of the price equation. In other words, they compute the fixed point of the equation

$$N^{RE} = \left(\frac{\exp(\gamma_p(w_t F N^{RE} - FQ))}{\delta w_t} \right)^{\frac{\delta}{\delta-1}}, \tag{6.27}$$

$$n = \left(\frac{\exp(\gamma_p(w_t F N^{RE} - F A N^{RE\frac{1}{\delta}}))}{\delta w_t} \right)^{\frac{\delta}{\delta-1}}. \tag{6.28}$$

3. A comparison between the behavior of the ABM with the RE solution regarding strategies that, in this simple model, are demands of labor.

In the following, we show two Monte Carlo simulations without and with the simple linear filter $\zeta_t = 4^{-1} \sum_{i=1}^{4} \Delta P_{HP,t-i}$ to approximate unbiased expectations. To perform the Monte Carlo analysis, the parameters of the model are set as follows: $\delta = 3/2$, $F = 200$, $\gamma_p = 0.01$, $\rho_w = 0.9$, $d = 0.1$, $\sigma_\varepsilon = 0.01$.

Fig. 6.1 shows $MC = 100$ Monte Carlo replications of 40-period simulations of the model with $F = 200$ firms. The figure describes the final (period $= 40$) distribution of the difference between the market price and average expectation with and without BCT. The figure shows the final distribution of percent errors (relative to the final market price) with BCT equal to the mean of four market price differentials (see above).

The average one-step-ahead percent error distribution without correction term has a mean -2.506% and standard deviation 0.119%. The distribution with simple time difference correction term has a mean 0.085% and standard deviation 0.123%.

As predicted by Palestrini and Gallegati [13], the mean error of corrected expectations is close to zero. How close to zero depends heavily on the persistence of the variable for which agents compute expectations and the correction mechanism used to evaluate local trend. In simulations, using the correction $\zeta_t = 4^{-1} \sum_{i=1}^{4} \Delta P_{t-i}$, we implicitly assume a local linear trend (or a local constant drift).

Regarding the error forecast, we obtain in simulations that the forecast error has a greater standard deviation compared to the rational expectation solution

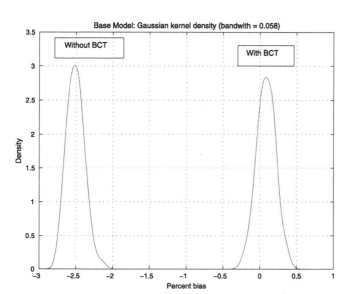

FIGURE 6.1 Error distribution with bias correction (kernel density estimation).

(which is related to the standard deviation of $\varepsilon_{P,t+1}$). This result is in line with the previous literature comparing adaptive expectations to rational expectations.[8] Note, however, that the forecast error is of the same order of magnitude: Around 0.12% with and without BCT versus the RE error forecast of 0.1%. This is due to the fact that we are aggregating heterogeneous agents. In other words, the average error forecast of heterogeneous agents may be compared to the representative agent's solution.

Coming to real quantities, Fig. 6.2 shows the ratio between the aggregate choice variable with adaptive agents (AE) and fully rational agents, that is,

$$\frac{N_t(AE)}{N_t(RE)}$$

is centered around 1 (the Monte Carlo mean is 0.997) when agents use the BCT and above 1 (with Monte Carlo mean equal to 1.079) with simple adaptive expectation. The reason simple adaptive agents tend to produce on average 8% more is that, with this specification, we have a decreasing price, so that agents underestimate price reduction and demand, on average, more labor compared to the optimal value.

---

8. See constant gain expectation schemes in [9].

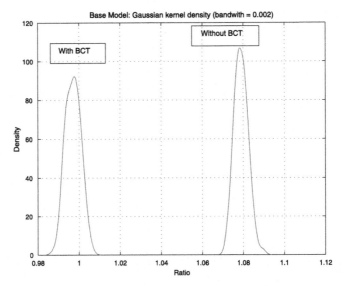

FIGURE 6.2 Ratio distribution with bias correction (kernel density estimation).

Summarizing this last analysis, the Monte Carlo simulations lead to the conclusion that when agents have a good estimation of variable drifts, the BCT produces on average the same solution of the fully rational case.

We would like to finish this work stressing that in explaining many economic phenomena the bias is important not only because the experimental economic literature shows that it is present [2], but also, and more importantly, because it allows us to enrich the economic analysis like in the De Grauwe [8] work, where the author is able to explain endogenous waves of optimism and pessimism ("animal spirits") exploiting the correlation between biased beliefs in order to identify conditions under which animal spirits arise.

6.6 CONCLUSIONS

In this chapter, we stress the fact that the focus on expectations is misleading since what economists want are agent's behavioral rules we can rely on. Optimization with rational expectations is simply a way to derive these behavioral rules. This poses many research questions: is this assumption too strong to produce a reasonable representation of actual behaviors? Is it necessary to compute rational solutions? What must be done when the economic environment is too complex to compute the unbiased minimum variance solution? The ABM approach, described in this chapter, is a way to answer such questions.

In an ABM, the rules (strategies, actions) are often not fixed. Agents search in a sufficiently rich *rule space* generated by combining a given set of possible actions. In a sense the task is similar to traditional approaches: learn the *value function of actions*. The approach differs once we understand that the learning process is made without assuming a complete knowledge of the objective function.

The learning process is made using variations of the switching rule decision described by Hommes [11] or modifications of the *reinforcement learning* suggested by Tesfatsion and Judd [16]. This implies that good agent-based models are more robust to the Lucas' critique compared to what non-agent-based economists usually think.

Moreover, ABM with heterogeneous (collectively) unbiased expectations can reproduce the rational solution showing that the minimum variance property, often rejected in empirical analysis, is not necessary.

Finally, unbiased properties are important in obtaining the rational solution but may be less important in explaining many economic phenomena. Not only because the experimental economic literature shows that a bias is often in every agent decision [2], but also, and more importantly, because the bias allows us to enrich the economic analysis like in the De Grauwe [8] work, in which the author is able to explain endogenous waves of optimism and pessimism ("animal spirits") exploiting the correlation between biased beliefs in order to identify conditions under which animal spirits arise.

REFERENCES

[1] M. Anufriev, C. Hommes, Evolutionary selection of individual expectations and aggregate outcomes in asset pricing experiments, American Economic Journal: Microeconomics 4 (4) (November 2012) 35–64.

[2] Dan Ariely, Simon Jones, Predictably Irrational, HarperCollins, New York, 2008.

[3] Robert Axelrod, The Evolution of Cooperation, vol. 5145, Basic Books, AZ, 1984.

[4] Gianni Bosi, Alessandro Caterino, Rita Ceppitelli, Existence of continuous utility functions for arbitrary binary relations: some sufficient conditions, Tatra Mountains Mathematical Publications 46 (1) (2010) 15–27.

[5] W.A. Brock, C. Hommes, A rational route to randomness, Econometrica 65 (5) (September 1997) 1059–1096.

[6] Alessandro Caiani, Alberto Russo, Antonio Palestrini, Mauro Gallegati, Economics with Heterogeneous Interacting Agents: A Practical Guide to Agent-Based Modeling, Springer, 2016.

[7] E. Catullo, M. Gallegati, A. Palestrini, Towards a credit network based early warning indicator for crises, Journal of Economic Dynamics and Control 50 (1) (2015) 78–97.

[8] Paul De Grauwe, Animal spirits and monetary policy, Economic Theory 47 (2–3) (2011) 423–457.

[9] George W. Evans, Seppo Honkapohja, Learning and Expectations in Macroeconomics, Princeton University Press, 2001.

[10] G. Gigerenzer, P.M. Todd, ABC Research Group, Simple Heuristics That Make Us Smart, Number 9780195143812 in OUP Catalogue, Oxford University Press, July 2000.

[11] Cars Hommes, Behavioral Rationality and Heterogeneous Expectations in Complex Economic Systems, Cambridge University Press, 2013.

[12] Robert E. Lucas Jr., Econometric policy evaluation: a critique, in: Carnegie-Rochester Conference Series on Public Policy, vol. 1, North-Holland, 1976, pp. 19–46.

[13] Antonio Palestrini, Mauro Gallegati, Unbiased adaptive expectation schemes, Economics Bulletin 35 (2) (2015) 1185–1190.

[14] Joseph E. Stiglitz, Bruce C. Greenwald, Financial market imperfections and business cycles, The Quarterly Journal of Economics 108 (1) (1993) 77–114.

[15] James Surowiecki, The Wisdom of Crowds, Random House Digital, Inc., 2005.

[16] Leigh Tesfatsion, Kenneth L. Judd, Agent-Based Computational Economics, Elsevier, 2006.

Chapter 7

Experimental Economics for ABM Validation

Annarita Colasante
Universitat Jaume I, Castellón de la Plana, Spain

7.1 INTRODUCTION

In the framework of Neoclassical Economics, the economic system is populated by a plurality of rational agents that make their decisions according to predetermined assumptions. This simplification permits us to investigate the process of decision making used by a *representative agent*, also called *Homo Economicus*. This agent is characterized by full rationality, and she takes this decision following an optimization process based on a utility function. This implies that this agent has specific preferences, and she is able to rank all possible choices, or outcomes, and, taking into account the budget constraint, she is able to find the optimal solution.

Driven by the Simon's critique ([47]), which discards the idea of perfect rationality, many economists have challenged the bearing wall of the mainstream economics. Thanks to these contributions, a new field in economics was born, Behavioral Economics. This approach was born by the intersection of psychology and economics, and it allows us to understand how agents characterized by human limitations behave in specific contexts. In this subfield, many researchers investigate the individual decision making, that is, the microaspect, and try to understand what factors influence agents' behavior. On the other hand, in recent years, some researchers try to investigate how agents interact in a market, that is, the macroaspect, and how their interaction leads to aggregate results.

In this chapter, we review the importance of this new field and investigate the interconnection with the Agent-Based Model (ABM) approach. As we will see, these approaches are, at the same time, substitutes and complements. Both approaches are useful to investigate the aggregate results of artificial economies in which the neoclassical assumptions do not hold, and, in this sense, they are substitute. Indeed, ABM is a computational method to create and analyze an artificial environment populated by virtual agents that interact. On the other hand, experiments allow us to investigate the impact of a certain policy in a controlled

Introduction to Agent-Based Economics. http://dx.doi.org/10.1016/B978-0-12-803834-5.00010-2

143

environment in which agents are human beings. The interesting thing is that they are also complement. Each of these approaches shows limitations, but we could integrate these methods to have complete results. The main disadvantage related to using experimental evidence is to have few observations due to the associated high cost, whereas the great drawback of the Agent-Based approach is connected with the implementation of baseless individual rules. Having an integrated approach could solve both of these problems. In this regard, we say that these approaches are complement.

In this chapter, we will see how the results from experiments are useful to calibrate and/or validate Agent-Based Models reviewing the main techniques usually adopted to make both of these procedures. At the end, we review some works that integrate ABM and Experimental Economics.

This chapter is structured as follows: in Section 7.2, we review the origin and the main features of Behavioral and Experimental Economics; in Section 7.3, we investigate how the results gathered from experiments can be used in an ABM; in Section 7.4, we conclude the analysis looking at some applications that combine Experimental Economics and ABM.

7.2 BEHAVIORAL AND EXPERIMENTAL ECONOMICS

Behavioral Economics (BE) is a field of economics that emphasizes the importance of how individuals behave in certain context. In particular, this approach takes into account the results from other disciplines, like Psychology, Sociology, and Computer Science, to improve the analysis of agents' choices. The main points of disagreement with the neoclassical approach concern the concept of perfect rationality and the fact that agents have only external constraints. In other words, agents have *internal constraints* such as limited capacity of calculus, which implies that, even if their goal is to reach the best solution, they are not able to obtain this result. Indeed, agents are classified as *boundedly rational*.

It is important to make a distinction between classical and modern BE. According to [33], the pioneer work of classical BE was [46], although the father of the modern BE was [17]. Both approaches rely on the evidence that agents are not fully rational, but the procedures they adopt are very different. On the one hand, the field of classical BE rejects totally the mainstream approach. Indeed, it is assumed that agents have limited information, and, as a consequence, they find the "satisficing solution" rather than the optimal solution. To find this solution, an algorithmic procedure is used in which players have limited information, and they decide step-by-step the best local solution. On the other hand, the modern BE follows an approach very close to the mainstream one. In this field, agents are optimizers, that is, they have a utility function to maximize and a constraint. The main difference with respect to the neoclassical model relies on the axioms on preferences. Indeed, in this field, some assumptions are relaxed, or they are substituted by less tighter hypothesis. The *Rank-Dependent Expected Utility* ([39]) and the *Case-Based Expected Utility* ([27]) are two of the many important theories in the field of BE in which the weight assigned to the utility function is subjective probability rather than the objective one.

In this chapter, we consider examples of both the classical and modern BE in order to understand how differently they work in a context of ABM.

Works in BE should be grouped into two "approaches": one based on the theoretical modeling and one built on experimental method. The *Experimental Economics* is a subfield of the BE. Experiments are used in Economic Science as a tool for the analysis of agents' behavior only in the last decade. Making an experiment means observing real behavior in a controlled setting in which it is possible to control all the variables except for that under observation, that is, the *control variable*. The key feature of experiments in economics is that all the participants are rewarded to give them a monetary incentive to reveal their true preferences. To gather data from experiments, we need two groups, the *control* and *treatment* groups. The latter receives the "treatment," whereas the former is used only for comparison. An example will clarify this concept. Consider, for example, the well-known Public Good Game [31] in which players are divided into groups, and they decide to put the share of their endowment in a public fund. The public good, which consists of the sum of the individual contributions in the same group, is split equally among participants. Suppose that you want to test the impact of inequality on the initial endowment. In this case the *control variable* is the degree of inequality, so in the *control group*, players receive the same amount, whereas in the *treatment group*, agents are endowed with different amount (see, e.g., the contribution by [9] and [12]).

Experiments could be conducted in the lab or in the field. The first one has the great advantage to guarantee the full control of the environment, whereas the field experiment is conducted in the same place where people live, but it ensures, in most of the cases, a representative sample. The majority of the researchers prefers to run lab experiment because it is simple to organize and it is cheap since they use a sample of undergraduate students. This is a weak point of this approach because, having a small sample of students, it undermines the external validity of the experimental results. As in [5], a possible solution to improve this weakness is to consider a large sample of heterogeneous people.

In the field of modern BE, we should identify different subfields: Experimental Microeconomics, Experimental Macroeconomics, and Experimental Finance. The Microeconomics analysis focuses on checking the validity of the neoclassical approach assumptions. One of the most investigated arguments in BE is the hypothesis that agents are selfish, that is, they take into account only their own monetary payoff and do not care about others' payoff. Many works have shown that agents consider also other nonmonetary factors, like altruism [1], reciprocity [20], or the importance of social norms [22]. Considering these aspects of human behavior should also have a great impact on economic policy decisions. Consider, for example, the contributions by [13] and [23], in which the behavior of employers and employees in an experimental asset market is analyzed. The results from these experiments highlight an important feature: the reciprocity between employers and employees plays a crucial role for determining the chosen effort and the wage. If we take into account this result, then we should improve the workers' productivity and so, in turn, foster the economic growth. As pointed out in [41], experiments in macroeconomics should be used to test the theory of general equilibrium or to analyze specific predictions on a single market. In this subfield, researchers try to reproduce a simplified economic system, and they observe the outcome without imposing any behavioral rules. Using this kind of experiments, it is possible to understand individual expectations and the impact of fiscal or monetary policies. One of the most meaningful experiments is that conducted by [24], in which they show that players are affected by *monetary illusion*. This means that, since there is individual money illusion, an anticipated shock generates a nominal inertia. The same conclusions are reached in the experiment by [38] about the money illusion. As suggested in [15], macroeconomic experiments are also very useful in a context with multiple equilibria. Indeed, in [35] an experiment with a simplified decentralized economy is proposed, in which there are two possible equilibria. The results of this experiment show that the equilibrium that emerges from the agents interaction is the Pareto-inferior solution. This lack of convergence to the best or rational equilibrium is confirmed also in an experiment by [10]. Also, in this case, players with their actions reach the suboptimal equilibrium. In the subfield of Experimental Finance the focus is to validate or discard the Efficient Market Hypothesis [21]. In particular, observing individual behavior in asset market is useful to understand if, and under which hypothesis, agents are able to update their initial belief with all available information. Also in this subfield, expectations play a crucial role. Indeed, many experiments have shown the fallacy of the Rational Expectation Hypothesis [36] and, moreover, that players follow some heuristics to make their investment choices (see, e.g., [2]). Experiments in finance also investigate other important features like bubble formation, which is usually related to the well-known *herding behavior* (see the contribution of [48] and [37]).

Why is it so important to take into account experimental methods? The main reason is that experiments allow researcher to observe the real individual behavior in specific context and to understand the micromechanism of agents' interaction, which explain, in turn, the aggregate outcome. Similarly, in ABM, we do not consider the representative agent, but the aggregate outcome emerges from the interaction of heterogeneous agents. In the next section, we analyze in depth how the experimental results are used to calibrate and validate an ABM.

7.3 THE LINKS BETWEEN EXPERIMENTAL ECONOMICS AND THE ABM APPROACH

Experimental Economics and ABM are two distinct research fields, but they have a lot of common features. In fact, both disciplines investigate the individual behavior in a dynamic context, and both take into account the heterogeneity of agents. In particular, ABMs are characterized by specific properties:

- These models follow a bottom-up approach [26,18], meaning that the aggregate results are given by the interaction of many heterogeneous agents. This approach is opposite to the top-down approach of mainstream models in which the behavior of a single agent is sufficient to reproduce the whole system.
- In the model, there are many heterogeneous interacting agents [25,7]. Including these features in a model allows us to have a more realistic approach, in which there is no space for the *representative agent*. Moreover, the interaction among agents leads to specific properties that are not deductible by a simple observation of aggregate behavior.
- Agents are characterized by bounded rationality, but they show cognitive capabilities [34,14]. Indeed, one of the main innovations of these models are that agents do not find their optimal solution by solving a maximization problem but using some heuristics, and they are able to learn different rules observing the environment.

Since ABMs are very different with respect to the standard macromodel, there are no standard methods to evaluate the results of this kind of models. The process of determining the degree to which a model is an accurate representation of the real world is called **validation**. Moreover, ABMs are based on a set of initial conditions and a set of individual rules, which implies that there are many degrees of freedom. The process by which researchers set these parameters is called **calibration**. From a particular point of view, calibration is a necessary step of validation.

There are many nonstandard techniques that should be used to calibrate and validate ABMs. As in [32], the main useful tools to calibrate the parameters of these models are: (i) empirical data (like financial market data), (ii) survey and/or interviews, and (iii) experiments. Empirical calibration that uses real data allows us to have a model with parameters and rules very close to the "real world." In the recent years, many data sets are becoming available for this use and some investigations based on ABM started to use these data (see, e.g., [40] and [6]). The disadvantage to use this calibration technique is that it is very difficult to extrapolate behavioral rules by observing data, and, usually, researchers must use very complex functions to extrapolate these rules. A great advantage deriving from the use of surveys is that data are gathered from a large and heterogeneous sample at a low cost. On the other hand, the drawback is that we obtain only responses to specific questions. This implies that this method does not allow us to understand the real agents' behavior and the dynamics under their decision processes. To improve the quality of the data, usually surveys are combined with face-to-face interviews. In [8], behavioral rules are extrapolated from survey data. The last method suggests to take information from experimental data. As we said in the previous section, experiments, both field and lab, are useful to observe directly the individual behavior in a controlled setting. Another interesting benefit we used in experiments is that it is possible to observe interactions and so to understand how the aggregate results emerge. In [4] and [43], an ABM starting from experimental data is calibrated. It is shown how it is possible to infer some behavioral rules by observing, for example, a Public Good Game and to construct a model that replicates both the structure of the game and the individual behavior. In the next section, we investigate in more detail this calibration procedure.

Before investigating the role of experiments in the process of validation, it is useful to specify what validation means. According to [45], we should consider that the model development process consists of different parts: the system that should be represented, the model that should be used to represent this system, and the computerized model. In [42], the importance of having a model that is "valid" under, at least, two aspects, *operational* and *empirical*, is underlined. Operational validity means verifying if the model's output has sufficient accuracy over the model's intended applicability. In [45], there are listed a lot of validation techniques that should be grouped into two main categories, *subjective* and *quantitative* methods. Some of the techniques that are included in the former set are: Turing test, with which it is possible to test the "intelligent behavior" of the computer system; internal validity the aim of which is to test, through a large number of replications, the magnitude of the internal variability; and face validity through the observation of which it is possible to understand if the model is "reasonable."

Empirical validity is strictly related to the comparison with real data. As explained in [19], it is possible to distinguish between *input* and *output* validation. Input validation is the process through which we select a list of parameters or behavioral rules consistent with the existent real data. The output validation process allows us to compare the results of the model with the real data. Obviously, input and output validations are strictly related. Experiments are usually adopted in the input validation. Indeed, there are a lot of parameters that should be calibrated or validated using real data, but it is very difficult to understand if the behavioral rules implemented in the ABM are in some sense realistic. The better way to gather this information is looking at the experimental evidence. For example, if we want to implement an expectation rule in the model, then it is very useful to take into account the results deriving from experiments on expectations (see, e.g., [29], [16]). Regarding the output validation, there are several well-known quantitative techniques that allow the comparison of summary statistics of both simulated and real data. In [50], two main instruments for validating a model are identified: the indirect calibration approach and the Werker–Brenner approach. The former procedure consists of four main steps: identifying the main stylized facts that the model should reproduce, constructing the model using the empirical/experimental data to choose realistic parameters and rules, running the simulation and trying to improve the set of initial conditions, and the last step consists of identifying the mechanism responsible for the emergence of the stylized facts. The latter approach is very close to the indirect calibration. Indeed, in the initial phase, it is important to calibrate the initial conditions using real data, and then, after having the simulated results, there is a procedure of output validation. In the final phase, this technique requires an exercise of validation for all the possible scenarios that we could obtain changing the initial conditions.

It is important to underline that we should use experiments also as an outcome validation. Indeed, we should construct an ad hoc experiment in which the underlying model is the same of the ABM, and we use human being choices as an input. We should consider that each ABM consists of two main components, the institutional structure, that is, the environment where agents act, and the behavioral decision rules that drive agents' actions. To test the validity of the behavioral rules implemented, we simply set an experiment with the same institutional context, and we ask subjects to take their decision in this context. This procedure allows us to directly compare the behavior of human beings and virtual agents. In other words, by implementing an experiment similar to the ABM we are able to collect a set of "real data" that are perfectly comparable with simulated data.

The relation between ABM approach and Experimental Economics is very strong even if only recent works combine results from these disciplines. As we see, it is possible to use experiments to elicit preferences or simply some heuristics that should be used to calibrate the model. Moreover, it is possible to mix, in the same experiment, inputs from human beings and artificial agents. This has been done in the so-called *participatory simulation* [28,11], in which the decisions in an ABM are taken at the same time by both human beings and virtual agents.

After listing the roles of experiments in the process of constructing an ABM, we briefly recall that these disciplines are *complementary*, and, before to analyze some practical examples, we explain the role of ABM in the experiments. One of the main disadvantages of running an experiment is the cost for paying participants. As a consequence, in many cases, the sample is small and composed by undergraduate students. This implies that the results collected could be biased or not fully representative of the agents behavior. Besides the use of a larger sample, another possible solution is to implement an ABM based on the same assumption of the experiment. If we are able to replicate experimental results using an ABM, then we should overcome the problem of external validity of the experimental results and replicate the results in a system with as many agents as we need.

7.4 APPLICATIONS: CALIBRATION AND VALIDATION OF AN ABM

In this section, we briefly explain how to implement a process of calibration or validation based on experimental data by reporting three different examples. The first one is an example of how to use experiments to calibrate the behavior of artificial automata. The second example shows how to construct an experiment to validate the results of a preexisting ABM. Finally, the third example is useful to explain a combination of calibration and validation process, and we will describe the validation procedure of a Learning to Forecast Experiment.

7.4.1 Example #1: Calibration Procedure

The first example explains how to calibrate the parameters of a model starting from an experiment in order to replicate human behavior. The experiment we consider is the two-choice bandit experiment. This experiment is very simple: it consists of a sequential choice in 100 trials between two actions, named A and B. In any trial, subjects have the possibility to gain a unit payoff. Usually, this kind of game is implemented to construct an algorithm able to find the best solution of an N-choice problem. This means that, in the economic context, this problem is used, for example, to realize the algorithm for profit maximization (see [44]). In contrast, the calibration procedure proposed in [4] and explained in the following, is dedicated to finding the algorithm able to reproduce human behavior characterized by limited rationality.

The experimental data considered by Arthur arise from an investigation conducted by Robillard at the Harvard university. In this experiment, the individual choice between A and B is driven by this expected payoff. Indeed, the probability to gain a unit payoff is expressed as $p_A:p_B$, where p_A represents the probability to gain a unit profit if the action A is chosen, and p_B is the probability to gain a unit profit if the action B is chosen. The experiments consisted in different sessions characterized by the following structure of the payoff: three sessions with 50:0, that is, 50% of probability to win if the option A is chosen and zero probability to gain if option B is chosen; one session 30:0; one session 80:0; one session 80:40; and one session 60:30. The outcome is expressed as the percentage of choice A over the total. Results show that, even if there is a process of learning, the individual behavior is not fully rational. One example to prove the bounded rationality is that the percentage of A choice is different from one even in the session 80:0.

In [4], these data were used to calibrate the behavior of artificial agents with the aim of replicate the real choices of human agents, that is, with the aim to model bounded rational automata. To calibrate the model, the author implemented a decision algorithm and then, starting from observed data, set the value of the parameters. The aim of the process is to take a decision among N alternatives. As in the experiment, the decision is driven by the profit, which, in turn, also influences the mechanism of learning. The algorithm implemented for modeling the behavior of the automata consists of:

- Agents face N alternatives; the vector S_0 contains the initial value of the strength of each alternative, whereas S_t is the vector of strength of the subsequent periods; C_t is the sum of the elements of S_t.
- In any period t, the probability associated with each alternative is given by $p_t = \frac{S_t}{C_t}$. According to this probability, the action j is chosen.
- Action j gives a profit $\Phi(j)$. This value is used to update the vector of strength, that is, $S_{t+1} = S_t + \beta_t$, where $\beta_t = \Phi(j)e_j$.
- The final step is to normalize the vector C_t in the following way: $C_t = Ct^v$, where v is the learning parameter.

In the last step, the vector C_t is normalized to include the mechanism of learning. Indeed, the parameter v measures the speed of learning, that is, it regulates how fast is the convergence to the optimal choice. This implies that in the vector C, there is information about both the payoff and the learning. Results presented in [3] show that the optimality condition is guaranteed under the condition $v = 1$, whereas in the case $v < 1$, agents choose inferior alternatives. The behavior of artificial agents pass through the calibration of the parameters C and v. The calibration process is based on the minimization of the sum of the squared errors between the frequency of choice of option A made by the automata and the human subjects. The results lead to $C = 31.1$ and $v = 0$. The behavior of the automata is closed to that of human beings, as shown in Fig. 7.1.

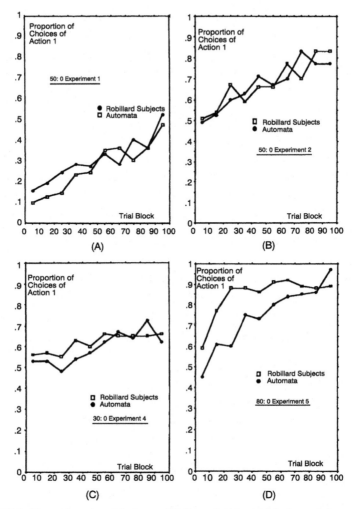

FIGURE 7.1 Figures from the original paper [4]. Share of choice A of the human beings compared with the choice of the automata.

By this exercise of calibration, Arthur showed that one of the reasons for the emergence of bounded rationality observed in the experiment is that they are not willing to explore all the feasible alternatives. This is reflected in the choice of inferior alternatives during the game.

This simple example highlights the impossibility to calibrate behavioral parameters without the use of data from experiments and underlines how it is possible to have a good reproduction of human behavior by a good calibration of only two parameters.

7.4.2 Example #2: Validation Procedure

Contrary to the previous example, the starting point in this case is the ABM in which there is implemented a series of rules to take a decision about the production. Indeed, this example is devoted to explain how to set an experiment to test if the behavioral rules implemented in a specific ABM are realistic. We consider the model proposed in [49], which is an economic long-wave model based on the self-ordering hypothesis. Before analyzing the experimental setting, we briefly describe the model to better understand the environment in which subjects interact.

The economy considered in the model has two sectors, consumer goods and capital good. The link between these sectors is quite ordinary: an increase in the demand for consumer goods leads to an increase of the capacity of firms, which, in turn, increase their need for capital. This implies that capital good producers increase their stock of capital, and, as a result, there is a positive feedback loop created by self-ordering. The more interesting aspect is that the firms' actions are modeled under the assumption of limited rationality and that the expectations about future orders are modeled as adaptive rather than rational expectations.

The production function of firms in the consumer good's side is given by the product of production capacity (PC) and the capacity utilization (CU), that is,

$$Q_t = PC_t * CU_t,$$

where $CU_t = f(IP_t/PC_t)$, so that the capacity utilization depends on the indicated production and on the production capacity as well. The indicated production, in turn, is a function of the backlog of unfilled orders and the time necessary to process. Production capacity depends on the capital stock (C) and on the constant capital-output ratio (COR), meaning that

$$PC_t = \frac{C_t}{COR_t}.$$

The capital stock is the accumulation of capital acquisition, net of the capital discards, which is determined according to sector's supply line. The supply line depends on the difference between capital order (CO) and capital acquisition. In particular, sector's supply line increases if the capital order is higher than the capital acquisition.

The capital order is the control variable of the firms, and it is determined as follows:

$$CO_t = C_t * COF_t,$$

PRODUCTION SECTOR: OVERVIEW

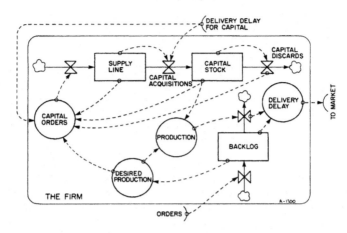

FIGURE 7.2   Figure from the original paper [49]. Structure of the simulation model.

$$COF_t = f\left(\frac{CD_t + CC_t + CSL_t}{C_t}\right),$$

where COF is the capital order fraction. The equation relative to COF suggests that the capital order takes place for three main reasons: for capital discard (CD), for correcting the discrepancy between actual and desired capital stock (CC), and for correcting the discrepancy between actual and desired supply line (CSL). Fig. 7.2 shows a graphical summary of the model.

The main goal of the firm is to eliminate or, at least, minimize the difference between actual and desired productions taking into account the time necessary to adjust the supply line. In other words, the objective is

$$\min_{C_t} CC_t = \frac{DC_t - C_t}{TAC}.$$

To test the behavior of firms, a shock on the demand side is introduced. The exogenous shock consists of the increase of orders. The simulation results show that firms need more than one period to adjust the production after the demand shock and the backlog and the level of production slowly converge to the equilibrium. The shapes of both capacity and production are displayed in Fig. 7.3.

To test the validity of the behavioral assumption implemented, an experiment based on the same framework was implemented. In particular, the author places the human subject in the same institutional context assumed in the model, and he gives the same information. The information available are both the history and

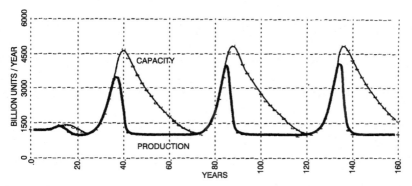

FIGURE 7.3 Figure from the original paper [49]. The shape of both capacity and production from the simulation model.

the current values of all the main variables like capacity, desired production and orders. This means that players have perfect and complete information about the market and that they just make their order decision for the current period. To mimic the structure of the simulation, an initial exogenous shock was introduced to analyze how subjects revise the capital order. Subjects are paid according to the absolute difference between desired and actual production to mimic the objective function of artificial agents in the simulation.

The results of the experiment are shown in Fig. 7.4. In panel (A), we show what should be the optimal behavior, whereas panels (B) and (C) show the experimental data. It is easy to see that subject choices are not fully rational. In fact, they overreact to the shock by increasing too much the order, and so they generate an excess of capacity. They need some periods of learning to correctly manage the orders. The author concludes that their assumptions about the limited rationality of firms are correct. Moreover, he adjusts the model by including the process of learning observed in the experiment.

Also, in this case, we can conclude that there are no alternative methods to directly test the correctness of assumptions in an ABM. This is particularly true in this model, in which one of the most important hypothesis is that firms are modeled as bounded rational agents.

7.4.3 Example #3: Validation and Calibration Procedure

This last example is useful to understand how it is possible to extrapolate information for calibrate parameters and then to validate the results of the simulation. We consider a model in which the data are collected by running a *Learning to Forecast Experiment*. This experiment is useful to observe individual expectations by asking to make forecast of the future price of an asset for 50 periods. In

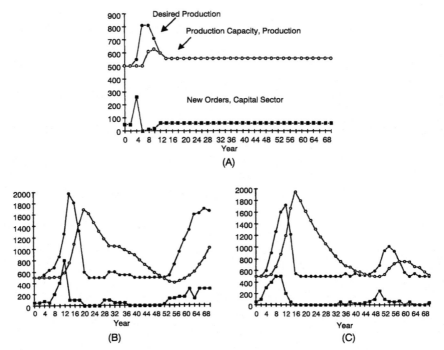

FIGURE 7.4 Figures from the original paper [49]. Results from the validation experiment with human beings. The picture shows: desired productions (black dotted line), production capacity (dotted line), and new orders from capital sectors (squared line).

this experiment, in fact, subjects do not directly trade, but they make just predictions, which then are used to compute the demand of the asset. This framework is very important to observe if the rational expectation hypothesis is a right representation of individual behavior. The experiment we describe is that proposed in [30], in which subjects make forecasts on a future price of an asset having only qualitative information about the market. To improve the individual performance in terms of predictions, subjects are paid according to the quadratic forecasting errors.

In the experiment, subjects are split in group of six and make individual predictions. Subjects have no information about the equation for demand and supply of assets, but they have access to the past information about both their own predictions and the market price. After collecting all the individual forecasts, the demand for the asset is computed, and, equating the demand to the given fixed offer, we obtain the standard equation for the realized price, that is,

$$p_t = \frac{1}{1+r}\left[(1-n_t)\bar{p}^e_{t+1} + n_t p^f_t + \bar{d} + \varepsilon_t\right], \tag{7.1}$$

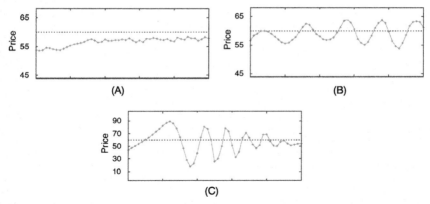

FIGURE 7.5 Figures from the original paper of [2]. Experimental market price in three different groups. (A) Slow monotonic convergence. (B) Small oscillations. (C) Large oscillations.

where r is the interest rate, $\bar{p}^e_{t+1} = \sum_{i=1}^{6} p^e_{it+1}$ is the average predicted price, $\bar{d}$ is the mean dividend, and ε_t is a small normal shock. In [30], there are also stabilizer robot traders, and n_t is the share of these robots in each period.

The results highlight that predictions are made using rules different from the rational expectations because none of the markets converges to the fundamental price. The shape of the observed market price in all experimental markets, shown in Fig. 7.5, can be summarized in three sets:

- slow monotonic convergence or converging pattern (Subfigure (A));
- persistent small oscillations around the fundamental (Subfigure (B));
- large initial oscillations dampening toward the end of the experiment (Subfigure (C)).

Starting from this evidence, in [2], it is suggested that a good description of the observed behavior can be explained by the implementation of the so-called *Heuristic Switching Model* (HSM). The HSM is based on the idea that each agent considers four rules and he/she switch among these rules according to a performance measure. First of all, authors use the collected data to calibrate the parameters of the model, that is, the parameters relative to the forecasting rules implemented. They take into account four specific rules:

- Adaptive rule (ADA):

$$p^e_{t+1} = \alpha p_{t-1} + (1-\alpha)p^e_{t-1}, \quad \alpha = 0.65.$$

- Weak trend following rule (WTR):

$$p^e_{t+1} = p_{t-1} + w(p_{t-1} - p_{t-2}), \quad w = 0.4.$$

- Strong trend following rule (STR):

$$p_{t+1}^e = p_{t-1} + s(p_{t-1} - p_{t-2}), \quad s = 1.3.$$

- Learning and Adjustment rule (LAA):

$$p_{t+1}^e = 0.5(p_{t-1}^{av} + p_{t-1}) + (p_{t-1} - p_{t-2}).$$

The calibrated parameters are $\alpha = 0.65$, $w = 0.4$, and $s = 1.3$.

As we said, agents evaluate the forecasting performance of each rule and then decide which is the best rule to implement in any period. The switching mechanism is based on the performance measure U, which, in turn, depends on the quadratic forecasting error. The measure U is given by

$$U_{h,t-1} = -\left(p_{t-1} - p_{h,t-1}^e\right)^2 + \eta U_{h,t-2}, \quad h = 1, \ldots, 4,$$

with $\eta = 0.7$. After computing the performance measure, the impact of each rule h is computed by using the discrete choice model with asynchronous updating, that is,

$$n_{h,t} = \delta n_{h,t-1} + (1 - \delta) \frac{\exp(\beta U_{h,t-1})}{Z_{t-1}},$$

$$Z_{t-1} = \sum_{h=1}^{H} \exp(\beta U_{h,t-1}).$$

Z_{t-1} is a normalization factor. In the model, $\delta = 0.9$ and $\beta = 0.4$.

Once computed the performance measure and thus the impact of each forecasting rule, we compute the average forecasting as

$$\bar{p}_{t+1}^e = \sum_{h=1}^{H} n_{h,t} p_{h,t+1}^e.$$

The model described makes one step-ahead predictions and takes as an input the realized price of the first and second periods. The other parameters (s, w, δ, η, β) are calibrated to reproduce the experimental results. The results of this process are shown in Fig. 7.6.

Looking at the results, the in-sample forecast works well. This implies that agents use a mix of adaptive expectations rules and trend following rules to make their forecasts. The analysis concludes with the out-of-sample predictions. To make those predictions for different time horizons, that is, from one to seven periods ahead, the parameters are set according to the grid search procedure. The implemented values for the parameters δ, η, and β are those that minimize the

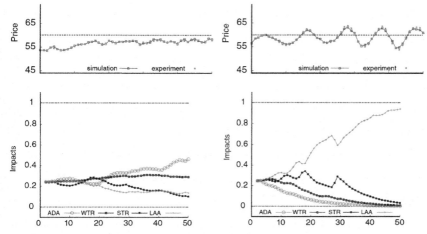

FIGURE 7.6 Figures from the original paper [2]. On the top panel the experimental market price (red line, in web version) and the simulated price (blue line, in web version). On the bottom panel the impact of different rules.

mean squared error. The best performance of the out-of-sample predictions is in replicating the so-called converging groups in which the mean squared error remains more or less stable during the whole simulation.

This last example is very useful to understand the importance of the information gathered by experiments. We have seen how from a very simple prediction task it is possible to extrapolate forecasting rules that can be implemented in any ABM of financial markets.

7.5 CONCLUSIONS

In this chapter, we review the link between the ABM approach and the field of Experimental Economics. Since the approach of ABM is not based on a standard economic maximization procedure, it is necessary to have data to confirm the accuracy of the results. There are many techniques to calibrate and/or validate an ABM, but the experimental approach is one of the best approaches for these purposes. We propose three examples to show how ABM and Experimental Economics are strictly related. The first example is devoted to explain how to calibrate the behavior of artificial agents starting from experimental results. The second one explains the procedure of validation of an ABM by setting an ad hoc experiment. Finally, we resume a work that uses experimental results for both validation and calibration procedures. In all of these examples, the parameters considered are behavioral ones. This means that it is very difficult to estimate these values starting from empirical data or surveys, and so we believe that the experimental economics is the prominent approach, which can be considered for validation and calibration.

REFERENCES

[1] J. Andreoni, Giving with impure altruism: applications to charity and Ricardian equivalence, Journal of Political Economy (1989) 1447–1458.

[2] M. Anufriev, C. Hommes, Evolutionary selection of individual expectations and aggregate outcomes in asset pricing experiments, American Economic Journal: Microeconomics 4 (4) (2012) 35–64.

[3] W.B. Arthur, A Learning Algorithm That Mimics Human Learning, Working paper, Standford University, 1990.

[4] W.B. Arthur, Designing economic agents that act like human agents: a behavioral approach to bounded rationality, The American Economic Review 81 (2) (1991) 353–359.

[5] N. Berg, G. Gigerenzer, As-if behavioral economics: neoclassical economics in disguise?, History of Economic Ideas 18 (1) (2010) 133–166.

[6] T. Berger, P. Schreinemachers, Creating agents and landscapes for multiagent systems from random samples, Ecology and Society 11 (2) (2006) 19.

[7] R. Blundell, T.M. Stoker, Heterogeneity and aggregation, Journal of Economic Literature 43 (2) (2005) 347–391.

[8] D.G. Brown, D.T. Robinson, Effects of heterogeneity in residential preferences on an agent-based model of urban sprawl, Ecology and Society 11 (1) (2006) 46.

[9] E. Buckley, R. Croson, Income and wealth heterogeneity in the voluntary provision of linear public goods, Journal of Public Economics 90 (4) (2006) 935–955.

[10] C.M. Capra, T. Tanaka, C.F. Camerer, L. Feiler, V. Sovero, C.N. Noussair, The impact of simple institutions in experimental economies with poverty traps, The Economic Journal 119 (539) (2009) 977–1009.

[11] J.-C. Castella, T.N. Trung, S. Boissau, Participatory simulation of land-use changes in the northern mountains of Vietnam: the combined use of an agent-based model, a role-playing game, and a geographic information system, Ecology and Society 10 (1) (2005) 27.

[12] A. Colasante, A. Russo, The Impact of Inequality on Cooperation: An Experimental Study, Tech. rep., 2014.

[13] A. Colasante, A. Russo, Reciprocity in the Labour Market: Experimental Evidence, Tech. rep., 2014.

[14] G. Dosi, O. Marsili, L. Orsenigo, R. Salvatore, Learning, market selection and the evolution of industrial structures, Small Business Economics 7 (6) (1995) 411–436.

[15] J. Duffy, Agent-based models and human subject experiments, Handbook of Computational Economics 2 (2006) 949–1011.

[16] G.P. Dwyer, A.W. Williams, R.C. Battalio, T.I. Mason, Tests of rational expectations in a stark setting, The Economic Journal (1993) 586–601.

[17] W. Edwards, The theory of decision making, Psychological Bulletin 51 (4) (1954) 380.

[18] J.M. Epstein, R. Axtell, Growing Artificial Societies: Social Science from the Bottom Up, Brookings Institution Press, 1996.

[19] G. Fagiolo, A. Moneta, P. Windrum, A critical guide to empirical validation of agent-based models in economics: methodologies, procedures, and open problems, Computational Economics 30 (3) (2007) 195–226.

[20] A. Falk, U. Fischbacher, A theory of reciprocity, Games and Economic Behavior 54 (2) (2006) 293–315.

[21] E.F. Fama, Efficient capital markets: a review of theory and empirical work, The Journal of Finance 25 (2) (1970) 383–417.

[22] E. Fehr, U. Fischbacher, Social norms and human cooperation, Trends in Cognitive Sciences 8 (4) (2004) 185–190.

[23] E. Fehr, G. Kirchsteiger, A. Riedl, Gift exchange and reciprocity in competitive experimental markets, European Economic Review 42 (1) (1998) 1–34.

[24] E. Fehr, J.-R. Tyran, Does money illusion matter? The American Economic Review (2001) 1239–1262.

[25] M. Gallegati, A. Kirman, Reconstructing economics: agent based models and complexity, Complexity Economics 1 (1) (2012) 5–31.

[26] D.D. Gatti, S. Desiderio, E. Gaffeo, P. Cirillo, M. Gallegati, Macroeconomics from the Bottom-up, vol. 1, Springer Science & Business Media, 2011.

[27] I. Gilboa, D. Schmeidler, Case-based decision theory, The Quarterly Journal of Economics (1995) 605–639.

[28] P. Guyot, S. Honiden, Agent-based participatory simulations: merging multi-agent systems and role-playing games, Journal of Artificial Societies and Social Simulation 9 (4) (2006).

[29] J.D. Hey, Expectations formation: rational or adaptive or...? Journal of Economic Behavior & Organization 25 (3) (1994) 329–349.

[30] C. Hommes, J. Sonnemans, J. Tuinstra, H. Van de Velden, Coordination of expectations in asset pricing experiments, The Review of Financial Studies 18 (3) (2005) 955–980.

[31] R.M. Isaac, J.M. Walker, A.W. Williams, Group size and the voluntary provision of public goods: experimental evidence utilizing large groups, Journal of Public Economics 54 (1) (1994) 1–36.

[32] M.A. Janssen, E. Ostrom, Empirically based, agent-based models, Ecology and Society 11 (2) (2006) 37.

[33] Y.-F. Kao, K.V. Velupillai, Behavioural economics: classical and modern, The European Journal of the History of Economic Thought 22 (2) (2015) 236–271.

[34] A. Kirman, The economy as an evolving network, Journal of Evolutionary Economics 7 (4) (1997) 339–353.

[35] V. Lei, C.N. Noussair, Equilibrium selection in an experimental macroeconomy, Southern Economic Journal (2007) 448–482.

[36] R.E. Lucas, T.J. Sargent, Rational Expectations and Econometric Practice, vol. 2, University of Minnesota Press, 1981.

[37] C. Noussair, S. Robin, B. Ruffieux, Price bubbles in laboratory asset markets with constant fundamental values, Experimental Economics 4 (1) (2001) 87–105.

[38] C.N. Noussair, G. Richter, J.-R. Tyran, Money illusion and nominal inertia in experimental asset markets, The Journal of Behavioral Finance 13 (1) (2012) 27–37.

[39] J. Quiggin, A theory of anticipated utility, Journal of Economic Behavior & Organization 3 (4) (1982) 323–343.

[40] M.C. Recchioni, G. Tedeschi, M. Gallegati, A calibration procedure for analyzing stock price dynamics in an agent-based framework, Journal of Economic Dynamics and Control 60 (2015) 1–25.

[41] R. Ricciuti, Bringing macroeconomics into the lab, Journal of Macroeconomics 30 (1) (2008) 216–237.

[42] M.G. Richiardi, R. Leombruni, N.J. Saam, M. Sonnessa, A common protocol for agent-based social simulation, Journal of Artificial Societies and Social Simulation 9 (2006).

[43] A.E. Roth, I. Erev, Learning in extensive-form games: experimental data and simple dynamic models in the intermediate term, Games and Economic Behavior 8 (1) (1995) 164–212.

[44] M. Rothschild, A two-armed bandit theory of market pricing, Journal of Economic Theory 9 (2) (1974) 185–202.

[45] R.G. Sargent, Verification and validation of simulation models, Journal of Simulation 7 (1) (2013) 12–24.

[46] H.A. Simon, Birth of an organization: the economic cooperation administration, Public Administration Review 13 (4) (1953) 227–236.

[47] H.A. Simon, A behavioral model of rational choice, The Quarterly Journal of Economics (1955) 99–118.

[48] V.L. Smith, G.L. Suchanek, A.W. Williams, Bubbles, crashes, and endogenous expectations in experimental spot asset markets, Econometrica (1988) 1119–1151.

[49] J.D. Sterman, Testing behavioral simulation models by direct experiment, Management Science 33 (12) (1987) 1572–1592.

[50] P. Windrum, G. Fagiolo, A. Moneta, Empirical validation of agent-based models: alternatives and prospects, Journal of Artificial Societies and Social Simulation 10 (2) (2007) 8.

Chapter 8

Econometric Methods for Agent-Based Models

Leonardo Bargigli
University of Florence, Florence, Italy

8.1 INTRODUCTION

A significant achievement of ABMs is that they are able to replicate stylized facts, in particular, those that are resistant to an explanation in terms of mainstream theory. For instance, thanks to the introduction of agent heterogeneity, bounded rationality and learning, decentralized out-of-equilibrium interactions, ABMs were able to replicate some fundamental features of financial markets such as non-Gaussianity and volatility clustering [9], or business fluctuations and distribution of the firm size and their growth rate [13].

In the last few years, a growing number of contributions suggests that ABMs should move from ad hoc calibration toward the consistent estimation of models [15,22]. The purpose of this chapter is to provide a representation of the state-of-the-art in this field and then to give a contribution on the two specific issues of parameter calibration and sensitivity analysis. In particular, in Section 8.2, I present a review of the literature on ABM estimation. In Section 8.3, I provide an example of parameter calibration with reference to a random network model of the credit market. In Section 8.4, I compare a number of alternative statistical models, which could serve as "reduced form" of a financial accelerator ABM, and, after having selected our model of choice, I analyze the role of each parameter. In Section 8.5, I provide some conclusions.

8.2 LITERATURE REVIEW

From the onset it is important to underline the specificity of ABMs within the larger field of simulated models. In particular, ABMs cannot be likened to simulated statistical models. Indeed, the mathematical structure of the latter is completely specified by the modeler, for example, by choosing regressors, functional shapes, lags, and by making assumptions on the structure of errors. ABM modelers instead have no equivalent control over the properties of their model.

Introduction to Agent-Based Economics. http://dx.doi.org/10.1016/B978-0-12-803834-5.00011-4

Not coincidentally, unexpected simulation results are a common experience for researchers in this field. Moreover, once statistical models are estimated, they can be used to provide computationally inexpensive predictions over the expected value of endogenous variables conditioned to variations of the exogenous variables. Instead, ABM modelers are always bound to replicate computationally expensive simulation runs over each point of the parameter space to provide such predictions. This necessity follows from the fact that the functional form of the relationship between endogenous and exogenous variables in ABMs is unknown.

8.2.1 Estimation of Agent-Based Models

In a classical statistical framework, the estimation problem for an ABM can be formulated in general as follows:

$$\theta^* = \underset{\theta \in \Theta}{\arg\min}\ F\big(h(x), h\big(y(\theta)\big)\big), \tag{8.1}$$

where F is a criterion function, x is a vector of observations from real data, $y(\theta)$ is a vector of observations produced from a simulated model characterized by the parameter vector θ, and h is a vector function defined over x and y. A frequent choice for F, in case of overidentified models, is a quadratic loss function with an optimal weighting matrix, that is, one minimizing the uncertainty of estimation.

In general, Eq. (8.1) defines a class of methods, denoted as "simulated minimum distance" methods [22]. If h results from the estimation of the same "auxiliary" statistical model over real and simulated data, this approach is usually termed "indirect inference"; if h stands for a set of moments computed over x and y, we obtain the method of simulated moments (MSM) [19]. The approach of "moment estimation" contrasts with that of "path calibration," whereby θ is chosen to make x and y as close as possible. The latter does not lend itself to econometric estimation in a frequentist framework since generally the resulting estimator is inconsistent [19]. The idea of path calibration comes close to the notion of a "history-friendly approach" in modeling [15] although the latter escapes inconsistency since it does not rely on econometric estimation but on a qualitative approach. More generally, if the fitness of the model is the only preoccupation, even inconsistent econometric estimates might be accepted. Indeed, a disregard for the structural estimation of models, that is, for the correct estimation of their structural parameters, is what is most often intended with "calibration" in the mainstream literature. This view is consistent with an instrumentalist approach, which disregards the plausibility of models (Section 8.2.2).

The appeal of SMD for ABMs is straightforward to explain since the possibility of writing down the likelihood function of an ABM is circumscribed to a subset of relatively simple models of the financial markets [1,31]. For instance, Lux [29] estimates numerically the likelihood of a model of market sentiment formation, in which agents switch between optimistic and pessimistic attitudes with a given exponential transition rate. Using this specification, it is possible to write down the time evolution equation of the conditional density of the relevant time series by means of the Fokker–Planck equation and obtain the conditional density as a numerical solution of this equation.

An early example of application of SMD is provided by Bianchi et al. [4], who use as moments the sequence of parameters of the cross-sectional distributions of total assets and net-worth over different years. This choice follows the idea of path calibration, raising the problems of consistency mentioned before. Franke [16] instead applies consistently MSM for the estimation of the exchange rate model of Manzan and Westerhoff [30] by choosing a set of longitudinal moments defined over stationary time series (returns and absolute returns). By reestimating the structural parameters from simulated data the author shows that the objective function is insensitive to changes in the parameter weighting the impact of fundamentalists over the market, so that this parameter cannot be identified. Then he estimates the parameters from real market data, coming to the conclusion that the model is rejected as misspecified by means of the J test although some moments are well reproduced in terms of t-statistics. While elaborating this point, the author takes an instrumentalist stance by underlining that since no model can be regarded as true, this matching may well suffice for accepting the model. On the other hand, since estimation is performed with a numerical algorithm that might not provide global optima and no systematic study of the objective function is performed, we lack the certainty of the correct identification of the parameters. Winker et al. [43] employ a composite objective function involving seven moments, studying its behavior over a grid of parameter values for two ABMs and two time series models (GARCH and stochastic volatility) and finding that at least some of the parameters might be unidentifiable. The distribution of values of the objective function for the purpose of inference is obtained by block bootstrapping the real data to preserve their autocorrelation. A similar systematic analysis is performed by Franke and Westerhoff [17], who employ a different bootstrapping procedure, finding a statistically significant fitness for a herding model of the stock market with respect to the daily returns of the S&P 500 stock market index.

If the model has a well-defined reduced form, then a simulated maximum likelihood (SML) estimation may be performed using a consistent simulator of the conditional loglikelihood, which depends on the distribution of the errors appearing in the reduced form. Otherwise, the joint loglikelihood must be simulated [19] (these limits, of course, also affect Bayesian estimation). In both cases, we need to simulate the likelihood of $y(\theta)$ for each θ from a large set of values, a procedure that is computationally intensive except for the simplest models. This task can be made relatively easier by efficient sampling techniques like importance sampling, sequential Monte Carlo, or Markov Chain Monte Carlo [26].

Grazzini et al. [21] review alternative methods for estimating the likelihood function from simulations in a Bayesian context. These include nonparametric kernel density estimation, parametric estimation via pseudomaximum likelihood (PML), and likelihood-free methods such as approximate Bayesian computation (ABC). PML relies on a family of misspecified densities, which nevertheless ensures the consistency of the estimators, once we have at disposal a tractable function $m(\theta)$ for the moments satisfying the identification condition for θ. Although this function generally is not available ex ante for ABMs, it is nevertheless possible to estimate it from simulations, obtaining what is called a metamodel of the ABM (see below). With ABC the Bayesian approach comes close to SMD since the method is based on the choice of a set of summary statistics and of a distance function, although in this case there is no optimization involved.

We might also consider filtering theory to obtain the sequence of conditional distributions of observables. In general, resorting to hidden state variables allows greater flexibility since it allows us to estimate the time-varying parameters of the DGP if any. Unfortunately, neither the Kalman filter nor the extended Kalman filter, which rely respectively on linearity or linearization around a steady-state solution of the model, is readily applicable to ABMs. Indeed, up to now, no one has provided a state space representation of this kind of models. Since it is very unlikely that such a representation may be derived analytically in general, resorting to the estimation of a metamodel (see below) might be the only general recipe for ABMs. Otherwise, more complex nonlinear particle filters may be employed; see the discussion by Grazzini and Richiardi [22].

Standard numerical algorithms are bound to fail on ABMs unless the seed for the generation of pseudorandom terms in the simulations is kept fixed during optimization [19]. On the other hand, if the ABM is nonergodic, fixing the random seeds may lead the model to a specific equilibrium in such a way that the structural parameters remain unidentified. Alternatively, we can employ adapted optimization algorithms, such as that proposed by Gilli and Winker [18], who compute the surface response of the objective function with noisy inputs. A shortcoming of this option is that we cannot avoid extensive Monte Carlo replications. Otherwise, we may replace the ABM with a deterministic counterpart, which can be obtained, for example, if the expected distribution of agents over different types is known [37].

Grazzini and Richiardi [22] discuss the restrictions that make an ABM econometrically tractable. Their approach contrasts with the more skeptical stance of Fagiolo et al. [15], who underline that the world is intrinsically indeterminate and nonlinear and thus are dubious regarding the possibility that ABMs might be consistently identified from actual data. Moreover, these authors warn against the risk of conservativeness framing ABMs on the basis of estimation restrictions or depending on the availability of data implies.

To apply SML and MSM, it is required that both the endogenous and exogenous variables follow a stationary process [19]. At least weak stationarity is usually required instead to apply II since this condition is necessary for the auxiliary models, for example, VAR models. Since ABMs do no necessarily converge to a unique and stable equilibrium, we need to choose carefully a set of observables that display this property. If the model is not ergodic, that is, equilibria change depending on initial conditions, then the latter should be estimated, or otherwise the observed initial conditions should be used as inputs for simulations [22]. Since it is not possible to know in advance if the ABM is stationary and ergodic, these conditions must be tested through simulations. In particular, since we do not know the distribution of moments, a nonparametric estimation approach should be preferred. The power limitation of such tests may be overcome by increasing the number of observations in simulated data. Grazzini [20] proposes to employ the Wald–Wolfowitz or runs test to check the stationarity of moments and their ergodicity. In the former case, the null hypothesis of equal population is checked across different time windows; in the latter case, it is checked across simulation runs with different initial conditions (which include different random seeds for the generation of pseudorandom numbers). Alternatively, other nonparametric tests like KS may be employed [23].

A comparative approach is of fundamental importance for ABMs. To strengthen our confidence in these models, we need to compare their forecasting power with that of other, incompatible, assumptions, for example, those underlying DSGE models. In this sense, estimation should be regarded as a stage of a more general procedure of model selection, by which we try to detect the best model among a set of alternatives according to some criterion, like goodness-of-fit measures and/or information criteria.

Model selection should be made consistent with the assumption that agents do not know the true model of the economy, in contrast, for example, to the standard assumption of rational expectations. Indeed, all models at hand for comparison might be misspecified. Model uncertainty, as defined by Hansen and Sargent [24], is consistent with a pluralist approach, which takes into account the ubiquitous problem of "observational equivalence" between different models and the existence of different research traditions, that is, of different prior beliefs regarding the phenomena under study. Model uncertainty has broad policy implications since according to the minimax principle, the least favorable model, and not the most likely one, should be preferred by the policy maker since we have no guarantee that the "best model" is correctly specified. Indeed, the notion of a single best model might be replaced by the weaker notion of a model confidence set, that is, a set of models constructed so that it contains the best model with a given level of confidence [25].

Barde [2] provides an example of this approach by comparing the fitness of three AB herding models of financial markets with a set of ARCH/GARCH processes. The author follows a nonparametric approach that requires to map the DGP of a set of candidate models to a set of standardized Markov processes whose conditional likelihoods can be computed and then compared. Each model is simulated: ARCH/GARCH processes using parameters that are estimated on real data and ABMs using a discretionary set of values (no optimization is involved). The procedure requires that the state space is bounded and discretized in an optimized way that ensures that the loss of information does not affect the comparison of models. Once this is obtained, the transition matrix is computed with a suitable algorithm, and the (discretized) log-likelihood of real data provides the fitness of models. The results show that one of the AB models performs comparably to the best ARCH/GARCH models, notwithstanding the fact that the parameters of the former are not optimized. Furthermore, a model confidence set is built by block bootstrapping the simulated series [25], showing that a number of the best ABMs fall into the 90% confidence level. In particular, AB models perform better than ARCH/GARCH model during turbulent market events. The main limitation of this approach in its current form is that it is univariate.

8.2.2 Estimation, Validation, Calibration

In the ABM literature, the term validation is used in a broader meaning than in the current statistical literature, where it is mostly considered as equivalent to forecasting. This is consistent with the assumption of a "realist" approach as opposed to an "instrumentalist" and "apriorist" one [15,27]. According to the former, any model should be an accurate description of reality, and strong "as if" a priori assumptions, which are typical of mainstream economics (e.g., full information, full foresight, optimizing behavior), should be avoided. This means that validation requires, in the first place, the selection of "valid" hypotheses, that is, hypotheses which are consistent, or at least not at odds with our prior knowledge of the phenomenon under consideration. If we assume model uncertainty (see above), then realism implies that the prior probability of alternative models is biased in favor of those with the "best" combination of simplicity and degree of accurateness of their hypotheses. Whereas the former may be quantified by the number of parameters, the latter can only be evaluated on the grounds of plausible arguments since they logically precede the formalization of the model. Indeed, under this perspective, realism is fully consistent with pluralism since the accurateness of any model is intrinsically debatable and provisional.

Fagiolo et al. [15] propose to define *empirical* validation as the comparison between simulated outputs and real world observables, within this realist and pluralist framework. In this sense, empirical validation may be conceived as a synonym of "model estimation" as intended by the econometricians, unless we accept that this comparison is performed loosely, without a rigorous statistical inference. In the latter case, it is indeed more common to speak of "calibration" [11]. An example of the former, more rigorous approach is provided by Guerini and Moneta [23], who propose a validation procedure based on the comparison of the causal structures underlying the ABM and the real DGP. These follow from an Indirect Inference estimation. Indeed, they are obtained as a result of the same identification procedure, involving causal dependency, applied to two SVAR models, which are estimated respectively on simulated and real data. The authors propose a measure to assess the similarity between causal structures but make no attempt to maximize the similarity of the two models by means of parameter estimation.

Fagiolo et al. [15] define instead "parameter calibration" as the choice of parameter values with the goal of stylized fact replication. Curiously enough, this terminology is inherited from mainstream macroeconomic theory [28]. The first vintages of RBC and DSGE models were usually "calibrated," that is, the parameters were chosen with reference to some prior belief or some external knowledge. This approach was used as a substitute for full blown estimation since these models systematically failed likelihood-based tests.

A standard example concerns the calibration of investment adjustment costs in business cycle models, where the parameters are sometimes calibrated to match the model-predicted investment volatility with observed investment volatility. Examples of this sort make calibration much like to an estimation by eye. More rigorously, calibration may refer to the imposition of a restriction over the domain of parameters, which is derived from a statistical estimation or from prior assumptions to be specified *in advance of* model estimation [5]. In this sense, the calibration of parameters is intended to make the estimation of the model more challenging since the number of free parameters is reduced. For instance, in the field of macroeconomics, we may fix the value of parameter on the basis of prior microeconomic evidence and then compare the macromodel predictions with the data conditional to these values.

8.2.3 Efficient Sampling

Random sampling from a uniform distribution, which is a common choice in Monte Carlo exercises, is inefficient because it generates a high number of redundant sampling points (points very close to each other), leaving some parts of the parameter space unexplored. A common alternative is importance sampling, which however requires prior information. A proper "design of experiment" (DOE) delivers instead a parsimonious sample, which is nevertheless representative of the parameter space. In particular, representative samples are said to be "space filling" since they cover as uniformly as possible the domain of variation [41]. Parsimonious schemes are getting more and more popular among AB modelers because of the computational time they allow one to save in Monte Carlo simulations.

There are of course many alternative DOEs available, with different strengths and weaknesses. A popular class of efficient DOEs is represented by Orthogonal Latin Hypercubes (OLH). In the context of sampling theory, a square grid representing the location of sample points for a couple of parameters is a Latin square if there is only one sample point in each row and each column. A Latin hypercube is a generalization of this concept to an arbitrary number of dimensions, whereby each sample point is the only one in each axis-aligned hyperplane containing it. This property ensures that sample points are noncollapsing, that is, that the one-dimensional projections of sample points along each axis are space filling. In fact, with this scheme, the sampled values of each parameter appear once and only once.

Basic Latin Hypercube schemes may display correlations between the columns of the $k \times n$ design matrix X, where k is the number of parameters, and n is the sample size for each parameter, especially when $k \lesssim n$. Instead, an orthogonal design is convenient because it gives uncorrelated estimates of the coefficients in linear regression models and improves the performance of statistical estimation in general. In practice, in orthogonal sampling, the sample space is divided into equally probable subspaces. All sample points in the orthogonal LH scheme are then chosen simultaneously, making sure that the total ensemble of sample points is a Latin Hypercube and that each subspace is sampled with the same density. The NOLH scheme of Cioppa and Lucas [10], which is becoming increasingly popular [41,14], improves the space filling properties of the resulting sample when $k \lesssim n$ at the cost of introducing a small maximal correlation of 0.03 between the columns of X. Furthermore, no assumptions regarding the homoskedasticity of errors or the shape of the response surface (like linearity) are required to obtain this scheme.

8.2.4 Identification, Metamodeling, and Sensitivity Analysis

In general, we cannot exclude that ABMs are unidentifiable. Indeed, even linear or linearized DSGE models exhibit a number of pathologies in estimation due to the flatness of the objective function or to the existence of multiple maxima [7]. ABMs entail additional difficulties due to the possible nonlinearity of moments in the parameters. On the other hand, the existence of nonlinearities in the model is usually presupposed but not proved, so we cannot exclude either that the ABM may be characterized by linear relationships between variables.

To address the identification issue, the parameter space should be explored systematically before any estimation exercise. In this context, it is useful to estimate the influence of θ over a function y of the endogenous variables of the model by means of a *metamodel*, that is, a statistical auxiliary model of the following form:

$$y(\theta) = f(\theta) + u, \tag{8.2}$$

where $f(\theta)$ is a deterministic, possibly nonlinear, term, and u is a second-order stationary, zero mean, potentially heteroskedastic random term with given covariance matrix [41]. This approach is widely used for ABM metamodeling in various fields (see, e.g., Salle and Yildizoglu [41], Dancik et al. [12], and references therein). The metamodel is estimated from a sample of points in the parameter space, which still represents a computationally costly exercise for ABMs that can be made more efficient by an appropriate choice of evaluation points, for example, with Latin Hypercube designs or other parsimonious sampling designs (see above). Furthermore, the parameter space may be eventually restricted through the calibration of at least some of them, following the suggestion of Brenner and Werker [5].

We remark that the result obtained in this way represents the analogue, for a simulated model, of the reduced form of an analytically solvable model. We can employ this reduced form if its fitness with respect to the original ABM is good for a variety of purposes, like sensitivity analysis [6] and even model estimation.

For the purpose of estimating metamodels, Kriging spatial models, which are generalized regression models, potentially allowing for heteroskedastic and correlated errors, are widely employed. The Kriging approach [40] resorts to feasible generalized least squares by assuming a stationary correlation kernel $K(h) = K(\theta_i - \theta_j)$, where θ_i, θ_j are points in the parameter space Θ, which takes the following general form:

$$K(h) = \prod_{j=1}^{d} g(h_j, \lambda_j), \tag{8.3}$$

TABLE 8.1 Covariance Kernels [40]

K1	Matérn ($\nu = 5/2$)	$g(h) = \left(1 + \frac{\sqrt{5}\lvert h \rvert}{\lambda} + \frac{5h^2}{3\lambda^2}\right)\exp\left(-\frac{\sqrt{5}\lvert h \rvert}{\lambda}\right)$
K2	Matérn ($\nu = 3/2$)	$g(h) = \left(1 + \frac{\sqrt{3}\lvert h \rvert}{\lambda}\right)\exp\left(-\frac{\sqrt{3}\lvert h \rvert}{\lambda}\right)$
K3	Gaussian	$g(h) = \exp\left(-\frac{h^2}{2\lambda^2}\right)$
K4	Power-exponential	$g(h) = \exp\left(-\left(\frac{\lvert h \rvert}{\lambda}\right)^t\right)$
K5	Exponential	$g(h) = \exp\left(-\frac{\lvert h \rvert}{\lambda}\right)$

where d is the dimension of Θ, and $\lambda = (\lambda_1, \ldots, \lambda_d)$ is a vector of parameters to be determined. In particular, the specifications represented in Table 8.1 are usually employed for g.

Since ABM simulations provide noisy, potentially heteroskedastic observations, the covariance matrix is determined as follows:

$$C = \sigma^2 R + \text{diag}(\tau), \qquad (8.4)$$

where R is the correlation matrix with elements $R_{ij} = K(\theta_i - \theta_j)$, and $\tau = (\tau_1^2, \ldots, \tau_n^2)$ is the vector containing the observed variance of model output at n fixed points of the parameter space. The ML estimation is performed on the "concentrated" multivariate Gaussian log-likelihood, obtained by substituting the vector of coefficients β with its generalized least square estimator. The "concentrated" log-likelihood is a function of σ and λ, which are the optimization variables of the estimation.

Campolongo et al. [6] define sensitivity analysis (SA) as the study of how uncertainty in the output of a model can be apportioned to different sources of uncertainty in the model input. With this respect, SA techniques should satisfy the two main requirements of being global and model free. By global we mean that SA must take into consideration the entire joint distribution of parameters. Global methods are opposed to local methods, which take into consideration the variation of one parameter at a time, for example, by computing marginal effects of each parameter. By model free we mean that no assumptions on the model functional relationship with its inputs, such as linearity, are required. Campolongo et al. [6] propose a global approach based on the decomposition of variance:

$$V(y) = \sum_i^k V_i + \sum_{i<j} V_{ij} + \sum_{i<j<m} V_{ijm} + \cdots + V_{12\ldots k},$$
$$V_i = \mathbb{V}\left[\mathbb{E}\left(y \vert \theta_i = x_i\right)\right],$$

$$V_{ij} = \mathbb{V}\left[\mathbb{E}\left(y|\theta_i = x_i, \theta_j = x_j\right)\right] - \mathbb{V}\left[\mathbb{E}\left(y|\theta_i = x\right)\right] - \mathbb{V}\left[\mathbb{E}\left(y|\theta_j = x\right)\right],$$

$$\cdots$$

We see that V_i represents the variance of the main effect of parameter i, whereas all the other terms are related to interactions effects. From this general formula we can obtain the contribution of interaction effects S_{Ii} involving the parameter θ_i in $y = f(\theta)$, with f square integrable, as

$$S_{Ii} = S_{Ti} - S_i,$$
$$S_i = \frac{\mathbb{V}_{\theta_i}\left[\mathbb{E}_{\theta_{-i}}(y|\theta_i)\right]}{V},$$
$$S_{Ti} = \frac{\mathbb{E}_{x_{-i}}\left[\mathbb{V}_{x_i}(y|x_{-i})\right]}{V} = 1 - \frac{\mathbb{V}_{\theta_{-i}}\left[\mathbb{E}_{x_i}(y|x_{-i})\right]}{V}.$$

The multidimensional integral of the last line can be evaluated numerically using the extended FAST method described in Campolongo et al. [6]. This method requires a specific sampling scheme, typically involving a large number of model runs than the optimal designs described in Section 8.2.3. To overcome this problem, Dosi et al. [14] employ a Kriging metamodel with the purpose of testing the robustness of an ABM reproducing the fat-tailed distribution of the growth rates of firms. The metamodel is estimated on an NHL design of the space of parameters, and subsequently it is employed instead of the ABM itself for a variance-based global SA. The main result is that the ABM, as approximated from the metamodel, is robust since the growth of the rate distribution, as measured by the value of the appropriate parameter of the Subbotin distribution, is fat-tailed over most of the domain range and for different assumptions regarding the innovation shocks.

Alternatively, AB modelers might be interested in SA methods that may work with any given sampling scheme, like that proposed by Plischke et al. [36], at the cost of losing some precision of estimates. These authors introduce a global, moment independent, uncertainty indicator, whose definition, to the contrary of the previous example, is well posed also in the presence of correlations among the parameters since their distributions are not required to be independent. This indicator is always between 0 and 1; it equals 0 if the output is not dependent upon a parameter, it is readily defined for parameter groups, and it equals unity if the group of all inputs is considered. It is defined as follows:

$$d(\theta_i) = \frac{1}{2}\mathbb{E}_{\theta_i}\left[s(\theta_i = x)\right], \tag{8.5}$$

$$s(\theta_i = x) = \int \left| f\left[y(\theta)\right] - f\left[y(\theta)|\theta_i = x\right] \right| p(\theta)d\theta, \qquad (8.6)$$

where f is the probability density of y. Eq. (8.6) provides the variational distance between the unconditional density of y and its conditional density once θ_i is fixed; $d(\theta_i)$ can be viewed as the reduction of uncertainty regarding the model output that is consequent to knowing the value of θ_i. Plischke et al. [36] provide an estimator for this quantity. Using this approach, it is possible to compare the response of the metamodel and of the ABM to check for their mutual consistency or otherwise apply global sensitivity directly to simulations performed over an efficient sampling scheme.

8.3 ESTIMATION OF A NETWORK MODEL OF CREDIT MARKET INTERACTION

In this section, following Bargigli et al. [3], we provide a representation of credit market interactions by means of a random network model. Agents with a high number of neighbors, that is, agents with a high degree value, called *hubs*, are typically conducive of large systemic effects; in particular, they can potentially trigger bankruptcy avalanches, if affected by external shocks, through balance-sheet effects on many other agents [42]. Indeed, real credit markets display a high fraction of such agents since their degree distributions are typically right-skewed. We wish to replicate this property of real credit markets in our model. A well-known solution for this task in network theory is to build a statistical ensemble of random networks for which the average degree of each node is equal to the degree of the same node in the real network [35]. Random networks drawn from this ensemble trivially replicate the degree distribution of nodes in the original network. Here we follow a different route because we wish to connect the degree distribution of nodes with economic variables. In particular, we assume that the degrees depend on the net-worth of banks and firms.

Once obtained a model for the activation of a link between firm i and bank j, conditioned on their respective net-worth, we need also a model to determine the size of the loan L_{ij}, conditioned on the same variables, with the ambition to replicate the debt and loan size distributions of some real market. To control for topological properties and assign loan amounts at the same time, we need to follow an approach in two stages, that is, we constrain L_{ij} to be positive only whenever a link between i and j has been activated (see Section 8.3.2). In fact, random weighted network models that replicate only the strength distribution of some real network are not bound to follow any topological property, including the degree distribution. Recent papers [32,33] have highlighted that random networks in these ensemble are dense with high probability.

To sum up, the purpose of the estimations presented in the following sections is to calibrate our simulated credit market with real markets taking as reference a set of properties of choice (degree, debt distributions). For this exercise, we employ the dataset for the banks–firms lending–borrowing links from 1980 to 2012 in Japan, maintained by the Econophysics Group at the University of Kyoto. The dataset includes balance sheet data on commercial banks and other credit institutions, as well as on listed companies.[1]

8.3.1 Links

We suppose that connections between banks and firms on the credit market are binary random variables dependent on respective equity:

$$a_{fb} \sim F(E_f, E_b). \tag{8.7}$$

From network theory [35] we know that the maximum entropy distribution of the value of the link between nodes i, j in a statistical ensemble of binary networks $\mathcal{G}$ is associated with an expectation of the following form:

$$\mathbb{E}\left[a_{ij}\right] = \frac{1}{1 + \exp(-\epsilon_{ij})}, \tag{8.8}$$

where ϵ_{ij} embodies a set of constraints imposed on $\mathcal{G}$. Then it is natural to explore relationship (8.7) by means of a logistic regression model. In practice, we make the following specification in (8.8):

$$\epsilon_{fb} = \alpha + \beta \log E_f + \gamma \log E_b, \tag{8.9}$$

where f, b stand for firms and banks indices, respectively.

We estimate three models using the most recent data available in the dataset (2011): model 1 is given by Eqs. (8.8)–(8.9); model 2 adds firm-specific random effects; model 3 includes both firm- and bank-specific random effects. We have opted for random effects instead of fixed effects because the conditional log-likelihood estimation method of Chamberlain [8] for logistic models with fixed effects does not provide the coefficients of the latter, which are needed for simulations (see Section 8.4.2). From Table 8.2 we see that the coefficients of the three models are always significant and their magnitude is similar. From the goodness-of-fit measures in the table we see that the introduction of random effects improves the estimation. Table 8.3 compares the distribution of degrees in actual data with that obtained from a sample of 1000 random networks simulated with calibrated parameters by means of the two-sample KS. We see that

---

1. For more details, see http://www.econophysics.jp/foc_kyoto/index.php?FOC%20Kyoto.

TABLE 8.2 Logistic Estimation on the Japanese Credit Market Data (2011)

	Model 1	Model 2	Model 3
(Intercept)	-3.95951^{***}	-4.20761^{***}	-4.35155^{***}
$\log E_f$	1.53145^{***}	1.62358^{***}	1.60026^{***}
$\log E_b$	0.19733^{***}	0.17885^{***}	0.18615^{***}
Firms RE	No	Yes	Yes
Banks RE	No	No	Yes
Null Dev.	75,004		
Resid. Dev.	53,576	51,686	49,750
AIC	53,582	51,694	49,760
Pseudo R^2	0.286	0.312	0.337

*** $(p < 0.01)$.

TABLE 8.3 Kolmogorov–Smirnov Two-Sample Test for Real and Simulated Degree Distributions

	×	Model 1	Model 2	Model 3
k_f	KS stat.	0.111	0.021	0.016
×	p-value	0.000	0.460	0.804
k_b	KS stat.	0.081	0.067	0.035
×	p-value	0.410	0.643	0.998

the null hypothesis of equal degree distributions cannot be rejected for models 2 and 3, and that the latter provides the best approximation for both the out- and in-degree distributions.

8.3.2 Loans

We want to employ the same regressors in order to explain the value of loans *conditioned* to the existence of a link between a firm f and a bank b (all log-variables are rescaled):

$$\log(L_{fb}|a_{fb} = 1) = \alpha + \beta \log E_f + \gamma \log E_b + u. \qquad (8.10)$$

With standard tests, we detect both firm and bank specific effects in the data. To take these into account, we estimate distinct models with clustered errors. Finally, we add an interaction term between regressors. From Table 8.4 we see that the coefficients are always significant with expected sign. We also detect a significant influence of the interaction term. The inclusion of random effects improves the fitness of the estimation, as shown by the decrease of the AIC

TABLE 8.4 Loan Estimation (2011)

×	M1	M2	M3	M4	M5	M6
(Int.)	0.000	−0.000	0.010	0.009	0.010	0.000
$\log E_f$	0.564***	0.571***	0.587***	0.560***	0.591***	0.580***
$\log E_b$	0.234***	0.236***	0.225***	0.241***	0.227***	0.228***
$\log E_f \times$ $\log E_b$		0.126***	–	–	–	0.095***
Firms RE	no	no	yes	no	yes	yes
Banks RE	no	no	no	yes	yes	yes
AIC	22,562	22,306	19,844	22,416	19,664	19,485
marg. R^2	0.374	0.391	0.381	0.371	0.383	0.384
cond. R^2	–	–	0.655	0.391	0.670	0.667

*** $(p < 0.01)$.

TABLE 8.5 Kolmogorov–Smirnov Two-Sample Test for Real and Simulated Distributions

	×	Model 2	Model 5	Model 6
D	KS stat.	0.094	0.017	0.019
×	p-value	0.000	0.714	0.560
S	KS stat.	0.060	0.084	0.042
×	p-value	0.784	0.367	0.981

measure and by the increase of the conditional R^2 proposed by Nakagawa and Schielzeth [34], which is equal to the proportion of variance explained by both the fixed and random factors, whereas the marginal R^2 accounts for the variance explained by fixed factors alone.

From Table 8.5 we see that the hypothesis of equal distribution cannot be rejected for models 5 and 6, with the latter providing a significantly better agreement with data for S.

8.4 METAMODELING OF A FINANCIAL ACCELERATOR ABM

In this section, we extend the "Network-based financial accelerator" model of Riccetti et al. [39], allowing firms to have multiple credit suppliers. Firms' financial structure adjusts toward a time-dependent, endogenous, leverage target, assuming that firms follow a sort of Dynamic Trade-off Theory. The main aim is methodological: we want to show that it is possible to derive from simulations a statistical model representing the ABM and consequently to employ this model for the purpose of a global sensitivity analysis.

8.4.1 Model Description

Firms produce their output with a linear production function where labor is the only input. They set their production plans at the maximum level allowed by their target leverage $\lambda_i = \frac{D_i}{E_i}$. We can use the balance sheet constraint $(1 + \lambda_i)E_i = W_i = wN_i$ and the production function $Y_i = \alpha N_i$ to obtain[2]

$$\hat{Y}_i = \frac{1 + \lambda_i}{c} E_i, \qquad (8.11)$$

where $c = w\alpha^{-1}$ is the unit labor cost. The effective production of final firm i is $Y_i = \min(\hat{Y}_i, \check{Y}_i)$, where $Y_i = \check{Y}_i$ in case of credit rationing, that is, $\check{Y}_i$ represents the maximal production level of i that can be financed by the credit sector. Agents are matched on the credit markets by means of a random network model, which can be calibrated with real data as shown in Section 8.3. The extension to multiple connections, indeed, allows us to calibrate our model with respect to fundamental network observables like degrees, that is, the number of first neighbors. The actual leverage of firms in each simulation period is endogenously determined as the outcome of calibrated interactions on the credit market. In particular, following empirical data (see Section 8.3), we assume that firms' debt is proportional to their equity $D_f \propto E_f$. The interest rate charged from banks to firm f is set in the following manner:

$$r_f = r_{cb}\left(1 + \delta\lambda_f\right), \qquad (8.12)$$

where r_{cb} is the benchmark policy rate, and $\delta \geqslant 0$ is a parameter that reflects the sensitivity of lenders to borrowers creditworthiness. Firms are subject to a random price shock defined with respect to labor unit cost:

$$p_f = c\left(1 + \epsilon_f\right), \qquad (8.13)$$

where $\epsilon_f \sim N(\mu, \sigma)$. In general, we may view the distribution of price shocks as reflecting demand conditions, within a framework of price adjustment to market imbalances. Thus, a higher μ and a lower σ stand, ceteris paribus, for a stronger final demand. Firms' equity is updated according to profits, assuming that no dividends are distributed:

$$E_f^{t+1} = E_f^t + \pi_f. \qquad (8.14)$$

---

2. Time indices are omitted whenever they are not strictly necessary.

The profits of firms π_f are given by the following equation

$$\Pi_f = \left[p_f - \left(c + r_f \frac{D_f}{Y_f} \right) \right] Y_f, \qquad (8.15)$$

where $D_i = \sum_b L_{fb}$ is the total debt of firm f, and L_{fb} is the amount of loan extended from bank b to firm f. Substituting Y_f, p_f, and r_f, respectively, into Eqs. (8.11), (8.13), and (8.12), after some simplifications, we obtain

$$\pi_f = \frac{\Pi_f}{E_f + D_f} = \epsilon_f - r_{cb} \frac{D_f}{E_f} \frac{(E_f + \delta D_f)}{(E_f + D_f)} = \epsilon_f - r_{cb} \frac{1 + \delta \lambda_f}{\lambda_f^{-1} + 1}. \qquad (8.16)$$

From this expression we see that the profit rate of firms is independent of c. Instead, it depends positively on the parameters of the price shock μ, σ, negatively on the parameters of the interest rates r_{cb}, δ and on λ_f, which is an endogenous variable since D_f depends on the net-worth of f and on the net-worth of banks. Thus all the relevant economic variables for firms (expected profits, loss risk, bankruptcy risk) depend on a firm specific, time-varying endogenous component. For instance, bankruptcy risk may be written as

$$P\left(\Pi_f + E_f \leqslant 0\right) = P\left(\pi_f + \frac{1}{1 + \lambda_f} \leqslant 0\right) = \Phi\left(r_{cb} \frac{1 + \delta \lambda_f}{\lambda_f^{-1} + 1} + \frac{1}{1 + \lambda_f}\right),$$
$$(8.17)$$

where Φ is the normal cdf. The profits of bank are computed as follows:

$$\Pi_b = \sum_f H(E_f + \Pi_f) r_f L_{fb} - \sum_f \left[1 - H(E_f + \Pi_f)\right] L_{fb}, \qquad (8.18)$$

where $H(E_f + \Pi_f) = 1$ if $E_f + \Pi_f > 0$ and $H(E_f + \Pi_f) = 0$ otherwise. We also assume that the supply of credit is proportional to banks' equity $S_b \propto E_b$ and that banks do not distribute dividends:

$$E_b^{t+1} = E_b^t + \pi_b. \qquad (8.19)$$

We have introduced some changes with respect to the original formulation to make the model more parsimonious in terms of parameters, thereby making our metamodeling exercise and sensitivity analysis easier. On the other hand, our setting is indeed simplistic from an economic point view, and it is easy to argue that a more realistic model is likely to be required to obtain convincing results with respect to empirical data.

TABLE 8.6 Parameter Space Explored in the Simulations

r_{cb}	$[0.001, 0.05]$
δ	$[0.1, 1]$
μ	$[0.001, 0.1]$
σ	0.001
c	0.8

8.4.2 Simulation Setting

The initial conditions of the model are given by the equity of firms and banks. For our simulations, we employ as initial conditions the observed values of both variables taken from the Japanese dataset in 2011, which includes $n = 1572$ firms and $m = 117$ banks.[3] During simulations, the equity of agents evolves endogenously according to Eqs. (8.14)–(8.19). When a firm/bank goes bankrupt, it is reinitialized with the median equity of survived firms/banks. The parameters needed for credit market interactions are fixed at the values estimated respectively from model 3 of Section 8.3.1 and model 6 of Section 8.3.2. In the simulations, we draw samples from the distribution of the estimated random effects from these models to take into account their influence over market interaction.

The range of the remaining parameters is presented in Table 8.6. In general, the dynamics of the model is determined by the losses of firms and the resulting bankruptcies. For each firm, the probability of bankruptcy depends, on the one hand, on an endogenous threshold, which is independent of c but dependent on r_{cb} and δ, and, on the other hand, on the parameters of the distribution of price shocks (see Eq. (8.17)), that is, the probability increases if the probability mass that falls below the endogenous threshold increases. So if, for example, we decrease μ, then the distribution of price shocks moves leftward, and bankruptcies increase ceteris paribus. Otherwise, if we increase σ, then the probability mass in the tails increases, and the effect is the same. However, the interpretation is different since in the former case the increase in bankruptcies is associated with a decrease in the expected profit at constant uncertainty, which we may call a "first-order" effect of price shocks; in the latter case, instead, uncertainty increases with expected profit unchanged, which we may call a "second-order" effect of price shocks. Mixing the two effects would make the results more difficult to interpret. Thus, for simplicity, we confine ourselves to first-order effects of price shocks by varying μ while keeping σ constant.

---

3. For a detailed explanation of the dataset, see http://www.econophysics.jp/foc_kyoto/index.php?FOC%20Kyoto.

The sampling scheme we adopt for the subspace of varying parameters (r_{cb}, δ, μ) is that suggested by Cioppa and Lucas [10] and described above. For each of the 17 points of the NOLH scheme, we replicate 10 simulations over $T = 500$ periods, after an initial run of 200 periods. For each simulation run, we compute the average and standard deviation of the time log-differences of the following aggregate variables: production (y), firms' equity (feq), banks' equity (beq), firms' debt (dbt), firms' leverage (lev). Furthermore, we compute the average of firms' and banks' bankruptcies by simulation step (fbkr and bbkr, respectively).

8.4.3 Selection of Metamodels and Sensitivity Analysis

The purpose of this section is firstly to estimate a metamodel for the ABM described in Section 8.4.1 and simulated according to the settings described in Section 8.4.2. Then we employ the metamodel for the purpose of a global sensitivity analysis and to check for identifiability of parameters. To achieve the first goal, we compare a number of metamodels. In particular, we compare the fitness of the same metamodel specification estimated with different Kriging kernels (see Section 8.2.4)[4] and with weighted OLS. With respect to the deterministic component of the model, we compare a constant, a linear, and a second-order polynomial trend. With these three different specifications, we arrive at a total of 18 models to be estimated for each of the variables listed at the end of the previous section. The general form of the metamodels, following Eq. (8.2), is as follows:

$$y = \beta f(\theta) + u(\theta), \tag{8.20}$$

$$\theta = (r_{cb}, \delta, \mu), \tag{8.21}$$

where f take the constant, linear, and polynomial forms mentioned above. In a preliminary exercise, we compute a simple OLS regression with the specifications introduced above for each model output. Since the hypothesis of constant variance is rejected by the Breusch–Pagan test, we introduce robust weights computed from the interquartile distance of model outputs at fixed values of the parameters and observe an improved fitness of the estimation. These results justify our choice of a weighted OLS estimation.

The fitness of alternative estimations is computed by means of k-fold cross validation, that is, the models are used to predict the response variables on k random sections of the experiment design after being estimated on the rest of it. In particular, we set $k = 5$. Fitness is compared through RMSE, MAE, and Q^2,

---

4. The ML estimation is obtained numerically through the quasi-Newton algorithm provided by the DiceKriging R [38] package [40].

TABLE 8.7 Cross k-Validation of Metamodels, $k = 5$

(a) bbkr

Trend	WLM	K1	K2	K3	K4	K5
Constant	−0.204	0.379	0.376	0.294	0.451	0.408
	(0.000)	(0.010)	(0.010)	(0.011)	(0.008)	(0.004)
Linear	0.526	0.194	0.189	0.192	0.184	0.190
	(0.000)	(0.006)	(0.006)	(0.006)	(0.007)	(0.006)
Polynomial	0.894	0.564	0.603	0.544	0.455	0.618
	(0.000)	(0.014)	(0.010)	(0.016)	(0.055)	(0.009)

(b) fbkr

x	WLM	K1	K2	K3	K4	K5
Constant	−0.531	0.185	0.218	0.208	0.279	0.202
	(0.000)	(0.008)	(0.008)	(0.010)	(0.008)	(0.005)
Linear	−0.249	−0.335	−0.360	−0.396	−0.420	−0.463
	(0.001)	(0.013)	(0.012)	(0.017)	(0.013)	(0.013)
Polynomial	0.763	0.280	−0.141	0.360	0.201	0.037
	(0.001)	(0.024)	(0.091)	(0.023)	(0.038)	(0.051)

(c) std_y

x	WLM	K1	K2	K3	K4	K5
Constant	−0.604	0.502	0.519	0.387	0.477	0.467
	(0.000)	(0.004)	(0.003)	(0.006)	(0.003)	(0.002)
Linear	0.735	0.508	0.519	0.501	0.507	0.522
	(0.000)	(0.004)	(0.004)	(0.004)	(0.004)	(0.004)
Polynomial	0.955	0.617	0.624	0.626	0.610	0.573
	(0.000)	(0.010)	(0.010)	(0.010)	(0.013)	(0.021)

Values are average Q^2 over 100 replications (standard errors in parentheses). WLM = weighted OLS estimation; K1 = Kriging est., Matern(5/2); K2 = Kriging est., Matern(3/2); K3 = Kriging est., Gaussian; K4 = Kriging est., power-exponential; K5 = Kriging est., exponential.

which is an R^2 statistics computed out of sample (thus, it can take negative values). The results for most endogenous variables display very low, if not negative, values of Q^2. Then we choose to focus on a subset of three variables for which the fit is high: std_y, fbkr, and bbkr. The values of Table 8.7 for these variables are means over 100 replications of the procedure of cross-validation. We see that the polynomial trend, combined with weighted OLS estimation, performs better with respect to the alternatives. This is our model of choice for the three variables under consideration. Since using a simplified trend function is a typical strategy of Kriging analysis, we show that, at least in our case, this strategy does not provide the best fit.

We apply the approach of Campolongo et al. [6] to the metamodels, finding that the policy rate r_{cb} and demand conditions as reflected by μ are the most important factors affecting the variance of firms' and banks' scaled defaults (Fig. 8.1). Credit market conditions are instead most influential on the volatility of growth. Moreover, we see that interactions between factors play a significant role, consistently with the nonlinearity of the metamodels.

The results of variance decomposition are vindicated by the graphical representation of the effect of parameters, displayed in Fig. 8.2. We see that the effect on both the conditional average (continuous line) and conditional variance (dashed line) of the dependent variables, estimated with a nonparametric regression, are more pronounced when the weight of the same factors in Fig. 8.1 are larger. The direction of effects is consistent with expectations: the policy rate has an (apparently weak) stabilizing effect at the cost of increasing firm bankruptcies, which are transmitted to the banking sector; strong demand conditions (high μ) lower the number of firms' defaults but increase the volatility of production; tighter credit market conditions make production more volatile too. On the other hand, we also see that both the flatness of the trend and the scale of volatility in outcomes make it uncertain, at first sight, that the parameters might be identified using the moments under consideration.

To evaluate the identifiability of parameters, we introduce the following simple loss function:

$$g(\bar{x}, \theta) = \left| E[\text{std\_y}|\theta] - x_1 \right| + \left| E[\text{fbkr}|\theta] - x_2 \right| + \left| E[\text{bbkr}|\theta] - x_3 \right|,$$

$$(8.22)$$

where x is a triplet of arbitrary values for the moments. In particular, we consider three different set of values: high volatility and (scaled) bankruptcies, $x = (3, 1, 1)$; average volatility and bankruptcies, $x = (2, 0, 0)$; low volatility and bankruptcies, $x = (1, -1, -1)$. The predictions of the metamodels are computed over a Latin Hypercube design with 1000 points. From Fig. 8.3 we see that a high-volatility (low) regime is associated with a higher (lower) policy rate, stronger (weaker) demand conditions, and looser (tighter) credit policies. We may read this result as a sign of the effectiveness of monetary policy in cooling the economy (at the cost of increased volatility and failures) when demand is hot and credit is abundant, and in stabilizing it when demand is weak and credit is tight. In general, we can consider all the parameters reasonably well identified under the three scenarios, although the minimal value of g in the high volatility scenario is much larger than zero, showing that the model is less effective in reproducing these circumstances.

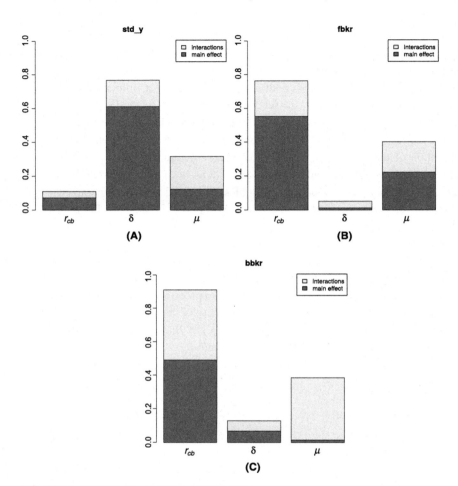

FIGURE 8.1 Variance decomposition of metamodel response.

8.5 SUMMARY

In the first part of this chapter, I have reviewed the recent developments of the AB literature with respect to empirical estimation. A growing number of contributions in this field employ statistical and econometric methods to estimate models. These methods include Bayesian estimation, simulated minimum distance, simulated maximum likelihood, which are largely employed also in the mainstream literature. This convergence potentially lays the foundation for a more consistent comparison between the two approaches. At the same time, model comparison is naturally consistent with the idea that agents do not know the true model of the economy, in contrast to the standard assumption of rational

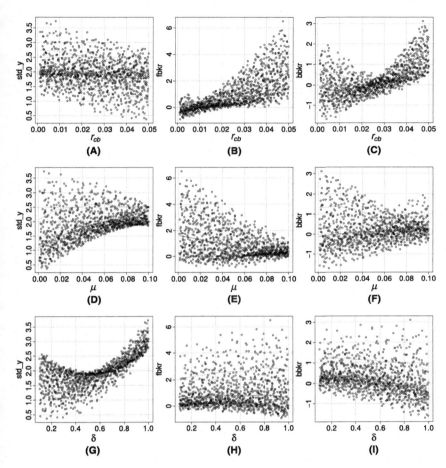

FIGURE 8.2 Global effect of parameters.

expectations. Indeed, economics may benefit from a pluralist approach, which takes into account the ubiquitous problem of observational equivalence between different models and the existence of different research traditions, which translate into different prior beliefs regarding the phenomena under study. Under this perspective, the ABM approach, which seeks to validate its assumptions with a stronger degree of realism, seems to be better equipped than the mainstream approach.

In the second part, we have focused on two distinct problems. The first one is parameter calibration. In particular, we have showed that it is possible to estimate a network model of market interactions from the data, thereby restricting the space of parameters of a larger ABM involving credit market interaction.

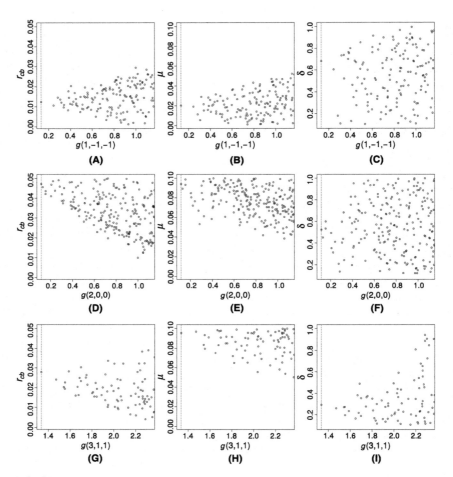

FIGURE 8.3 Parameter identification.

This approach is indeed useful since ABMs have typically a large parameter space. The second one regards the possibility of replacing the ABM with a metamodel, that is, a statistical model linking the value of parameters to a set of model outputs, moments of simulated data. The metamodels provide a conditional expectation of the moments, which may be used for a variety of purposes, including estimation. In particular, we have focused on sensitivity analysis, using the global approach suggested by Campolongo et al. [6], and on the problem of parameter identification, showing that, notwithstanding the nonlinear form of moments, the parameters of a financial accelerator ABM can be correctly identified with respect to a set of moment conditions.

ACKNOWLEDGMENTS

We thank the Kyoto node of the FOC project and, in particular, Yoshi Fujiwara for making available the Japanese bank-firm dataset. All the usual disclaimers apply.

REFERENCES

[1] S. Alfarano, T. Lux, F. Wagner, Estimation of agent-based models: the case of an asymmetric herding model, Computational Economics 26 (1) (2005) 19–49.

[2] Sylvain Barde, Direct Calibration and Comparison of Agent-Based Herding Models of Financial Markets, Studies in Economics 1507, School of Economics, University of Kent, 2015.

[3] Leonardo Bargigli, Luca Riccetti, Alberto Russo, Mauro Gallegati, Network calibration and metamodeling of a financial accelerator agent based model, Available at SSRN, http://ssrn.com/abstract=2712715 or http://dx.doi.org/10.2139/ssrn.2712715, January 8, 2016.

[4] C. Bianchi, P. Cirillo, M. Gallegati, P.A. Vagliasindi, Validating and calibrating agent-based models: a case study, Computational Economics 30 (3) (2007) 245–264.

[5] T. Brenner, C. Werker, A taxonomy of inference in simulation models, Computational Economics 30 (3) (2007) 227–244.

[6] F. Campolongo, A. Saltelli, S. Tarantola, Sensitivity analysis as an ingredient of modeling, Statistical Science 15 (4) (2000) 377–395.

[7] F. Canova, L. Sala, Back to square one: identification issues in DSGE models, Journal of Monetary Economics 56 (2009) 431–449.

[8] G. Chamberlain, Analysis of covariance with qualitative data, The Review of Economic Studies 47 (1) (1980) 225–238.

[9] S.-H. Chen, C.-L. Chang, Y.-R. Du, Agent-based economic models and econometrics, Knowledge Engineering Review 27 (6) (2012) 187–219.

[10] T.M. Cioppa, T.W. Lucas, Efficient nearly orthogonal and space-filling Latin hypercubes, Technometrics 49 (1) (2007) 45–55.

[11] Pasquale Cirillo, Mauro Gallegati, The empirical validation of an agent based model, Eastern Economic Journal 38 (2012) 525–574.

[12] G.M. Dancik, D.E. Jones, K.S. Dorman, Parameter estimation and sensitivity analysis in an agent-based model of Leishmania major infection, Journal of Theoretical Biology 262 (3) (2010) 398–412.

[13] D. Delli Gatti, E. Gaffeo, M. Gallegati, G. Giulioni, A. Palestrini, Emergent Macroeconomics, Springer, Milan, 2008.

[14] G. Dosi, M.C. Pereira, M.E. Virgillito, On the Robustness of the Fat-Tailed Distribution of Firm Growth Rates: A Global Sensitivity Analysis, LEM Working Papers, 12, 2016.

[15] G. Fagiolo, A. Moneta, P. Windrum, A critical guide to empirical validation of agent-based models in economics: methodologies, procedures, and open problems, Computational Economics 30 (3) (2007) 195–226.

[16] Reiner Franke, Applying the method of simulated moments to estimate a small agent-based asset pricing model, Journal of Empirical Finance 16 (2009) 804–815.

[17] R. Franke, F. Westerhoff, Why a simple herding model may generate the stylized facts of daily returns: explanation and estimation, Journal of Economic Interaction and Coordination 11 (2016) 1–34.

[18] M. Gilli, P. Winker, A global optimization heuristic for estimating agent based models, in: Computational Econometrics, Computational Statistics & Data Analysis 42 (3) (2003) 299–312.

[19] C. Gouriéroux, A. Monfort, Simulation-Based Econometric Methods, CORE Lectures, Oxford University Press, Oxford, 1996.

[20] Jakob Grazzini, Analysis of emergent properties: stationarity and ergodicity, Journal of Artificial Societies and Social Simulation 15 (2) (2012) 7.

[21] Jakob Grazzini, Matteo G. Richiardi, Mike Tsionas, Bayesian Estimation of Agent-Based Models, LABORatorio R. Revelli Working Papers Series 145, LABORatorio R. Revelli, Centre for Employment Studies, 2015.

[22] Jakob Grazzini, Matteo Richiardi, Estimation of ergodic agent-based models by simulated minimum distance, Journal of Economic Dynamics and Control 51 (February 2015) 148–165.

[23] Mattia Guerini, Alessio Moneta, A Method of Agent-Based Model Validation, LEM Working Paper Series, 2016/16, April 2016.

[24] Lars Peter Hansen, Thomas J. Sargent, Robustness, Oxford University Press, 2008.

[25] Peter R. Hansen, Asger Lunde, James M. Nason, The model confidence set, Econometrica 79 (2) (March 2011) 453–497.

[26] F. Hartig, J.M. Calabrese, B. Reineking, T. Wiegand, A. Huth, Statistical inference for stochastic simulation models: theory and applications, Ecology Letters 14 (2011) 816–827.

[27] S. Hassan, J. Arroyo, J.M. Galán, M. Antunes, J. Pavón, Asking the oracle: introducing forecasting principles into agent-based modelling, Journal of Artificial Societies and Social Simulation 16 (3) (2013) 13.

[28] Finn E. Kydland, Edward C. Prescott, The computational experiment: an econometric tool, The Journal of Economic Perspectives 10 (1) (1996) 69–85.

[29] T. Lux, Estimation of an agent-based model of investor sentiment formation in financial markets, Journal of Economic Dynamics & Control 36 (2012) 1284–1302.

[30] S. Manzan, F. Westerhoff, Representativeness of news and exchange rate dynamics, Journal of Economic Dynamics & Control 29 (2005) 677–689.

[31] S. Manzan, F.-H. Westerhoff, Heterogeneous expectations, exchange rate dynamics and predictability, Journal of Economic Behavior & Organization 64 (1) (2007) 111–128.

[32] I. Mastromatteo, E. Zarinelli, M. Marsili, Reconstruction of financial networks for robust estimation of systemic risk, Journal of Statistical Mechanics: Theory and Experiment 3 (2012) 11.

[33] N. Musmeci, S. Battiston, G. Caldarelli, M. Puliga, A. Gabrielli, Bootstrapping topological properties and systemic risk of complex networks using the fitness model, Journal of Statistical Physics 151 (3–4) (2013) 720–734.

[34] S. Nakagawa, H. Schielzeth, A general and simple method for obtaining R^2 from generalized linear mixed-effects models, Methods in Ecology and Evolution 4 (2) (2013) 133–142.

[35] J. Park, M.E.J. Newman, Statistical mechanics of networks, Physical Review E 70 (2004) 066117.

[36] E. Plischke, E. Borgonovo, C.L. Smith, Global sensitivity measures from given data, European Journal of Operational Research 226 (3) (2013) 536–550.

[37] M.C. Recchioni, G. Tedeschi, M. Gallegati, A calibration procedure for analyzing stock price dynamics in an agent-based framework, Journal of Economic Dynamics and Control 60 (2015) 1–25.

[38] R Core Team, R: A Language and Environment for Statistical Computing, R Foundation for Statistical Computing, Vienna, Austria, 2015.

[39] L. Riccetti, A. Russo, M. Gallegati, Leveraged network-based financial accelerator, Journal of Economic Dynamics and Control 37 (8) (2013) 1626–1640.

[40] O. Roustant, D. Ginsbourger, Y. Deville, DiceKriging, DiceOptim: two R packages for the analysis of computer experiments by Kriging-based metamodeling and optimization, Journal of Statistical Software 51 (1) (2012) 1–55.

[41] I. Salle, M. Yildizoglu, Efficient sampling and meta-modeling for computational economic models, Computational Economics 44 (4) (2014) 507–536.

[42] H.S. Shin, Risk and liquidity in a system context, Journal of Financial Intermediation 17 (3) (2008) 315–329.

[43] P. Winker, M. Gilli, V. Jeleskovic, An objective function for simulation based inference on exchange rate data, Journal of Economic Interaction and Coordination 2 (2) (2007) 125–145.

Chapter 9

Modeling the Joint Distribution of Income and Consumption in Italy

A Copula-Based Approach With κ-Generalized Margins

Fabio Clementi* and Lisa Gianmoena[†]
*University of Macerata, Macerata, Italy
[†]Marche Polytechnic University, Ancona, Italy

9.1 INTRODUCTION

The focus of this chapter is on developing and fitting a flexible parametric model for the bivariate distribution of income and consumption in Italy. Since the independence between income and consumption is not the most appropriate assumption to work with, we study the joint distribution of the two variables by separately estimating the univariate marginal distribution models for income and consumption and by estimating a parametric copula function to capture information about the dependence between the two dimensions. This approach is appealing since copulas are easily estimated using maximum likelihood techniques, and there are many alternatives available in the literature that capture a wide range of dependence structures beyond simply correlation. In addition, copulas are flexible in that they can be applied to any specification of the marginal distributions, including allowing for the latter to have different specifications. This provides an attractive method for capturing the dependence structure contained in the joint distribution of income and consumption of actual samples.

Using copulas to model multivariate distributions is extremely popular in the finance and actuarial context, particularly for capturing dependence among stocks. However, copula-based approaches have rarely been applied in welfare economics—see [3] on potential applications. There are some notable exceptions: the approach used by Burtless [12] and Fournier [33] to analyze the correlation between the incomes of spouses is (implicitly) copula-based; Dar-

Introduction to Agent-Based Economics. http://dx.doi.org/10.1016/B978-0-12-803834-5.00012-6

191

danoni and Lambert [25] use a copula-based framework to measure the extent of re-ranking through taxation; Bonhomme and Robin [9] estimate a parametric copula to describe individual earnings trajectories and income mobility in France; Quinn [70,71] and Wu et al. [84] utilize copulas to measure association between income and health, whereas Kennickell [50] and Jäntti et al. [36] take advantage of the copula paradigm to analyze the dependence between income and wealth; a copula-based approach was also considered, inter alia, by Vinh et al. [81], Decancq [26], Pérez and Prieto [69], and Atkinson and Lakner [4] for assessing inequality and poverty under dependent dimensions of well-being.

As far as income and consumption are concerned, the only attempt that we are aware of in the current literature is by Domma and Giordano [28,29], who apply a copula-based approach to the measurement of household financial fragility in Italy. However, our work is different from their approach because of the distinctive parametric assumptions we make for both the univariate margins and the copula function that summarizes the existing dependence structure. Furthermore, we are better positioned to take a long-term perspective since we use the same data but for a longer time span than the single appraisal period as in [28] and [29].

The organization of the chapter is as follows. In Section 9.2.1, we describe the data set used and provide a preliminary inspection of the degree of dependence between income and consumption in Italy. In Section 9.2.2, we motivate the choice of κ-generalized models for the income and consumption distributions, whereas in Section 9.2.3, we briefly review the theory of copulas and discuss the reasons of our interest in the "symmetrized Joe–Clayton" specification for modeling the association between the two variables. Estimation results and analysis of the parametric model for the bi-variate distribution of income and consumption are presented in Section 9.3. Finally, in Section 9.4, we conclude and point to possible extensions of this work for the future.

9.2 DATA AND METHODOLOGY

9.2.1 The Italian Personal-Income and Consumption Data

Income and consumption data are drawn from the Survey on Household Income and Wealth (SHIW), a representative survey of the Italian resident population conducted by the Bank of Italy since the mid-1960s to gather data on income, saving, consumption expenditure, wealth, demographics, and labor force participation of Italian households.[1]

---

1. The data (with documentation in English) are freely available at https://www.bancaditalia.it/ statistiche/tematiche/indagini-famiglie-imprese/bilanci-famiglie/index.html. We refer the reader to the works of Brandolini and Cannari [11] and Brandolini [10] for details on design of the

The SHIW was carried out yearly until 1987 (except for 1985) and every two years thereafter (the survey for 1997 was shifted to 1998). The sample used in the most recent waves comprises about 8,000 households (20,000 individuals), distributed over around 300 Italian municipalities.

The dataset employed in this chapter includes fourteen independent cross sections of Italian households covering the period 1987–2014, for a total of 111,118 observations. Although income and consumption data are available also for years prior to 1987, we choose to focus on data collected from 1987 onwards because of a major overhaul of the survey that took place in 1986–7, when the design of the questionnaire was entirely revised, the sample size was raised to double that of previous waves, and the income definition underwent significant changes that hinder temporal comparisons (income from financial assets started to be recorded only in 1987).

The basic definition of income provided by the SHIW is net of taxation and social security contributions. It is the sum of four main components: compensation of employees, pensions and net transfers, net income from self-employment, and property income (including income from buildings and income from financial assets). The SHIW variable recording household consumption expenditure, in turn, is obtained by aggregating household expenditures for durable and nondurable goods. According to the definition of the Bank of Italy, expenditures for nondurable goods correspond to all spending on both food and nonfood items, plus nonmonetary income integrations (fringe benefits) and imputed rents.[2] Household expenditures for durable goods correspond to items belonging to the following categories: means of transport, furniture, and precious objects.

The variables analyzed here focus on total income and consumption of the households surveyed. Since in some waves there were cases of zero and/or negative figures, we dropped such observations and kept only strictly positive amounts of income and consumption.[3] Furthermore, income and consumption figures have been adjusted for differences in household size using the "modified

survey, data quality, and main changes in the sample and variable definitions. See also the *Supplement to the Statistical Bulletin* available from https://www.bancaditalia.it/pubblicazioni/indagine-famiglie/index.html, which sets out the main results of the survey waves that the Bank of Italy has carried out.

2. If a household dwelling is neither owned nor rented, but occupied in usufruct or free of charge, the total consumption expenditure for that household includes an imputed rent, that is, an amount corresponding to the rent that could be charged for such a dwelling.

3. This exclusion affected only a tiny fraction of the data—on average, 0.28% and 0.01% of the observations on income and consumption, respectively—and left us with a total of 110,870 observations. Accordingly, the sampling weights of households have been recalibrated in such a way that estimates from the samples after deletion of nonpositive records are forced to fit the initial population-level distribution of certain characteristics known from external sources. The external information used in calibration is: gender, age group (under 26, 26–45, 46–65, and over 65),

OECD" equivalence scale and weighted by the provided sampling weights.[4,5] Finally, we deflated all monetary aggregates (expressed in Euros) so as to obtain *real* distributions of income and consumption. To do so, we employed the consumption deflator for resident households provided by the Italian statistical office (ISTAT).[6] The base year for the deflator is 2010.

Information on the association between income and consumption in our samples is shown in Fig. 9.1, where we plot summary indicators of correlation such as Pearson's ρ, Spearman's ρ_s, and Kendall's τ. The Pearson's correlation coefficient gives us an indication of the linear relationship between income and consumption. The others—Spearman's ρ_s and Kendall's τ—are rank correlation indicators that are often preferred to Pearson's ρ for non-normal data, since they are less sensitive to extreme data (e.g., [56] and [23]; see also discussion in Section 9.2.3). Overall, we observe a strong positive dependence between income and consumption in Italy that is generally greater than 0.5 in all samples, but that dependence varied considerably over time. Indeed, regardless of the indicator used, two regime changes of temporal evolution are clearly identified: correlation was high in the early part of the period, then lowered in central years, and raised at last during the recent economic crisis.

To test for the presence of time-varying dependence, we perform a structural change analysis of correlation coefficients over the whole period using the procedure proposed by Bai and Perron [5,6], henceforth BP. A key feature of the methodology developed by these authors is that it allows to test for multiple breaks at unknown dates. The model considered here is the linear regression model with m breaks (or, equivalently, with $m + 1$ regimes):

$$y_t = \beta_j + u_t, \quad t = T_{j-1} + 1, \ldots, T_j, \quad j = 1, \ldots, m + 1, \qquad (9.1)$$

geographical area (North, Center, South, and Islands) and size of the municipality of residence (under 20,000 inhabitants, 20,000–40,000, 40,000–500,000, and over 500,000). Weighting adjustments have been implemented using the R function calib from the library sampling [79].

4. The "modified OECD" equivalence scale allocates points to each person in a household by taking the first adult as having a weight of 1 point, whereas each additional person who is 14 years or older is allocated 0.5 points, and each child under the age of 14 is allocated 0.3 points [35]. Equivalized household figures are derived by dividing total household income and consumption by a factor equal to the sum of the equivalence points allocated to household members. Unlike the old OECD scale, the modified one gives less weight to any additional household member, allowing for higher economies of scale.

5. We use person-level adjusted weights (the product of household weights and the number of household members) when generating income and consumption indicators for the total population. The results from estimation of distributional parameters, presented in Section 9.3, have also been weighted to obtain population-level estimates and account for the SHIW survey design.

6. Available at https://www.bancaditalia.it/statistiche/tematiche/indagini-famiglie-imprese/bilanci-famiglie/tavole-principali-risultati/index.html.

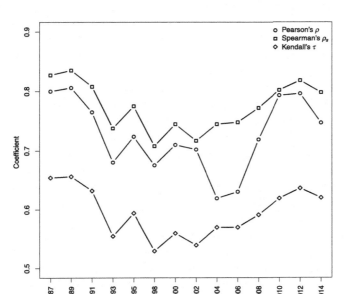

FIGURE 9.1 The association between income and consumption in Italy, 1987–2014.

where $T_0 = 0$ and $T_{m+1} = T$ by convention (T is the number of yearly observations).[7] In other words, within the regime j, Pearson's ρ, Spearman's ρ_s, or Kendall's τ equals the regime-specific mean β_j plus a stationary error term u_t, which may have a different distribution across regimes. The goal of the analysis is to determine the optimal number and location of the structural break points T_j, $j = 1, \ldots, m$, by minimizing the within-regime sums of squares. By default, our implementation of BP's technique derives the appropriate number of breaks as the one achieving the lowest Bayesian information criterion score [75].[8]

The results can be visualized in Fig. 9.2, which shows time series plots for any of the three measures of dependence stated previously (gray solid lines) along with the estimated break points (black dashed lines) and the regime-specific means in each resulting data segment (black solid lines). As can be seen, the period under consideration has two clear breaks, which correspond to

---

7. To increase significance of findings, we use linear interpolation to estimate missing data for years in which the SHIW waves are not available. This leads us to enlarge sample size from 14 to 28 time observations.

8. When implementing the BP procedure for structural change, the maximal number of breaks to be calculated is a parameter to be fixed by the researcher. For our data, we allow simultaneous calculation for up to $m = 2$ breaks. The technique suggested by BP has been implemented in a unified way in the package strucchange [87,86,85] for the statistical software R [72], which is the one we rely upon in the present study.

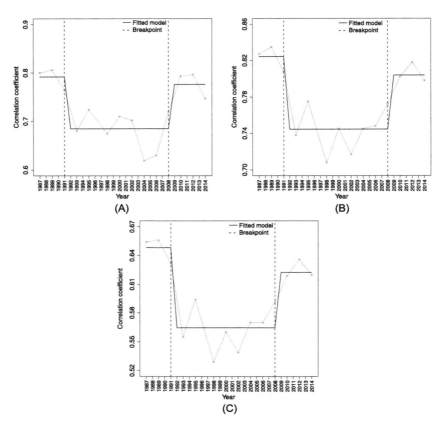

FIGURE 9.2 Structural breaks in correlation coefficients, 1987–2014. (A) Pearson's ρ. (B) Spearman's ρ_S. (C) Kendall's τ.

1991 and 2008. For all correlation indicators, we find statistically significant evidence of a break in the earlier two dates, with a p-value lower than 0.05.[9]

Thus, we can conclude that there is evidence against constant dependence structure over time for the SHIW income-consumption data. This provides a solid motivation for considering copula-based multivariate models that are able to reproduce the analyzed pattern of time-varying dependence. However, as it will be shown in Section 9.2.3, the association between income and consumption in any single year is more complex than can be captured by single summary measures like linear correlation or rank correlation because the strength of de-

---

9. The values of the F statistic for testing against a single-shift alternative of known timing—the so-called "Chow test" [14]—amounted in fact to 12.58, 19.66, and 23.02 in 1991 and to 8.39, 6.55, and 5.51 in 2008 for, respectively, Pearson's ρ, Spearman's ρ_S, and Kendall's τ, which in all cases exceed their respective 5% critical values.

pendence between the two variables in the bottom tail of their joint distribution is different from what comes out of the upper tail. Hence, our "ideal" copula-based model should also be able to accommodate asymmetric dependence in the tails of the bivariate distribution of income and consumption.

9.2.2   The κ-Generalized Distribution for Margins

The interest in finding parametric models for the size distribution of income has a long history. A natural starting point in this area of inquiry was the observation that the number of persons in a population whose incomes exceed x is often well approximated by $Cx^{-\alpha}$ for some real C and positive α, as Pareto argued over 100 years ago [63,64,66,65]. Since the early studies of Pareto, numerous empirical works have shown that the power-law tail is a ubiquitous feature of income distribution. However, even 100 years after Pareto's observation, the understanding of the shape of income distribution is still far to be complete and definitive. This reflects the fact that there are two distributions, one for the rich, following the Pareto power law, and one for the vast majority of people, which appears to be governed by a completely different law.

Over the years, research in the field has considered a wide variety of functional forms as possible models for the size distribution of income, some of which aim at providing a unified framework for the description of real-world data—including the heavy tails present in empirical income distributions [52]. Among these, the "κ-generalized distribution" was found to work remarkably well [17,15,18–20,16,22]. First proposed in 2007 and further developed over successive years, this model finds its roots in the context of generalized statistical mechanics [43–48]. Within this theoretical framework, the ordinary exponential function $\exp(x)$ generalizes into the function $\exp_\kappa(x)$ defined as

$$\exp_\kappa(x) = \left(\sqrt{1+\kappa^2 x^2} + \kappa x\right)^{\frac{1}{\kappa}}, \quad x \in \mathbb{R}, \quad \kappa\,[0, 1). \tag{9.2}$$

We recall briefly that in the limit as $\kappa \to 0$ the function (9.2) reduces to the ordinary exponential, that is, $\exp_0(x) = \exp(x)$, and for $x \to 0$—independently on the value of κ—behaves very similarly to the ordinary exponential. On the other hand, the most interesting property of $\exp_\kappa(x)$ for modeling the size distribution of income and wealth is the power-law asymptotic behavior

$$\exp_\kappa(x) \underset{x \to \pm\infty}{\sim} |2\kappa x|^{\pm\frac{1}{|\kappa|}}. \tag{9.3}$$

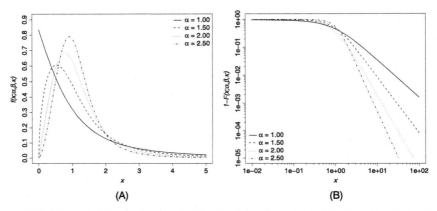

FIGURE 9.3 Plot of the κ-generalized PDF (A) and complementary CDF (B) for some different values of α ($= 1.00, 1.50, 2.00, 2.50$) and fixed β ($= 1.20$) and κ ($= 0.75$). The complementary CDF is plotted on doubly-logarithmic axes, which is the standard way of emphasizing the right-tail behavior of a distribution. Notice that the curvature (shape) of the distribution becomes less (more) pronounced when the value of α decreases (increases). The case $\alpha = 1.00$ corresponds to the standard exponential distribution.

Given (9.2), the κ-generalized distribution is defined in terms of the following cumulative distribution function (CDF):

$$F(x; \alpha, \beta, \kappa) = 1 - \exp_\kappa\left[-\left(\frac{x}{\beta}\right)^\alpha\right], \quad x > 0, \quad \alpha, \beta > 0, \quad \kappa \in [0, 1),$$
(9.4)

where $\{\alpha, \beta, \kappa\}$ are parameters. The corresponding probability density function (PDF) reads as

$$f(x; \alpha, \beta, \kappa) = \frac{\alpha}{\beta}\left(\frac{x}{\beta}\right)^{\alpha-1} \frac{\exp_\kappa\left[-\left(\frac{x}{\beta}\right)^\alpha\right]}{\sqrt{1 + \kappa^2\left(\frac{x}{\beta}\right)^{2\alpha}}}.$$
(9.5)

The distribution defined through (9.4) and (9.5) can be viewed as a generalization of the Weibull distribution, which recovers in the limit as $\kappa \to 0$. Consequently, the exponential law is also a special limiting case of the κ-generalized distribution since it is a particular case of the Weibull with $\alpha = 1$. As $x \to 0^+$, the κ-generalized distribution behaves similarly to the Weibull distribution, whereas for large x, it presents a Pareto's power-law tail and hence satisfies the weak Pareto law [55].

Figs. 9.3 to 9.5 illustrate the behavior of the κ-generalized PDF and complementary CDF, $1 - F(x; \alpha, \beta, \kappa)$, for various parameter values. The exponent

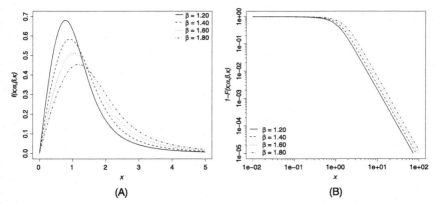

(A)   (B)

FIGURE 9.4 Plots of the κ-generalized PDF (A) and complementary CDF (B) for some different values of β (= 1.20, 1.40, 1.60, 1.80) and fixed α (= 2.00) and κ (= 0.75). The complementary CDF is plotted on doubly logarithmic axes, which is the standard way of emphasizing the right-tail behavior of a distribution. Notice that the distribution spreads out (concentrates) as the value of β increases (decreases).

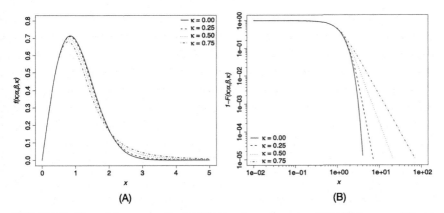

(A)   (B)

FIGURE 9.5 Plots of the κ-generalized PDF (A) and complementary CDF (B) for some different values of κ (= 0.00, 0.25, 0.50, 0.75) and fixed α (= 2.00) and β (= 1.20). The complementary CDF is plotted on doubly logarithmic axes, which is the standard way of emphasizing the right-tail behavior of a distribution. Notice that the upper tail of the distribution fattens (thins) as the value of κ increases (decreases). The case $\kappa = 0.00$ corresponds to the Weibull (stretched exponential) distribution.

α quantifies the curvature (shape) of the distribution, which is less (more) pronounced for lower (higher) values of the parameter, as seen in Fig. 9.3.[10] The constant β is a characteristic scale since its value determines the scale of the

---

10. It should be noted that, for $\alpha = 1$, the density exhibits a pole at the origin, whereas for $\alpha > 1$, there exists an interior mode.

probability distribution: if β is small, then the distribution is more concentrated around the mode; if β is large, then it is more spread out (Fig. 9.4). Finally, as Fig. 9.5 shows, the parameter κ measures the fatness of the upper tail: the larger (smaller) its magnitude, the fatter (thinner) the tail.

Expressions that facilitate the analysis of the associated moments and various tools for the measurement of inequality have been reported for the κ-generalized distribution [15,18–20,16,22]. These expressions are functions of the parameters in the model and prove useful in the analysis of population characteristics.

The κ-generalized distribution was also successfully used in a three-component mixture model for analyzing the singularities of survey data on *net* wealth, that is, the value of gross wealth minus total debt, which present highly significant frequencies of households or individuals with null and/or negative wealth [21,16,22]. The support of the κ-generalized mixture model for net wealth distribution is the real line $\mathbb{R} = (-\infty, \infty)$, thus allowing to describe the subset of economic units with nil and negative net worth. Furthermore, there exist four-parameter variants that contain as a particular case the κ-generalized model for income distribution [61].

During the last decade, there have been several applications of κ-generalized models to real-world data on income and wealth distribution. Of special interest are papers fitting several distributions to the same data, with an eye on relative performance. From comparative studies such as [19], who considered the distribution of household income in Italy for the years 1989 to 2006, it emerges that model (9.5) typically outperforms its three-parameter competitors such as the Singh–Maddala [77] and Dagum type I [24] distributions, apart from the generalized beta II (GB2), which has an extra parameter.[11] The model was also fitted by [20] to data from other household budget surveys, namely Germany 1984–2007, Great Britain 1991–2004, and the United States 1980–2005. In a remarkable number of cases, the distribution of household income follows the κ-generalized distribution more closely than the Singh–Maddala and Dagum type I distributions. In particular, the fit is statistically superior in the right tail of data with respect to the other competitors in many instances. Another example of comparative study is [60], who considered US and Italian income data for the 2000s. He found the three-parameter κ-generalized model to yield better estimates of income inequality even when the goodness-of-fit is inferior to that of distributions in the GB2 family. The excellent fit of the κ-generalized distribution and its ability in providing relatively more accurate estimation of income

---

11. The GB2 is a quite general family of parametric models for the size distribution of income that nests most of the functional forms previously considered in the size distributions literature as particular or limiting cases [58]. In particular, both the Singh–Maddala and Dagum type I distributions are particular cases of the GB2.

inequality have recently been confirmed in a book by Clementi and Gallegati [16], who utilize household income data for 45 countries selected from the most recent waves of the LIS Database (http://www.lisdatacenter.org/).

The previously mentioned works were mainly concerned with the distribution of household incomes. In an interesting contribution by Clementi et al. [21] the κ-generalized distribution was used in a three-component mixture to model the US net wealth data for 1984–2011. Both graphical procedures and statistical methods indicate an overall good approximation of the data. The authors also highlight the relative merits of their specification with respect to finite mixture models based upon the Singh–Maddala and Dagum type I distributions for the positive values of net wealth. Similar results were recently obtained by Clementi and Gallegati [16] when analyzing net wealth data for nine countries selected from the most recent waves of the LWS Database (http://www.lisdatacenter.org/).

Finally, four-parameter extensions of the κ-generalized distribution were used by Okamoto [61] to analyze household income/consumption data for approximately 20 countries selected from Waves IV to VI of the LIS Database. To provide a comparison with alternative four-parameter models of income distribution, the GB2 and double Pareto-lognormal (dPlN) distribution introduced by Reed and Jorgensen [74] were also fitted to the same data sets. In almost all cases, the new variants of the κ-generalized distribution outperform the other four-parameter models for both the income and consumption variables. In particular, they show an empirical tendency to estimate inequality indices more accurately than they counterparts do.

Given the excellent performance of the κ-generalized family of distributions, documented through several years of research, we assume in the following that consumption and income data can be modeled by nonidentical three-parameter κ-generalized distributions, henceforth denoted by $F_c(x_c; \alpha_c, \beta_c, \kappa_c)$ and $F_i(x_i; \alpha_i, \beta_i, \kappa_i)$, where the subscripts c and i clearly refer to consumption and income, respectively.

Parameter estimation will be performed using the maximum goodness-of-fit (MGF) estimation method [54], also known as the "minimum distance estimation method" [42,82,83]. MGF estimation consists of maximizing goodness of fit—or minimizing a goodness-of-fit distance—between the empirical distribution function (EDF) of the sample and the CDF of the specified distribution. This method is suitable for estimating distribution parameters of data characterized by both skewness and heavy tails since in such cases other commonly used estimation techniques (e.g., maximum likelihood approach) can lose their optimality properties [54].

In what follows, the distance measure that will be minimized to fit the κ-generalized distribution to the SHIW microdata on income and consumption is the so-called "right-tail Anderson–Darling statistic of second degree" defined as

$$\text{AD2R} = 2\sum_{j=1}^{n} \ln\left(1 - z_j\right) + \frac{1}{n}\sum_{j=1}^{n} \frac{2j-1}{1 - z_{n+1-j}}, \tag{9.6}$$

where $z_j = F\left(x_j; \boldsymbol{\gamma}\right)$ is the pointwise κ-generalized CDF of income or consumption, $\boldsymbol{\gamma} = \{\alpha, \beta, \kappa\}$ is the unknown parameter vector, and n is the sample size. The AD2R, one of the variants of the Anderson and Darling's distance [2] proposed by Luceño [54], assigns more weight to the right tail of the distribution and thus is particularly indicated to accommodate both heavy-tailedness and positive skewness in data.

Minimization of the AD2R statistics with respect to the unknown parameters of the κ-generalized CDF (9.4) are performed by numerical methods using optimization routines from the fitdistrplus package [27] implemented in the R programming language [72].

9.2.3 The Symmetrized Joe–Clayton Copula

Often the issue of dependence between random variates is addressed through the concept of correlation. However, for nonnormal variables, more complex, nonlinear dependence structures can arise when considering their joint distributions (see, e.g., [80]).[12] Copula-based multivariate models are becoming an increasingly popular approach to modeling joint distributions since for a wide range of dependence structures, they make it possible to be captured beyond simply correlation.

Popularized by Sklar [78], copula-based models allow the researcher to specify the models for the marginal distributions separately from the dependence structure (copula) that links these distributions. In particular, a substantial advantage of copula-based methods is that the models for the marginal distributions may come from different families. This frees researchers from considering only existing multivariate distributions and allows for a much greater degree of flexibility in forming the joint distribution.

---

12. Nonnormality is usually the case when analyzing income and consumption data because of skewness and fat tails (kurtosis) in their distributions. An obvious consequence is that the correlation can be misleading when analyzing their degree of association. For example, Pearson's correlation coefficient—by far the most widely applied correlation concept in statistics—is known to be sensitive toward extreme events, which are more likely to occur with fat tails than predicted by normal distribution (see, e.g., [56] and [23]). Furthermore, Pearson's correlation coefficient measures the degree of linear association between two random variates, but usually this does not sufficiently describe association between nonnormally distributed random variables [32]. In particular, the concept of correlation is not defined for some heavy-tailed distributions whose second moments do not exist (see, e.g., [73]).

In more detail, a copula is a multivariate distribution defined on the $[0, 1]^d$ hypercube, where each of the d marginal variates is uniformly distributed,[13] that is, given a set of d random variates $X_1, \ldots, X_d$ with cumulative distribution function $F_1(x_1), \ldots, F_d(x_d)$, each can be transformed into marginal variates defined on the unit interval $[0, 1]$ using $u_i \sim F_i(x_i)$ for $i = 1, \ldots, d$. Each variate also has an inverse cumulative distribution function such that, for $i = 1, \ldots, d$, $x_i \sim F_i^{-1}(u_i)$.

Under Sklar's theorem [78], if the joint cumulative distribution of $X_1, \ldots, X_d$ is given by some function $H(x_1, \ldots, x_d)$, then there exists a copula function $C(u_1, \ldots, u_d)$ with margins $F_1(x_1), \ldots, F_d(x_d)$ such that

$$\begin{aligned} H(x_1, \ldots, x_d) &= H\left(F_1^{-1}(u_1), \ldots, F_d^{-1}(u_d)\right) \\ &= C\left(F_1(x_1), \ldots, F_d(x_d)\right) \\ &= C(u_1, \ldots, u_d). \end{aligned} \tag{9.7}$$

Thus, the joint distribution is expressed in terms of its respective marginal distributions and a function C that binds them together. This makes modeling the dependence between the uniformly distributed margins equivalent to modeling the dependence between the variates themselves. In case the multivariate distribution has an available density h, it further holds that

$$h(x_1, \ldots, x_d) = c(u_1, \ldots, u_d) \times f_1(x_1) \times \cdots \times f_d(x_d), \tag{9.8}$$

where

$$c(u_1, \ldots, u_d) = \frac{\partial^d C(u_1, \ldots, u_d)}{\partial u_1 \cdots \partial u_d} \tag{9.9}$$

is the density of the copula.

If the marginal distributions $F_1(x_1), \ldots, F_d(x_d)$ are continuous, then the corresponding copula in Eq. (9.7) is unique. If $F_1(x_1), \ldots, F_d(x_d)$ are not all continuous, then the joint distribution function can always be expressed as (9.7), although in such a case, the copula is not unique [76, Ch. 6].

There exist many copula functions that could be used in dependence modeling, especially for the bivariate case—a fairly exhaustive list is contained, e.g., in [40, Ch. 4].[14] All these functions depend on one or more parameters, say θ, which are called association parameters and are related

---

13. [38] and [59] are the two comprehensive treatments on this topic. A detailed review and discussion of copula theory is also given, among others, in [31], [80], [1], [7], [68], and [40].

14. Henceforth, we will concentrate on the bivariate case, that is, where $d = 2$, since it will be later considered in the empirical analysis. Accordingly, by "copula" we always mean bivariate copulas for modeling the dependence between income and consumption distributions.

to the degree of dependence between margins. Common measures of the amount of association between two variables, such as Kendall's τ and Spearman's ρ_s among others, are usually expressed as function of the association parameters. For instance, Kendall's τ can be written as $\tau(\theta) = 4 \int_0^1 \int_0^1 C(u_c, u_i; \theta) c(u_c, u_i; \theta) \, du_c \, du_i - 1$, whereas Spearman's ρ_s is written in terms of copula as $\rho_s(\theta) = 12 \int_0^1 \int_0^1 C(u_c, u_i; \theta) \, du_c \, du_i - 3$ [59, Ch. 5]. In particular, these measures do not depend on parameters of the marginal distributions but on the association parameters only.[15]

It is worth noticing, however, that the values of τ and ρ_s corresponding to the θ domain do not necessarily cover the whole dependence interval $[-1, 1]$, and the range of dependence that can be really achieved varies for different copulas. Therefore, a key point to consider should be choosing an appropriate copula from the competitive functions whose association parameter lies within a range that allows τ and ρ_s to cover at least their empirical values or, more generally, the positive dependence domain $[0, 1]$.[16]

Information on "tail dependence" is also useful for making initial decisions on the types of copulas that may be suitable for a given data set, since many copula models—such as the normal and Frank ones—impose zero tail dependence in both tails, whereas other copulas impose zero tail dependence in one of their tails (e.g. right for the Clayton copula and left for the Gumbel copula).[17] Tail dependence is a measure of the strength of dependence in the joint upper (lower) tail of a bi-variate distribution. Informally, in our application it measures the probability that large (or small) values of consumption appear with large (or small) values of income.

Tail dependence in the income-consumption data for the 2014 wave of the SHIW can be seen in Fig. 9.6, where we show the cross-tabulation of the quin-

---

15. The Pearson's correlation coefficient is a poor measure of the association between two variables. In particular, it is not invariant under general nonlinear, strictly increasing transformations of the variables—for example, $\rho(X_c, X_i) \neq \rho[\exp(X_c), \exp(X_i)]$—and is affected by the marginal distributions of the data (see, inter alia, [49], [32], [80], and [68]). This is equivalent to imposing that a better measure of dependence should be obtained as a function of the *ranks* of the data only, which is in turn equivalent to it being a function solely of the copula, and not the marginal distributions. Both Kendall's τ and Spearman's ρ_s are invariant under nonlinear, strictly increasing transformations, and, as it is seen in the main text, they can be expressed in terms of the associated copula.

16. For instance, the Farlie–Gumbel–Morgenstern copula allows only for a limited degree of dependence (Kendall's τ is restricted to $\left[-\frac{2}{9}, \frac{2}{9}\right]$ and Spearman's ρ_s to $\left[-\frac{1}{3}, \frac{1}{3}\right]$), which reduces its appeal for use in applications (see, e.g., [40, p. 213]). Similar considerations hold also for the Ali–Mikhail–Haq copula, one of the members of the so-called Archimedean family of copulas, whose range for Kendall's τ is restricted to $[-0.18, 0.33]$ and for Spearman's ρ_s to $[-0.27, 0.48]$, so that it can only model weak dependence (see, e.g., [59]).

17. For more on this issue, see [59, Ch. 4], [40, Ch. 2], and [68].

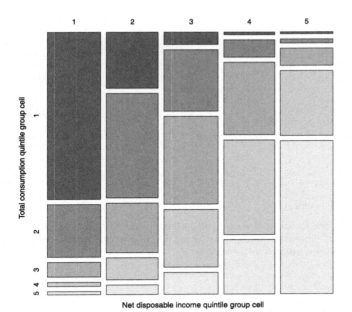

FIGURE 9.6 Distribution across quintile groups of total consumption and net disposable income for the 2014 wave of the SHIW.

tile groups of both resource variables.[18] The bars denote the proportion of households found in the quintile groups of both the income and consumption distributions. The most striking feature is that for households in the top quintile group of disposable income (the five stacked bars that are furthest to the right in the figure) the probability of being in a particular quintile group of total consumption increases very quickly—that is, it is more likely that a household in the top-income quintile group is also in the top consumption group rather than in one of the other four. Likewise, the probability that a lowest-income quintile group household is in the lowest consumption group is higher than such a household being in the second to fifth groups of consumption (see the five stacked bars that are furthest to the left). Thus total consumption and disposable income are highly associated, particularly at the top and bottom of the distribution.

In the SHIW income-consumption data we also find evidence of *asymmetric tail dependence*, in that observations in the lower tail of the bi-variate distribution are somewhat more dependent than observations in the upper tail. This can be seen from Fig. 9.7, where panel (A) presents the estimated quantile dependence plot and panel (B) displays the difference between the upper and

---

18. The plots for the other waves resemble to Fig. 9.6, therefore they are not shown here but are available from the authors upon request.

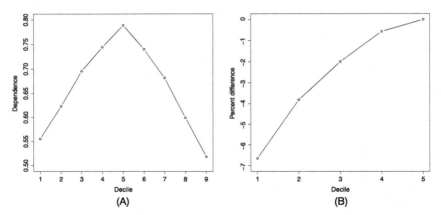

FIGURE 9.7 Asymmetric tail dependence for the 2000 wave of the SHIW: (A) estimated quantile dependence between income and consumption data; (B) percent difference between corresponding upper and lower quantile dependence estimates.

lower portions of this plot, respectively.[19] "Quantile dependence" measures the strength of the dependence between two variables in the joint lower or upper tails of their support—see [68, p. 909] for a more formal definition. By estimating the strength of the dependence between two variables as we move from the center to the tails, and by comparing the left tail to the right tail, we are thus provided with a richer description of the dependence structure of the two variables. The figure clearly shows that income-consumption pairs at the bottom of the joint distribution are more dependent than observations in the upper tail, with the relative difference between corresponding quantile dependence estimates being as high as nearly 7%.

The above evidence compels us to be flexible in selecting the copula function to use in our empirical analysis. In particular, it should allow for asymmetric positive dependence in either direction. Since some of the copulas presented in the statistics literature impose zero tail dependence in one or both of the tails (e.g., normal, Frank, Clayton, and Gumbel), whereas other copulas such as the Student's t allow for positive and symmetric dependence in both tails, these functions are not considered in this chapter. Rather, our choice falls on the "symmetrized Joe–Clayton" copula used in [67]. The symmetrized Joe–Clayton

---

19. The results depicted in the figure focus on the 2000 wave of the SHIW and use deciles as the quantiles of choice—hence the differences are calculated as $\frac{q_u - q_l}{q_l} \times 100$ for $\{(u, l)\} = \{(90, 10),\ (80, 20),\ (70, 30),\ (60, 40),\ (50, 50)\}$. The results for the other waves (not shown) are pretty similar and can be obtained on request.

(SJC) copula is given by

$$
C_{SJC}\left(u_c, u_i; \tau^U, \tau^L\right) = \frac{1}{2} \times \left[C_{JC}\left(u_c, u_i; \tau^U, \tau^L\right)\right.
$$
$$
\left. + C_{JC}\left(1 - u_c, 1 - u_i; \tau^L, \tau^U\right) + u_c + u_i - 1\right], \tag{9.10}
$$

where $C_{JC}\left(u_c, u_i; \tau^U, \tau^L\right)$ is the Joe–Clayton copula defined as

$$
C_{JC}\left(u_c, u_i; \tau^U, \tau^L\right)
$$
$$
= 1 - \left(1 - \left\{\left[1 - (1 - u_c)^k\right]^{-r} + \left[1 - (1 - u_i)^k\right]^{-r} - 1\right\}^{-\frac{1}{r}}\right)^{\frac{1}{k}} \tag{9.11}
$$

with $k = \frac{1}{\log_2(2-\tau^U)}$ and $r = -\frac{1}{\log_2(\tau^L)}$ [38].

The copula functional form (9.10) has two parameters, τ^U and τ^L, which are measures of tail dependence. The SJC copula exhibits lower tail dependence if $\tau^L \in (0, 1]$ and no lower tail dependence if $\tau^L = 0$; similarly, it exhibits upper tail dependence if $\tau^U \in (0, 1]$ and no upper tail dependence if $\tau^U = 0$. By construction, the SJC copula also nests symmetry as a particular case, which occurs when $\tau^U = \tau^L$. From an empirical perspective, the fact that this copula is flexible enough to allow for both upper- and lower-tail asymmetric dependence— with symmetric dependence as a particular case—makes it a more interesting specification than many other copulas.[20]

A commonly used procedure will be adopted for estimating the parameters τ^U and τ^L of the SJC copula. The method is called "inference functions for margins" (IFM) and was introduced by Joe and Xu [41]. It consists of two steps: the parameters of the marginal distributions are estimated separately in the first step, and then, given these, the procedure calculates the estimate of the association parameters of the copula function. Here, this means that the MGF estimates $\hat{\gamma}_c$ and $\hat{\gamma}_i$ of the κ-generalized distributions for consumption and income margins are provided in the first step. They are then plugged into the log-likelihood function

$$
l\left(u_c, u_i; \tau^U, \tau^L\right) = \sum_{j=1}^{n} \ln\left[c_{SJC}\left(u_c^j, u_i^j; \tau^U, \tau^L\right)\right], \tag{9.12}
$$

---

20. Unfortunately, there is no simple closed-form expression for Kendall's τ and Spearman's ρ_s in terms of the SJC copula parameters. In the following, the accuracy of the chosen copula will be thus assessed by comparing the actual measures of association to their values computed from observations drawn at random from the SJC-copula-based joint distribution of income and consumption (see Section 9.3.2).

which is maximized with respect to τ^{U} and τ^{L}, where

$$
\begin{aligned}
c_{\mathrm{SJC}}\left(u_c, u_i; \tau^{\mathrm{U}}, \tau^{\mathrm{L}}\right) &= \frac{\partial^2 C_{\mathrm{SJC}}\left(u_c, u_i; \tau^{\mathrm{U}}, \tau^{\mathrm{L}}\right)}{\partial u_c \partial u_i} \\
&= \frac{1}{2} \left[\frac{\partial^2 C_{\mathrm{JC}}\left(u_c, u_i; \tau^{\mathrm{U}}, \tau^{\mathrm{L}}\right)}{\partial u_c \partial u_i} \right. \\
&\quad \left. + \frac{\partial^2 C_{\mathrm{JC}}\left(1-u_c, 1-u_i; \tau^{\mathrm{U}}, \tau^{\mathrm{L}}\right)}{\partial\left(1-u_c\right)\partial\left(1-u_i\right)} \right]
\end{aligned}
\tag{9.13}
$$

is the density of the SJC copula (9.10), and $u_c = F_c\left(x_c; \hat{\boldsymbol{\gamma}}_c\right)$ and $u_i = F_i\left(x_i; \hat{\boldsymbol{\gamma}}_i\right)$ are the estimated κ-generalized cumulative probabilities of consumption and income, respectively.[21] Joe [39] showed that the traditional asymptotic properties of the maximum likelihood estimates still hold for the IFM estimates.

9.3 RESULTS

9.3.1 Parametric Marginal Distributions of Income and Consumption

Estimates by MGF of the parameters of the two marginal distributions for each wave are shown in Table 9.1. Also, there are displayed the estimated standard errors, obtained by numerically evaluating the Hessian of the negative log-

---

21. In Eq. (9.13), the expression for $\dfrac{\partial^2 C_{\mathrm{JC}}\left(1-u_c, 1-u_i; \tau^{\mathrm{U}}, \tau^{\mathrm{L}}\right)}{\partial\left(1-u_c\right)\partial\left(1-u_i\right)}$ is the same as

$$
\begin{aligned}
\frac{\partial^2 C_{\mathrm{JC}}\left(u_c, u_i; \tau^{\mathrm{U}}, \tau^{\mathrm{L}}\right)}{\partial u_c \partial u_i} &= (AB)^{-r-1}\left(1-u_c\right)^{k-1}\left(1-u_i\right)^{k-1}\left\{\left[1-\left(A^{-r}+B^{-r}-1\right)^{-\frac{1}{r}}\right]^{-1+\frac{1}{k}}\right. \\
&\quad \left(A^{-r}+B^{-r}-1\right)^{-2-\frac{1}{r}}(1+r)k+\left[1-\left(A^{-r}+B^{-r}-1\right)^{-\frac{1}{r}}\right]^{-2+\frac{1}{k}} \\
&\quad \left. \left(A^{-r}+B^{-r}-1\right)^{-2-\frac{2}{r}}(k-1)\right\},
\end{aligned}
$$

where $A = 1-\left(1-u_c\right)^k$ and $B = 1-\left(1-u_i\right)^k$, but we substitute u_c and u_i in the latter with $1-u_c$ and $1-u_i$ to get the former. Also note that $k = \frac{1}{\log_2\left(2-\tau^{\mathrm{L}}\right)}$ and $r = -\frac{1}{\log_2\left(\tau^{\mathrm{U}}\right)}$ for the former.

TABLE 9.1 Estimated κ-Generalized Distributions of Income and Consumption for SHIW Data, 1987–2014[a]

Wave	Total consumption						Net disposable income					
	$\hat{\alpha}_c$		$\hat{\beta}_c$		$\hat{\kappa}_c$		$\hat{\alpha}_i$		$\hat{\beta}_i$		$\hat{\kappa}_i$	
1987	2.34	(0.03)	13,403	(98)	0.63	(0.03)	2.20	(0.05)	16,892	(93)	0.61	(0.03)
1989	2.89	(0.04)	13,766	(87)	0.84	(0.03)	2.45	(0.06)	18,098	(87)	0.74	(0.03)
1991	2.54	(0.03)	13,669	(92)	0.72	(0.03)	2.41	(0.06)	17,987	(89)	0.68	(0.03)
1993	2.85	(0.04)	12,838	(88)	0.93	(0.03)	2.10	(0.06)	17,674	(91)	0.65	(0.03)
1995	2.65	(0.04)	13,306	(87)	0.75	(0.03)	2.32	(0.06)	16,690	(89)	0.79	(0.03)
1998	2.76	(0.04)	13,021	(100)	0.91	(0.03)	2.52	(0.07)	17,823	(96)	0.91	(0.03)
2000	2.49	(0.03)	13,950	(95)	0.69	(0.03)	2.46	(0.06)	18,569	(93)	0.81	(0.03)
2002	2.59	(0.04)	13,951	(96)	0.76	(0.03)	2.46	(0.06)	18,679	(92)	0.77	(0.03)
2004	2.63	(0.04)	14,913	(100)	0.76	(0.03)	2.78	(0.05)	18,706	(94)	0.99	(0.03)
2006	2.78	(0.04)	15,308	(99)	0.78	(0.03)	2.53	(0.06)	20,123	(98)	0.72	(0.03)
2008	2.90	(0.04)	14,884	(90)	0.76	(0.03)	2.64	(0.08)	19,489	(93)	0.82	(0.03)
2010	2.85	(0.04)	15,333	(99)	0.83	(0.03)	2.52	(0.06)	19,915	(103)	0.79	(0.03)
2012	2.61	(0.04)	15,190	(96)	0.67	(0.03)	2.35	(0.05)	18,426	(97)	0.71	(0.02)
2014	2.79	(0.04)	13,725	(86)	0.76	(0.03)	2.39	(0.08)	18,661	(91)	0.67	(0.03)

[a] *Numbers in parentheses: estimated standard errors.*

likelihood under both the data and the estimated κ-generalized parameters.[22] Convergence was achieved easily within a few iterations.

The model fit varied slightly across years but was generally excellent, as indicated by the small value of the errors. This is demonstrated by the plots shown in Figs. 9.8 and 9.9 for the most recent data available (for brevity, we do not report plots for each year, but they are available from the authors on request). In fact, the fitted cumulative function well approximates the empirical curve in panels (A); the κ-generalized and empirical densities match appropriately in panels (B), and the points in the Q–Q plots (C) comparing sample quantiles with the theoretical quantiles computed from the model lie extremely close to the 45° ray from the origin—except for a few extreme values—and much closer than is typically observed in plots of this type. Moreover, the double-logarithmic plots in panels (D) show how the κ-generalized distribution performs particularly well in the top part of the empirical distributions.

Thus, the overall fit of the κ-generalized distribution is extremely satisfactory.

9.3.2 The Joint Distribution of Income and Consumption

Table 9.2 presents the estimated parameters of the SJC copula along with asymptotic standard errors.[23] Given parameter estimates, the joint cumulative distribution of income and consumption is easily derived from Eq. (9.7) as

$$H\left(x_c, x_i; \hat{\boldsymbol{\gamma}}_c, \hat{\boldsymbol{\gamma}}_i, \tau^U, \tau^L\right) = C\left(F_c\left(x_c; \hat{\boldsymbol{\gamma}}_c\right), F_i\left(x_i; \hat{\boldsymbol{\gamma}}_i\right); \tau^U, \tau^L\right), \qquad (9.14)$$

---

22. The κ-generalized log-likelihood for a complete random sample of size n is

$$l\left(x; \alpha, \beta, \kappa\right) = n \ln\left(\alpha\right) - n\alpha \ln\left(\beta\right) + \left(\alpha - 1\right) \sum_{j=1}^{n} \ln\left(x_j\right)$$

$$+ \frac{1}{\kappa} \sum_{j=1}^{n} \ln\left[\sqrt{1 + \kappa^2 \left(\frac{x_j}{\beta}\right)^{2\alpha}} - \kappa \left(\frac{x_j}{\beta}\right)^{\alpha}\right] - \frac{1}{2} \sum_{j=1}^{n} \ln\left[1 + \kappa^2 \left(\frac{x_j}{\beta}\right)^{2\alpha}\right],$$

where the consumption and income subscripts have been omitted for notational convenience. By numerically evaluating the Hessian $H\left(\hat{\boldsymbol{\gamma}}\right)$ of the negative of $l\left(\mathbf{x}; \hat{\boldsymbol{\gamma}}\right)$ under both the data $\mathbf{x} = \{x_1, \ldots, x_n\}$ and the estimated κ-generalized parameters $\hat{\boldsymbol{\gamma}} = \left\{\hat{\alpha}, \hat{\beta}, \hat{\kappa}\right\}$, the sampling covariance of the MGF estimates has been estimated from the Fisher information as $V_{\hat{\boldsymbol{\gamma}}} = H^{-1}\left(\hat{\boldsymbol{\gamma}}\right)$. The standard errors for each unknown $\boldsymbol{\gamma} = \{\alpha, \beta, \kappa\}$ have been finally obtained as the square roots of the off-diagonal elements of $V_{\hat{\boldsymbol{\gamma}}}$. To calculate numerical approximations to the Hessian matrix $H\left(\hat{\boldsymbol{\gamma}}\right)$ at the estimated parameter values, we use here the R function hessian from the library numDeriv [34].
23. The SJC copula for all waves of the SHIW was estimated using MATLAB code provided by Andrew Patton to replicate the results presented by Patton [68]. The code is freely available at http://public.econ.duke.edu/~ap172/code.html.

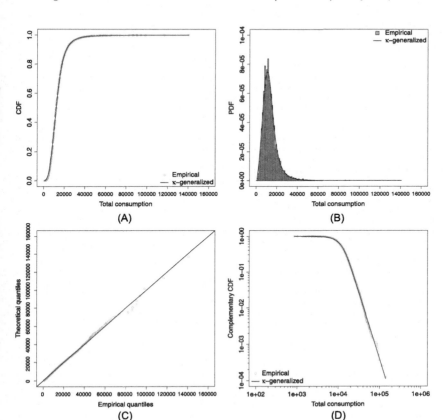

FIGURE 9.8 Adequacy of the κ-generalized distribution for the SHIW consumption data, 2014: (A) empirical and fitted CDFs; (B) empirical and fitted PDFs; (C) Q–Q plot; (D) empirical and fitted complementary CDFs.

that is, by coupling together the κ-generalized marginal distributions of income and consumption via the SJC copula estimation.

The overall goodness of fit of the bivariate model (9.14) can be gauged in two ways.

First, we compare measures of association derived from the parameter estimates to the statistics computed from the raw data. Since no closed-form expression exists for deriving various association measures from the SJC copula parameters, our estimation is based on Monte Carlo sampling using the parametric models and their estimated parameters. That is, we simulate pseudo-samples of income and consumption pairs for each wave of the SHIW based on the inverse sampling method (see, e.g., [59]): we first draw n correlated pairs of uniformly distributed variates (u_c, u_i), where n equals the original sample size, and the

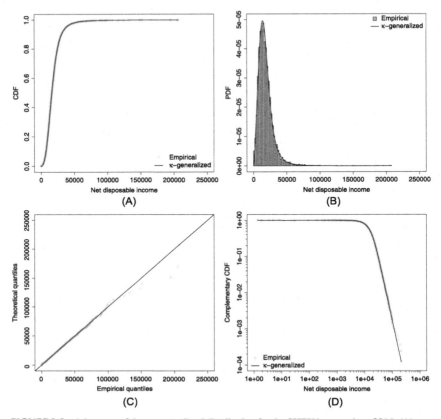

FIGURE 9.9 Adequacy of the κ-generalized distribution for the SHIW income data, 2014: (A) empirical and fitted CDFs; (B) empirical and fitted PDFs; (C) Q–Q plot; (D) empirical and fitted complementary CDFs.

correlation is determined by the SJC copula parameters, and then we generate the consumption and income pairs as $\left(x_c = F_c^{-1}\left(u_c; \hat{\boldsymbol{\gamma}}_c \right), x_i = F_i^{-1}\left(u_i; \hat{\boldsymbol{\gamma}}_i \right) \right)$, that is, the x_cth and x_ith theoretical quantiles implied by the parameter estimates of the marginal distributions. Model-based measures of association are finally obtained by performing standard calculations on the pseudo-samples.

Fig. 9.10 shows model-based predictions of Spearman's and Kendall's correlation coefficients. As can be seen, measures of association computed from simulated data reproduce well the time-varying profile of dependence observed in Fig. 9.1, confirming that the SJC copula can give an adequate description of the dependence structure in the Italian income-consumption data.

A second approach to assessing whether our model really conforms with data consists in generating a probability plot of the theoretical joint CDF given

TABLE 9.2 Parameter Estimates for the SJC
Copula, 1987–2014[a]

Wave	τ^U		τ^L	
1987	0.64	(0.01)	0.78	(0.00)
1989	0.63	(0.01)	0.79	(0.00)
1991	0.60	(0.01)	0.79	(0.00)
1993	0.57	(0.01)	0.62	(0.01)
1995	0.58	(0.01)	0.68	(0.01)
1998	0.57	(0.01)	0.45	(0.01)
2000	0.56	(0.01)	0.55	(0.01)
2002	0.56	(0.01)	0.55	(0.01)
2004	0.59	(0.01)	0.55	(0.01)
2006	0.57	(0.01)	0.63	(0.01)
2008	0.56	(0.01)	0.64	(0.01)
2010	0.65	(0.01)	0.61	(0.01)
2012	0.66	(0.01)	0.65	(0.01)
2014	0.65	(0.01)	0.57	(0.01)

[a] *Numbers in parentheses: estimated standard errors.*

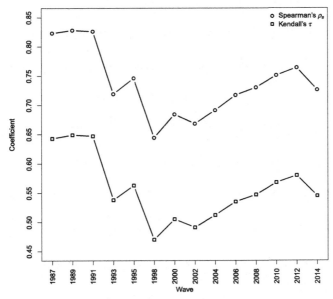

FIGURE 9.10 Model-based predictions of the Spearman's and Kendall's correlation coefficients, 1987–2014.

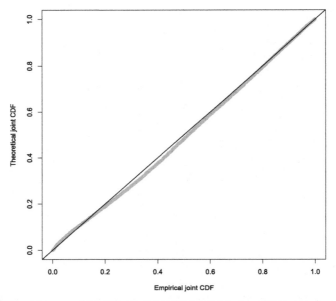

FIGURE 9.11 Adequacy of the SJC-copula-based joint distribution of income and consumption for the 2014 wave of the SHIW.

by Eq. (9.14) against the empirical copula,[24] as shown in Fig. 9.11 for the 2014 wave.[25] The 45° line from $(0, 0)$ to $(1, 1)$ is the comparison line: the cumulative distributions are equal if the plot falls approximately on this line, whereas any deviation from it indicates a difference between the theoretical and empirical joint distributions of income and consumption. As can be seen, the points almost coincide with the comparison line, and the majority of the probability plot is linear. Hence, the hypothesis that income and consumption can be modeled as nonidentically κ-generalized distributed variables, and their dependence by an SJC copula, is not rejected for the examined data.

---

24. Similarly to the empirical distribution, the empirical copula can be defined for multivariate data after a transform to ranks. Suppose that data are realizations from a continuous bivariate distribution of size n. The empirical copula is then the empirical distribution function corresponding to [59, p. 219]

$$C_n\left(\frac{j}{n}, \frac{k}{n}\right) = \frac{\text{number of pairs } (x_c, x_i) \text{ in the sample with } x_c \leq x_c^{(j)} \text{ and } x_i \leq x_i^{(k)}}{n},$$

for $1 \leq j, k \leq n$, where $x_c^{(j)}$ and $x_i^{(k)}$ denote order statistics from the sample.

25. Plots for the other waves of the SHIW are similar and can be obtained on request.

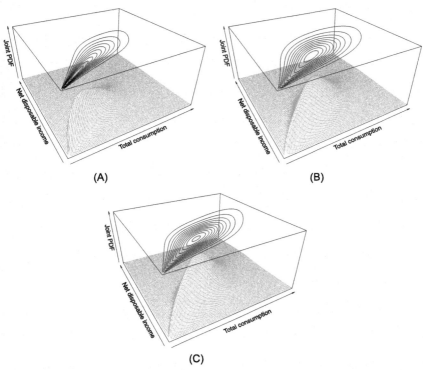

FIGURE 9.12 Joint PDF of the bivariate distribution of income and consumption in Italy: (A) 1987; (B) 2000; (C) 2014.

The estimated joint PDF of income and consumption

$$h\left(x_c, x_i; \hat{\boldsymbol{\gamma}}_c, \hat{\boldsymbol{\gamma}}_i, \tau^{U}, \tau^{L}\right)$$
$$= c\left(F_c\left(x_c; \hat{\boldsymbol{\gamma}}_c\right), F_i\left(x_i; \hat{\boldsymbol{\gamma}}_i\right); \tau^{U}, \tau^{L}\right) \times f_c\left(x_c; \hat{\boldsymbol{\gamma}}_c\right) \times f_i\left(x_i; \hat{\boldsymbol{\gamma}}_i\right), \quad (9.15)$$

obtained as the product of the SJC copula density (9.13) with the κ-generalized distribution for margins given by Eq. (9.5), is charted in Fig. 9.12 for 1987, 2000, and 2014. The contours of the joint densities are also shown at the top to help visualize the overall pattern. There are a number of interesting features revealed by the bivariate PDF graphs. The narrow profile of the contours of the distribution at the lower end of the income-consumption space suggests a strong positive dependence between the two variates for bottom-ranked households. By contrast, the round profile of the contours of the joint distribution at the upper end suggests a lesser degree of dependence between income and consumption for top-ranked households. Furthermore, there is a gradual evolution of the de-

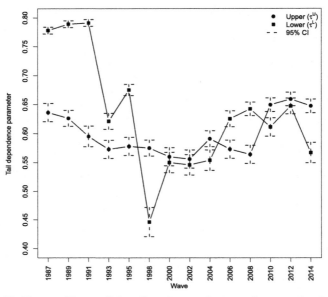

FIGURE 9.13 Upper and lower tail dependence between income and consumption from the SJC copula, 1987–2014. Vertical bars denote 95% pointwise confidence intervals based on the standard normal distribution.

pendence structure between income and consumption during the sample period, especially seen in the wider contours of the 2000 joint distribution: the dependence in the lower tail of the distribution is reduced compared to 1987 and 2014, although the contours remain narrower than those at the top-right corner; at the same time, by comparing contours of the joint distributions we note that also the dependence in the upper tail is somewhat lower in 2000 than in 1987 and 2014.

The above evidence suggests that the dependence structure between income and consumption in Italy varied *asymmetrically* over the sample period. Fig. 9.13 shows the degree of asymmetry implied by the SJC copula by plotting the upper and lower tail dependence estimates presented in Table 9.2 along with 95% (pointwise) confidence intervals for these estimates. The plot confirms that the change in dependence also took place in the tails of the joint distribution, with average tail dependence—defined as $\left(\tau^U + \tau^L\right)/2$—dropping from 0.71 in 1987 to 0.56 in 2000 and then rising to 0.61 in 2014. However, the level and the dynamics of dependence were both substantially different in the two tails of the income-consumption distribution: in the first part of the sample period, from 1987 to 2000, lower tail dependence was on average about 12% greater than upper tail dependence, and the average rate of decline for the former dependence was consistently higher than for the latter (respectively, an average decline of more than 2% per annum versus nearly 1%). By contrast, during the 2000s and

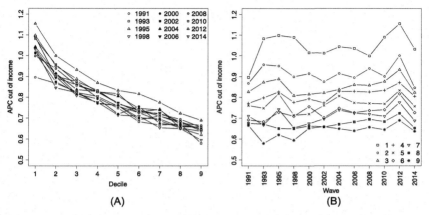

FIGURE 9.14   The average propensity to consume (APC) in Italy, 1991–2014. (A) By decile over time. (B) Over time by decile.

up to 2014, the asymmetry pattern is reversed and somewhat weaker: upper tail dependence was on average about 1% greater than lower tail dependence and also grew faster than the latter (respectively, an average yearly increase of about 1.3% versus nearly 0.3%). In particular, Fig. 9.13 shows quite clearly that the level of dependence between income and consumption increased markedly following the break that occurred around the Great Recession of 2008, and the dependence structure went from significantly asymmetric in one direction to weakly asymmetric in the opposite direction.

Overall, our results can be deemed to be consistent with compelling evidence that the propensity to consume declines as household income increases (e.g., [8], [51], [57], [13], [30], and [37]). This can be seen in panel (A) of Fig. 9.14, where we plot estimates of the average propensity to consume (APC) of Italian households for the years 1991–2014.[26] The figure shows quite clearly that the APC, which measures the average association between the total consumption and net disposable income, declines for all years when moving from the bottom toward the top of the income distribution, meaning that consumption and income are somewhat more dependent in the lower tail than in the upper tail. Furthermore, from panel (B) of the same figure we note that APC increased substantially for all income deciles around the outbreak of the 2008 crisis, following years of decline during the 1990s and of relative stagnation during the first half of the 2000s. Thus, it appears that consumption became more dependent on income toward the end of the sample period in all deciles of the distribution, thereby

---

26. Appendix 9.A provides a detailed specification and estimates of the consumption function used to gauge the propensity to consume based on the SHIW data.

reducing the degree of asymmetry in the dependence structure of the Italian income-consumption data.

9.4 CONCLUSIONS AND DIRECTIONS FOR FUTURE RESEARCH

The purpose of this work was to provide a contribution to the estimation of joint distributions where both the variables are dependent and parametrically distributed. Since the independence between household income and consumption variables is not the most appropriate assumption to work with, the approach concerned modeling the bivariate distribution of income and consumption in Italy with univariate margins belonging to a given parametric family and a copula function that summarizes the existing dependence structure. To do this, we applied the "symmetrized Joe–Clayton" copula to model the dependence between income and consumption margins whose nonidentical distributions belong to the κ-generalized family.

The proposed copula-based approach was found to capture well the complex dependence between income and consumption observed in our samples, but more needs to be done.

One clear extension of this work would be to extend the model to account for other measures of economic well-being, such as wealth. There can be indeed little dispute that wealth is a relevant measure of living standard too and one which is probably able to capture long-term economic resources better than income— as, over and above any income flow, it represents resources that people are able to draw upon to face adverse shocks. Thus, since both income and wealth may be used to finance current consumption, or retained to support future consumption, they can be thought of as alternative means of securing the living standards of individuals, families, or households. Information on household wealth holdings is also collected in the Bank of Italy's SHIW database.

Another aspect of interest is studying whether accounting for income and consumption jointly reveals a different pattern of economic inequality than the traditional "income only" approach.[27] To capture inequality in the joint distribution of income and consumption, we can rely on the bivariate Gini coefficient [53], which is determined by the degree of inequality in the two marginal distributions and by the association among the two variates. This would also allow us to compare overall inequality of income and consumption across time and examine if changes are driven by differences in the association between income and consumption or by differences in the marginal distributions. In our view,

---

27. Clearly, the same is true for the relationship between consumption and wealth or income and wealth.

the most straightforward way to attain this goal is to work with parametric estimates of our bivariate model to design a counter-factual analysis to assess the implications of variations in the model parameters on the bivariate version of the Gini coefficient: we would evaluate these implications by calculating what the bivariate Gini would be if the dependence structure of income and consumption was fixed but the parameter estimates of the marginal distributions changed over time, and by assessing how would bivariate inequality change if the relationship between income and consumption changed over time but the marginal distributions were fixed.

All these aspects are still open and in need of an in-depth study.

APPENDIX 9.A THE PROPENSITY TO CONSUME IN ITALY

To estimate the marginal propensity to consume at the household level and using cross-sectional information, we follow the empirical approach proposed by [62]. We consider a simple consumption function based on the life cycle model where individuals use income and wealth accumulation to smooth consumption over their life cycle. In this framework, current consumption is proportional to total net disposable income (i.e., the sum of total consumption and saving) and total net wealth (i.e., the sum of real and financial assets minus the financial liabilities).

We start with the following simple consumption function:

$$C_{it} = \beta_0 Y_{it} + \beta 1 W_{it}, \tag{9.A.1}$$

where each period of time t available in the SHIW survey is considered as a dynasty. Dividing Eq. (9.A.1) by the level of net income, we obtain the expression for estimating the average propensity to consume (APC) with respect to net income and net wealth as

$$\frac{C_{it}}{Y_{it}} = \beta_0 + \beta 1 \frac{W_{it}}{Y_{it}}, \tag{9.A.2}$$

where C_{it}, Y_{it}, and W_{it} denote, respectively, the total consumption, total income, and net wealth at time t for a given household i. In this model, β_0 and β_1 are the APC out of income (or "income effect") and the APC out of wealth (or "wealth effect"), respectively.[28]

The results of the microbased estimates are reported in Table 9.A.1. The results show a strong income effect and a limited wealth effect on consumption in Italy: the estimated APC out of income varies from 0.75 to 0.85, but overall it is

---

28. Eq. (9.A.2) is estimated taking into account the period 1991–2014, where data on net wealth are available.

TABLE 9.A.1 Linear Regression Estimates, 1991–2014

	1991	1993	1995	1998	2000	2002	2004	2006	2008	2010	2012	2014
						Dependent variable: C/Y						
Y/Y	0.754***	0.760***	0.803***	0.754***	0.773***	0.755***	0.793***	0.781***	0.789***	0.809***	0.854***	0.770***
	(0.003)	(0.005)	(0.004)	(0.005)	(0.004)	(0.004)	(0.004)	(0.004)	(0.003)	(0.004)	(0.003)	(0.003)
W/Y	0.005***	0.006***	0.003***	0.002**	0.001*	0.002***	0.000	0.000	−0.001***	−0.001***	0.000	0.000
	(0.000)	(0.000)	(0.000)	(0.000)	(0.001)	(0.000)	(0.000)	(0.000)	(0.000)	(0.000)	(0.000)	(0.000)
Obs	7763	7436	7510	6593	7427	7468	7467	7224	7357	7327	7428	7496

Notes: to reduce the impact of outliers, we drop the bottom 0.01% and the top 2%; numbers in parentheses: estimated standard errors; star codes for significance: *** = 1%, ** = 5%, * = 10%.

TABLE 9.A.2 Linear Regression Estimates by Income Decile, 1991–2014

						Dependent variable: $(C/Y)^d$						
	1991	1993	1995	1998	2000	2002	2004	2006	2008	2010	2012	2014
$(Y/Y)^{d1}$	0.896***	1.082***	1.098***	1.089***	1.014***	1.011***	1.043***	1.034***	0.998***	1.089***	1.155***	1.031***
	(0.006)	(0.019)	(0.013)	(0.018)	(0.015)	(0.015)	(0.015)	(0.013)	(0.011)	(0.014)	(0.012)	(0.015)
$(W/Y)^{d1}$	0.004***	0.008***	0.006***	0.003*	0.012***	0.008***	0.003*	0.002	0.003**	0.001	0.000	0.005**
	(0.001)	(0.002)	(0.001)	(0.002)	(0.002)	(0.002)	(0.002)	(0.002)	(0.001)	(0.001)	(0.000)	(0.001)
Obs	789	638	635	517	604	576	540	531	542	549	521	507
$(Y/Y)^{d2}$	0.868***	0.956***	0.950***	0.899***	0.914***	0.874***	0.914***	0.894***	0.938***	0.900***	0.999***	0.846***
	(0.008)	(0.013)	(0.012)	(0.015)	(0.013)	(0.012)	(0.011)	(0.011)	(0.011)	(0.012)	(0.012)	(0.013)
$(W/Y)^{d2}$	0.000	0.003*	0.007***	0.009***	0.004***	0.007***	0.003**	0.001	0.000	0.003*	0.001	0.007***
	(0.001)	(0.002)	(0.001)	(0.002)	(0.001)	(0.001)	(0.001)	(0.001)	(0.001)	(0.001)	(0.001)	(0.002)
Obs	755	740	726	637	654	698	623	650	615	665	602	560
$(Y/Y)^{d3}$	0.826***	0.872***	0.888***	0.808***	0.816***	0.821***	0.837***	0.860***	0.857***	0.876***	0.933***	0.823***
	(0.008)	(0.013)	(0.012)	(0.016)	(0.013)	(0.010)	(0.012)	(0.012)	(0.010)	(0.012)	(0.011)	(0.011)
$(W/Y)^{d3}$	0.005***	0.009***	0.008***	0.011***	0.007***	0.001*	0.005***	0.002	0.001	0.002*	0.000	0.006***
	(0.001)	(0.002)	(0.002)	(0.002)	(0.001)	(0.001)	(0.001)	(0.001)	(0.001)	(0.001)	(0.001)	(0.001)
Obs	820	746	744	655	695	731	759	682	761	678	664	697

(continued on next page)

TABLE 9.A.2 (continued)

							Dependent variable: $(C/Y)^d$					
	1991	1993	1995	1998	2000	2002	2004	2006	2008	2010	2012	2014
$(Y/Y)^{d4}$	0.771***	0.798***	0.826***	0.776***	0.793***	0.772***	0.828***	0.828***	0.825***	0.833***	0.870***	0.804***
	(0.009)	(0.013)	(0.011)	(0.013)	(0.011)	(0.010)	(0.009)	(0.011)	(0.011)	(0.011)	(0.011)	(0.010)
$(W/Y)^{d4}$	0.012***	0.010***	0.010***	0.005***	0.004***	0.003**	0.001	0.002	0.002	0.004***	0.004***	0.001
	(0.002)	(0.002)	(0.001)	(0.002)	(0.001)	(0.001)	(0.000)	(0.001)	(0.001)	(0.001)	(0.001)	(0.001)
Obs	727	728	763	672	744	767	789	760	769	768	746	792
$(Y/Y)^{d5}$	0.760***	0.747***	0.817***	0.714***	0.719***	0.761***	0.805***	0.773***	0.770***	0.768***	0.833***	0.756***
	(0.009)	(0.012)	(0.011)	(0.013)	(0.012)	(0.011)	(0.010)	(0.011)	(0.009)	(0.011)	(0.011)	(0.010)
$(W/Y)^{d5}$	0.0081***	0.015***	0.007***	0.007***	0.008***	0.005***	0.001*	0.001	0.003**	0.003**	0.005***	0.001
	(0.002)	(0.002)	(0.001)	(0.002)	(0.002)	(0.001)	(0.001)	(0.001)	(0.001)	(0.001)	(0.001)	(0.001)
Obs	741	783	782	626	751	809	835	740	791	751	825	803
$(Y/Y)^{d6}$	0.692***	0.683***	0.728***	0.709***	0.755***	0.701***	0.746***	0.726***	0.735***	0.739***	0.816***	0.726***
	(0.009)	(0.011)	(0.012)	(0.011)	(0.009)	(0.012)	(0.012)	(0.009)	(0.011)	(0.010)	(0.009)	(0.010)
$(W/Y)^{d6}$	0.010***	0.013***	0.007***	0.004***	0.003***	0.005***	0.005***	0.003***	0.003*	0.003*	0.002**	0.007***
	(0.002)	(0.001)	(0.002)	(0.001)	(0.001)	(0.001)	(0.001)	(0.001)	(0.001)	(0.001)	(0.001)	(0.001)
Obs	740	787	768	717	781	726	811	776	779	801	738	801

(continued on next page)

TABLE 9.A.2 (continued)

	Dependent variable: $(C/Y)^d$											
	1991	**1993**	**1995**	**1998**	**2000**	**2002**	**2004**	**2006**	**2008**	**2010**	**2012**	**2014**
$(Y/Y)^{d7}$	0.710	0.667***	0.742***	0.653***	0.674***	0.695***	0.738***	0.723***	0.718***	0.708***	0.775***	0.687***
	(0.009)	(0.012)	(0.012)	(0.014)	(0.014)	(0.012)	(0.012)	(0.011)	(0.008)	(0.012)	(0.011)	(0.011)
$(W/Y)^{d7}$	0.008***	0.009***	0.009***	0.004***	0.007***	0.005***	0.001	0.001	0.000	0.006***	0.003*	0.003**
	(0.001)	(0.001)	(0.002)	(0.002)	(0.001)	(0.001)	(0.001)	(0.001)	(0.001)	(0.001)	(0.001)	(0.001)
Obs	761	709	781	642	764	749	767	779	795	778	807	775
$(Y/Y)^{d8}$	0.675***	0.672***	0.651***	0.649***	0.663***	0.657***	0.670***	0.682***	0.694***	0.683***	0.722***	0.652***
	(0.010)	(0.014)	(0.011)	(0.013)	(0.012)	(0.012)	(0.013)	(0.011)	(0.009)	(0.012)	(0.011)	(0.010)
$(W/Y)^{d8}$	0.009***	0.005*	0.009***	0.004***	0.008***	0.007***	0.006***	0.005***	0.002*	0.006***	0.006***	0.004***
	(0.002)	(0.002)	(0.002)	(0.006)	(0.001)	(0.001)	(0.002)	(0.001)	(0.001)	(0.001)	(0.001)	(0.001)
Obs	780	695	747	671	795	827	793	834	831	819	851	806
$(Y/Y)^{d9}$	0.665***	0.579***	0.620***	0.594***	0.652***	0.658***	0.649***	0.639***	0.656***	0.645***	0.689***	0.636***
	(0.01)	(0.012)	(0.012)	(0.013)	(0.012)	(0.012)	(0.012)	(0.011)	(0.007)	(0.010)	(0.010)	(0.009)
$(W/Y)^{d9}$	0.007***	0.012***	0.008***	0.006***	0.004***	0.002*	0.004***	0.005***	0.000	0.005***	0.005***	0.001
	(0.002)	(0.001)	(0.001)	(0.002)	(0.001)	(0.001)	(0.001)	(0.001)	(0.000)	(0.001)	(0.001)	(0.001)
Obs	829	814	757	727	816	812	811	804	776	779	810	851

Notes: in order to reduce the impact of outliers, we drop the bottom 0.01% and the top 2%; numbers in parentheses: estimated standard errors; star codes for significance:
*** = 1%, ** = 5%, * = 10%.

increasing in the period 1991–2014, whereas the impact of wealth on consumption appears to be negligible, about 0.006, meaning that one additional euro of wealth would increase annual consumption by 0.6%.

We consider now a more flexible specification where we allow the APC to vary across the income distribution. We define income categories in which the household income composition is quite homogeneous. We introduce dummy variables accounting for the households belonging to the considered income position, which are interacted with the variables in Eq. (9.A.2). We consider nine income groups, defined according to the following income deciles: 0.0 to 0.10, 0.10 to 0.20, 0.20 to 0.30, 0.30 to 0.40, 0.40 to 0.50, 0.50 to 0.60, 0.60 to 0.70, 0.70 to 0.80, 0.80 to 0.90, and 0.90 to 1.00.

The results are presented in Table 9.A.2.

As expected, the impact of net wealth is still negligible, but remarkable differences of the impact of income among the different percentiles emerge. The APC out of income, which we consider as a proxy of the marginal propensity to consume, shows a decreasing trend when we move forward along the income distributions. Indeed, we obtain an APC decreasing from 0.8–1.1 cents of euro for households in the first decile to about 0.6 cent of euro for households at the top of the income distribution. This implies that the average APC out of income, estimated from the baseline model (9.A.2), is likely to be biased by the nonlinear effects arising along the income distribution.

REFERENCES

[1] C. Alexander, Practical Financial Econometrics, Market Risk Analysis, vol. II, John Wiley & Sons, Chichester, UK, 2008.

[2] T.W. Anderson, D.A. Darling, A test of goodness-of-fit, Journal of the American Statistical Association 49 (1954) 765–769.

[3] A.B. Atkinson, On lateral thinking, The Journal of Economic Inequality 9 (2011) 319–328.

[4] A.B. Atkinson, C. Lakner, Wages, capital and top incomes: the factor income composition of top incomes in the USA, 1960–2005, Mimeo, available at: http://www.ecineq.org/ecineq_lux15/FILESx2015/CR2/p196.pdf, 2016.

[5] J. Bai, P. Perron, Estimating and testing linear models with multiple structural changes, Econometrica 66 (1998) 47–78.

[6] J. Bai, P. Perron, Computation and analysis of multiple structural change models, Journal of Applied Econometrics 18 (2003) 1–22.

[7] N. Balakrishnan, C.-D. Lai, Continuous Bivariate Distributions, Springer, New York, NY, 2009.

[8] A.S. Blinder, Distribution effects and the aggregate consumption function, Journal of Political Economy 83 (1975) 447–475.

[9] S. Bonhomme, J.-M. Robin, Assessing the equalizing force of mobility using short panels: France, 1990–2000, The Review of Economic Studies 76 (2009) 63–92.

[10] A. Brandolini, The distribution of personal income in post-war Italy: source description, data quality, and the time pattern of income inequality, Giornale degli Economisti e Annali di Economia 58 (1999) 183–239.

[11] A. Brandolini, L. Cannari, Methodological appendix: the Bank of Italy's Survey of Household Income and Wealth, in: A. Ando, L. Guiso, I. Visco (Eds.), Saving and the Accumulation of Wealth: Essays on Italian Household and Government Saving Behavior, Cambridge University Press, New York, NY, 1994, pp. 369–386.

[12] G. Burtless, Effects of growing wage disparities and changing family composition on the U.S. income distribution, European Economic Review 43 (1999) 853–865.

[13] C.D. Carroll, Requiem for the representative consumer? Aggregate implications of microeconomic consumption behavior, The American Economic Review 90 (2000) 110–115.

[14] G.C. Chow, Tests of equality between sets of coefficients in two linear regressions, Econometrica 28 (1960) 591–605.

[15] F. Clementi, T. Di Matteo, M. Gallegati, G. Kaniadakis, The κ-generalized distribution: a new descriptive model for the size distribution of incomes, Physica A: Statistical Mechanics and its Applications 387 (2008) 3201–3208.

[16] F. Clementi, M. Gallegati, The Distribution of Income and Wealth: Parametric Modeling with the κ-Generalized Family, Springer International Publishing AG, Cham, 2016.

[17] F. Clementi, M. Gallegati, G. Kaniadakis, κ-Generalized statistics in personal income distribution, The European Physical Journal B 57 (2007) 187–193.

[18] F. Clementi, M. Gallegati, G. Kaniadakis, A κ-generalized statistical mechanics approach to income analysis, Journal of Statistical Mechanics: Theory and Experiment 2009 (2009) P02037.

[19] F. Clementi, M. Gallegati, G. Kaniadakis, A model of personal income distribution with application to Italian data, Empirical Economics 39 (2010) 559–591.

[20] F. Clementi, M. Gallegati, G. Kaniadakis, A new model of income distribution: the κ-generalized distribution, Journal of Economics 105 (2012) 63–91.

[21] F. Clementi, M. Gallegati, G. Kaniadakis, A generalized statistical model for the size distribution of wealth, Journal of Statistical Mechanics: Theory and Experiment 2012 (2012) P12006.

[22] F. Clementi, M. Gallegati, G. Kaniadakis, S. Landini, κ-generalized models of income and wealth distributions: a survey, The European Physical Journal Special Topics 225 (2016) 1959–1984.

[23] C. Croux, C. Dehon, Influence functions of the Spearman and Kendall correlation measures, Statistical Methods & Applications 19 (2010) 497–515.

[24] C. Dagum, A new model of personal income distribution: specification and estimation, Economie Appliquée 30 (1977) 413–436.

[25] V. Dardanoni, P.J. Lambert, Horizontal inequity comparisons, Social Choice and Welfare 18 (2001) 799–816.

[26] K. Decancq, Copula-based measurement of dependence between dimensions of well-being, Oxford Economic Papers 66 (2014) 681–701.

[27] M.L. Delignette-Muller, C. Dutang, fitdistrplus: an R package for fitting distributions, Journal of Statistical Software 64 (2015) 1–34.

[28] F. Domma, S. Giordano, A stress-strength model with dependent variables to measure household financial fragility, Statistical Methods & Applications 21 (2012) 375–389.

[29] F. Domma, S. Giordano, A copula-based approach to account for dependence in stress-strength models, Statistical Papers 54 (2013) 807–826.

[30] K.E. Dynan, J.S. Skinner, S.P. Zeldes, Do the rich save more?, Journal of Political Economy 112 (2004) 397–444.

[31] P. Embrechts, F. Lindskog, A. Mcneil, Modelling dependence with copulas and applications to risk management, in: S.T. Rachev (Ed.), Handbook of Heavy Tailed Distributions in Finance, vol. 1., North Holland, Amsterdam, 2003, pp. 329–384, Ch. 8.

[32] P. Embrechts, A.J. McNeil, D. Straumann, Correlation and dependency in risk management: properties and pitfalls, in: M.A.H. Dempster (Ed.), Risk Management: Value at Risk and Beyond, Cambridge University Press, New York, NY, 2002, pp. 176–223.

[33] M. Fournier, Inequality decomposition by factor components: a 'rank-correlation approach' illustrated on the Taiwanese case, Recherches économiques de Louvain 67 (2001) 381–403.

[34] P. Gilbert, R. Varadhan, numDeriv: accurate numerical derivatives, R package version 2016.8-1, https://CRAN.R-project.org/package=numDeriv, 2016.

[35] A.J.M. Hagenaars, K. de Vos, M.A. Zaidi, Poverty Statistics in the Late 1980s: Research Based on Micro-data, Office for Official Publications of the European Communities, Luxembourg, 1994.

[36] M. Jäntti, E. Sierminska, P. Van Kerm, Modelling the joint distribution of income and wealth, in: T.I. Garner, K.S. Short (Eds.), Measurement of Poverty, Deprivation, and Economic Mobility, vol. 23, Emerald Group, Bingley, UK, 2015, pp. 301–327.

[37] T. Jappelli, L. Pistaferri, Fiscal policy and MPC heterogeneity, American Economic Journal: Macroeconomics 6 (2014) 107–136.

[38] H. Joe, Multivariate Models and Dependence Concepts, Chapman & Hall, London, 1997.

[39] H. Joe, Asymptotic efficiency of the two-stage estimation method for copula-based models, Journal of Multivariate Analysis 94 (2005) 401–419.

[40] H. Joe, Dependence Modeling with Copulas, CRC Press, Boca Raton, FL, 2015.

[41] H. Joe, J.J. Xu, The Estimation Method of Inference Functions for Margins for Multivariate Models, Technical Report 166, Department of Statistics, University of British Columbia, Vancouver, BC, 1996. Available at: http://hdl.handle.net/2429/57078.

[42] M. Kac, J. Fiefer, J. Wolfowitz, On tests of normality and other tests of goodness of fit based on distance methods, The Annals of Mathematical Statistics 26 (1955) 189–211.

[43] G. Kaniadakis, Non-linear kinetics underlying generalized statistics, Physica A: Statistical Mechanics and its Applications 296 (2001) 405–425.

[44] G. Kaniadakis, Statistical mechanics in the context of special relativity, Physical Review E 66 (2002) 056125.

[45] G. Kaniadakis, Statistical mechanics in the context of special relativity. II, Physical Review E 72 (2005) 036108.

[46] G. Kaniadakis, Maximum entropy principle and power-law tailed distributions, The European Physical Journal B 70 (2009) 3–13.

[47] G. Kaniadakis, Relativistic entropy and related Boltzmann kinetics, The European Physical Journal A 40 (2009) 275–287.

[48] G. Kaniadakis, Theoretical foundations and mathematical formalism of the power-law tailed statistical distributions, Entropy 15 (2013) 3983–4010.

[49] J.N. Kapur, M. Dhande, On entropic measures of stochastic dependence, International Journal of Pure and Applied Mathematics 17 (1986) 581–591.

[50] A.B. Kennickell, Ponds and Streams: Wealth and Income in the U.S., 1989 to 2007, Finance and Economics Discussion Series 2009/13, Divisions of Research & Statistics and Monetary Affairs, Federal Reserve Board, Washington, DC, 2009. Available at: https://www.federalreserve.gov/pubs/feds/2009/200913/200913pap.pdf.

[51] A.H. Khan, Aggregate consumption function and income distribution effect: some evidence from developing countries, World Development 15 (1987) 1369–1374.

[52] C. Kleiber, S. Kotz, Statistical Size Distributions in Economics and Actuarial Sciences, John Wiley & Sons, New York, NY, 2003.

[53] G.A. Koshevoy, K. Mosler, Multivariate Gini indices, Journal of Multivariate Analysis 60 (1997) 252–276.

[54] A. Luceño, Fitting the generalized Pareto distribution to data using maximum goodness-of-fit estimators, Computational Statistics & Data Analysis 51 (2006) 904–917.

[55] B. Mandelbrot, The Pareto–Lévy law and the distribution of income, International Economic Review 1 (1960) 79–106.

[56] R.A. Maronna, D.R. Martin, V.J. Yohai, Robust Statistics: Theory and Methods, John Wiley & Sons, Chichester, UK, 2006.

[57] J. McCarthy, Imperfect insurance and differing propensities to consume across households, Journal of Monetary Economics 36 (1995) 301–327.

[58] J.B. McDonald, Some generalized functions for the size distribution of income, Econometrica 52 (1984) 647–665.

[59] R.B. Nelsen, An Introduction to Copulas, 2nd edition, Springer, New York, NY, 2006.

[60] M. Okamoto, Evaluation of the goodness of fit of new statistical size distributions with consideration of accurate income inequality estimation, Economics Bulletin 32 (2012) 2969–2982.

[61] M. Okamoto, Extension of the κ-Generalized Distribution: New Four-Parameter Models for the Size Distribution of Income and Consumption, Working Paper 600, Luxembourg Income Study, Luxembourg, 2013. Available at: http://www.lisdatacenter.org/wps/liswps/600.pdf.

[62] M. Paiella, Does wealth affect consumption? Evidence for Italy, Journal of Macroeconomics 29 (2007) 189–205.

[63] V. Pareto, La legge della domanda, Giornale degli Economisti 10 (1895) 59–68.

[64] V. Pareto, La courbe de la répartition de la richesse. Reprinted in: G. Busino (Ed.), Œuvres complètes de Vilfredo Pareto, Tome 3: Écrits sur la courbe de la répartition de la richesse, Librairie Droz, Geneva, 1965, pp. 1–15.

[65] V. Pareto, Aggiunta allo studio della curva delle entrate, Giornale degli Economisti 14 (1897) 15–26.

[66] V. Pareto, Cours d'économie politique, Macmillan, London, 1897.

[67] A.J. Patton, Modelling asymmetric exchange rate dependence, International Economic Review 47 (2006) 527–556.

[68] A.J. Patton, Copula methods for forecasting multivariate time series, in: G. Elliott, A. Timmermann (Eds.), Handbook of Economic Forecasting, vol. 2B, North Holland, Amsterdam, 2013, pp. 899–960.

[69] A. Pérez, M. Prieto, Measuring dependence between dimensions of poverty in Spain: an approach based on copulas, in: 2015 Conference of the International Fuzzy Systems Association and the European Society for Fuzzy Logic and Technology (IFSA-EUSFLAT-15), The Atlantis Press, 2015, pp. 734–741. Available at: http://www.atlantis-press.com/php/download_paper.php?id=23615.

[70] C. Quinn, Using Copulas to Measure Association Between Ordinal Measures of Health and Income, Econometrics and Data Group Working Paper 07/24, Department of Economics, University of York, York, UK, 2007. Available at: http://www.york.ac.uk/media/economics/documents/herc/wp/07_24.pdf.

[71] C. Quinn, Measuring Income-Related Inequalities in Health Using a Parametric Dependence Function, Econometrics and Data Group Working Paper 09/24, Department of Economics, University of York, York, UK, 2009. Available at: http://www.york.ac.uk/media/economics/documents/herc/wp/09_24.pdf.

[72] R Core Team, R: A Language and Environment for Statistical Computing, R Foundation for Statistical Computing, Vienna, 2016. Available at: https://www.R-project.org/.

[73] S.T. Rachev, S. Mittnik, Stable Paretian Models in Finance, John Wiley & Sons, Chichester, UK, 2000.

[74] W.J. Reed, M. Jorgensen, The double Pareto-lognormal distribution—a new parametric model for size distributions, Communications in Statistics – Theory and Methods 33 (2004) 1733–1753.

[75] G. Schwarz, Estimating the dimension of a model, The Annals of Statistics 6 (1978) 461–464.

[76] B. Schweizer, A. Sklar, Probabilistic Metric Spaces, North Holland, New York, NY, 1983.

[77] S.K. Singh, G.S. Maddala, A function for size distribution of incomes, Econometrica 44 (1976) 963–970.

[78] A. Sklar, Fonctions de répartition à n dimensions et leurs marges, Publications de L'Institut de Statistique de L'Université de Paris 8 (1959) 229–231.

[79] Y. Tillé, A. Matei, sampling: survey sampling. R package version 2.7, https:// CRAN.R-project.org/package=sampling, 2015.

[80] P.K. Trivedi, D.M. Zimmer, Copula modeling: an introduction for practitioners, Foundations and Trends in Econometrics 1 (2005) 1–111.

[81] A. Vinh, W.E. Griffiths, D. Chotikapanich, Bivariate income distributions for assessing inequality and poverty under dependent samples, Economic Modelling 27 (2010) 1473–1483.

[82] J. Wolfowitz, Estimation by the minimum distance method, Annals of the Institute of Statistical Mathematics 5 (1953) 9–23.

[83] J. Wolfowitz, The minimum distance method, The Annals of Mathematical Statistics 28 (1957) 75–88.

[84] X. Wu, A. Savvides, T. Stengos, The global joint distribution of income and health, in: J. Ma, M. Wohar (Eds.), Recent Advances in Estimating Nonlinear Models: With Applications in Economics and Finance, Springer, New York, NY, 2014, pp. 249–279.

[85] A. Zeileis, C. Kleiber, Validating multiple structural changes models—a case study, Journal of Applied Econometrics 20 (2005) 685–690.

[86] A. Zeileis, C. Kleiber, W. Krämer, K. Hornik, Testing and dating of structural changes in practice, Computational Statistics & Data Analysis 44 (2003) 109–123.

[87] A. Zeileis, F. Leisch, K. Hornik, C. Kleiber, strucchange: an R package for testing for structural change in linear regression models, Journal of Statistical Software 7 (2002) 1–38.

Chapter 10

A Networked Economy: A Survey on the Effect of Interaction in Credit Markets

Ruggero Grilli*, Giulia Iori†, Niccolò Stamboglis†, and Gabriele Tedeschi‡

*Marche Polytechnic University, Ancona, Italy
†City University, London, United Kingdom
‡Universitat Jaume I, Castellón de la Plana, Spain

10.1 INTRODUCTION

The 2007 credit market freeze drew new attention to the dynamics of financial markets [5,9,35,54,26]. These markets, recognized as highly efficient before the crisis, showed important phenomena of trust evaporation, which led to the well-known problems of credit-crunch (see [38,4,9,54]). As suggested by many authors, the credit squeeze phenomena have their origin in the problem of informational asymmetries among market participants (see [63,48,73], among many). This view has opened the way to an original interpretation of the "global financial crisis," which analyzes interlinkages among financial institutions, recognized as the main propagation channel of crises (see [29,42,56,83]). A proper understanding of the credit market dynamics, thus, requires models suited to study the interaction among heterogeneous agents operating in different market structures (see [23,22]). To this end, different techniques and approaches have been introduced. These range from microeconomic models à la Diamond and Dybvig [46] to network models, simulation methodologies of contagion, and agent-based computational models.

The aim of this chapter is to review the literature on credit market models by emphasizing the mechanisms able to generate financial crises and contagion.

Firstly, we present the main insights provided by the theoretical microeconomic literature. Starting from the fundamental analysis of Diamond and Dybvig [46] on rational bank runs and the analysis of systemic versus sharing risk of Allen and Gale [13], we provide important tools allowing us to detect contagion in the credit sector by analyzing the balance-sheet structure [47,6,7, 81].

Introduction to Agent-Based Economics. http://dx.doi.org/10.1016/B978-0-12-803834-5.00013-8

Secondly, we investigate the importance of credit relationships to fully understand the stability of the financial system adopting network theory. This approach studies how agents create and/or cut their credit relationships, thereby endogenously shaping the topology of the credit network [19]. Once detected the credit network structure, this methodology investigates how complex behavioral rules affect market dynamics and the stability of the credit system as a whole [2,39]. Finally, we introduce an agent-based methodology as a useful tool to understand the effect of interaction among heterogeneous agents in financial markets. We show that this approach can analyze more in detail the effect of the network structure on the stability of a simulated credit system. By simulating artificial credit markets we can explore, for example, how the interaction of heterogeneous agents might impact the stability of the system [68,49,53,32,89, 24], how information flows might influence the assets' price [85], and how the network structure might affect the flow of liquidity in the credit market [74].

The rest of the review is organized as follows. In Section 10.2, we present the main findings of the theoretical literature on credit markets. Here, the focus is on the identification of different sources of contagion. In Section 10.3, we illustrate theoretical and empirical credit network models. In Section 10.4, we consider simulation studies that investigate how systemic risk emerges in artificial financial networks. In the last part of Section 10.4, we illustrate additional agent-based models of credit markets. Finally, in Section 10.5, we draw conclusions.

10.2 THEORETICAL MODELS OF CREDIT MARKETS

The theoretical literature on the credit sector provides a number of important insights concerning the stability of financial markets. One of the main results of this approach is provided by Diamond and Dybvig [46], who develop a three-period model, where banks have to invest on behalf of their risk averse depositors. In period 0, banks invest their clients' deposits. Specifically, financial institutions have to decide how much capital to invest into a short-term investment, providing 1 in the next period, or into a long-term investment, providing $R > 1$ in period two. In period 1, depositors are subject to a noninsurable liquidity shock. After the shock realization, depositors discover if they are short- or long-term investors and, consequently, if they can withdraw in period 1 or 2. The payoff of agents' withdrawing in period 1 and 2 is defined as follows:

$$V_1(f_j, r_1) = \begin{cases} r_1 & \text{if } f_j < r_1^{-1}, \\ 0 & \text{if } f_j \geq r_1^{-1}, \end{cases} \tag{10.1}$$

$$V_2(f, r_1) = \max \left\{ R \frac{(1 - r_1 f)}{(1 - f)}, 0 \right\}, \tag{10.2}$$

where f_j is the number of withdrawers' deposits served before agent j as a fraction of total demand deposits, f is the total number of demand deposits withdrawn, and r_1 is the fixed claim provided to agents withdrawing in period 1. From the payoff functions, two equilibria can be reached. First, a pure strategy Nash equilibrium is reached when the optimal consumption of early consumers equals the fixed claim provided to agents in period 1, that is, $r_1 = c_1^* > 1$. This equilibrium condition leads to an optimal risk sharing. Second, a bank run equilibrium can arise when $r_1 = c_1^* > 1$. This equilibrium is due to exogenous negative news, that is, when all agents panic and try to withdraw their deposits in period 1. If agents anticipate that all other agents withdraw their capital in period one, then the only optimum equilibrium is an early deposit withdrawal regardless of individual consumption preferences. This occurs since the face value of deposits is larger than the liquidation value of the bank assets. In other words, the condition making bank payments higher than the initial endowment of depositors, $r_1 > 1$, is the condition allowing for bank runs, thus showing the intrinsic fragility of the banking system.

An important extension of the Diamond and Dybvig [46] model is obtained by Allen and Gale [13]. The authors, by introducing four identical regions in the Diamond and Dybvig [46] framework, each populated by a bank, show how a perfectly connected interbank market can reduce systemic risk in case of liquidity shocks. Each region i is hit by a liquidity shock, represented by the share of early consumers ω_i. The system is subject to two equally likely states of nature $S1$ and $S2$. In each state of nature, two regions face a shock, which is negatively correlated to the one faced by the other two. Systemic risk, thus, arises due to the unbalance of liquidity distribution in the different regions. In this setting, the development of interbank claims among the different regions may increase systemic stability.[1] The authors show that the structure of interbank relations becomes crucial when "the aggregate demand for liquidity is higher than the system ability to supply liquidity" [13]. Specifically, banks facing an extraordinary liquidity shock can become insolvent and, therefore, be forced to an early liquidation of their long-term assets. If the additional shock is high enough, then the single bank might go bankrupt and be forced to use the claims of other institutions, thus propagating the shock to other regions. Therefore, the interbank topology determines the chain of bankruptcies across regions. The authors show that a complete market structure circumscribes crisis to the sole banks facing an extraordinary liquidity shock, whereas an incomplete interbank structure can lead to the breakdown of the whole system.

---

1. Empirical studies show that banks develop lending agreements to ensure themselves against liquidity shocks (see [41]).

The impact of credit linkages on the systemic risk is also investigated by Freixas et al. [50]. In this model, depositors of one region decide to consume in another region. However, agents, not being sure of the consumption resources available in the new region, may withdraw their deposits at the home region, thus generating gridlocks in solvent banks. The authors show that interbank links, profitable during normal times, may become sources of contagion during bad times.

As the works previously mentioned, this model highlights the key role of bank liabilities in guaranteeing systemic stability. Liquidity unbalances, however, are not the only possible source of systemic instability. Many other models, which use the Diamond and Dybvig [46] framework, analyze contagion as arising from both the liability and the asset side of banks' balance sheet [88].

Important sources of contagion on the liability side are common pools of liquidity. For example, Aghion et al. [10] consider the possibility of contagion in an unregulated banking system with a centralized clearing mechanism. The authors show that a centralized clearing mechanism in a four-period Diamond and Dybvig [46] framework may induce a trade-off between the risk of moral hazard of a single institution and the fragility of the whole system in case of aggregate liquidity shortage.

The aim of the clearing house is to provide coinsurance to banks through interbank lending. In case there are no insolvent members, the clearing house can be an effective mechanism in coinsuring banks against idiosyncratic liquidity shocks. By introducing the hypothesis of a privately observable cash flow the authors introduce panic among financial institutions. In fact, solvent banks may assume that the default of at least one bank absorbs all the banking system liquidity. This might induce banks to an early withdrawal, thus leading to the collapse of an otherwise solvent banking system.

An interesting contribution to the theoretical microeconomic literature is the model of Diamond and Rajan [47]. The authors show that the bankruptcy of one single institution may reduce the pool of liquidity of other banks, thus amplifying the effect of liquidity shrinkages. In this paper, the authors show that the "bank run" is not a key ingredient to generate crisis, but rather contagion may arise from the general equilibrium of the system. The authors consider a framework where banks invest their own resources in a project. Each project repays back an interest after a given time horizon. If a small number of projects delays in repaying interests, then financial institutions can intermediate on these delayed projects and satisfy depositors' demands. On the contrary, if many projects are delayed, then the resources available to pay deposit back are not sufficient, and, consequently, banks are not able to intermediate. In this circumstance, liquidity shortages may force banks to increase their interest rates, thus generating possible insolvency of their borrowers and propagating contagion.

Last but not least, the paper of Acharya et al. [3] must be mentioned. The authors develop a model of interbank lending where surplus banks strategically act to under-provide interbank lending to demanding banks. The specific tiering structure of the banking system proposed by the authors shows that even regions without liquidity shortage can be converted into states of aggregate liquidity shortage, thus, generating contagion.

Many other important sources of contagion from the liability side have been investigated in the microeconomic literature. Among them, the effect of herding and fire-sale prices in generating financial instability has proven to be particularly important (see [6,7,44]).

Other studies consider the propagation of contagion starting from the asset side [81]. A famous contribution in this direction is the pioneering work of Angelini et al. [17], which analyzes interbank contagion via the payment system. The authors estimate the impact of a sudden liquidity problem of debtors on creditors' financial stance. In the model, banks have a positive probability of incurring into an exogenous default. The default of a single bank may draw other agents into default via the repercussion in the payment system.[2]

Maturity transformation, sharing risk, herding behavior, and interbank linkages are just some among the many components able to trigger instability or collapse in financial markets. The models presented so far, however, have proven to be unable to forecast, or even describe, the current global crisis. By focusing just on a single source of distress, they have been unable to identify the multiple contributing factors generating the present "depression" [42,88]. In the next sections, we present more sophisticated models embedding different sources of contagion.

10.3 NETWORK MODELS OF FINANCIAL STABILITY

The pioneering work by Allen and Gale [13] provided important insights on the effect of credit relationships on systemic stability. Nonetheless, this model presented only a stylized structure of interbank relations. An important branch of literature, thus, began to extend this framework in order to introduce more realistic network topologies to analyze different types of credit markets. Theoretical and empirical network models have become important techniques to study the nature of interrelations on credit markets and their effect on the systemic stability.

On the one hand, theoretical network models deal with the agent's incentives to create or destroy links and the overall impact of the resulting network structure on the credit system efficiency [20,90]. The idea is to analyze how agents'

---

2. The role of the payment system in generating contagion is also been considered in a game-theoretic framework; see [27].

behavioral rules affect the stability of the network [2,87] and how risk sharing and systemic risk emerge [39].

On the other hand, the empirical network literature aims at understanding the actual topology of credit markets, its characteristics and resilience [26,54, 43]. In the same spirit, same of the properties of empirical credit networks are adopted to control or predict systemic risk on markets [76]. Last but not least, the results provided by the empirical research on credit networks can be used to build more realistic computational models of the credit sector.

10.3.1   Theoretical Network Models

In an extensive review of networks in economics and finance, Allen and Babus [12] state that network theory can efficiently address the issue of systemic risk. According to the authors' view, the 2007 interbank market freezes should be studied using this approach, which describes network (in)stability using a bottom-up methodology. Clearly, network theory becomes increasingly important in a very interconnected world, which needs a high and constant level of monitoring [53].

A first theoretical model using this methodology is Babus [19]. The author proposes a model where banks develop mutual claims to share the losses of a defaulted bank with all other counterparties. Formally the work represents a network formation game[3] where banks minimize the risk of contagion. Financial institutions have to decide whether to create a new link by comparing the cost (i.e., risk of a loss in case of default) with the benefit. Specifically, agents form or sever links using the Loss Given Default (LGD), which expresses the excess of nominal liabilities over the value of the assets of the failed bank. The use of the LGD function allows the author to derive results similar to Allen and Gale [13], that is, the emergence of a positive correlation between the number of interbank links and the network stability. Specifically, the network resulting from the minimization of the LGD is pairwise stable and has a positive probability of contagion decreasing to zero when the number of banks increases to infinity.[4]

Also the model of [90] follows a game-theoretical approach to describe the evolution of the network. As the authors show, the dynamics of the credit network strongly depends on agents' utility maximization, incomplete information, and risk aversion. The authors consider a framework where the bank i forms a link with a random bank k or one of its neighbors. In the next period, the bank i

---

3. The use of a game theoretical model for detecting the evolution of credit relations is also the key ingredient of the work [20].
4. See Jackson and Wolinsky [71] for a definition of a pairwise stability in networks.

has to decide whether to continue its relationship with k, or with one of its neighbors, or to create a new link with another randomly chosen bank. The decision depends on expected benefit of the bank i to create or maintain a link, which, in turn, is a function of the bank risk aversion. On the one hand, the authors identify a positive relationship between risk aversion and the cluster coefficient. On the other hand, they find no relationship between the risk attitude and the bank degree. Interestingly, the authors show that the decision of agents to create new links depends on the degree of riskiness of the environment in which they operate. When the environment is very risky, the number of links of highly connected banks increases, whereas the number of links of less connected agents decreases.

In the same spirit of Allen and Gale [13] and Freixas et al. [50], Acemoglu et al. [1] show that a more uniform distribution of interbank liabilities leads to a more stable system. In a simple model where banks can invest in a risky asset and lend capital each other, the authors show that the stability of the network strongly depends on the intensity of the shock affecting the system. For a small shock, strongly connected networks are more stable and resilient than weakly connected networks, whereas for a strong shock, interbank links become channels of contagion propagation. Moreover, the authors identify the critical threshold of the shock inducing a phase transition in the stability and resilience of a perfectly connected network. Furthermore, by endogenizing banks' connection decision,[5] the authors find that the resulting financial structure is generally inefficient. This result arises because banks fail to internalize the externality of their possible default on the counterparties.[6]

Another important example of mechanism of financial-network endogenous formation is the model of Castiglionesi and Navarro [39]. In this work, banks strategically create preliminary lending agreements able to provide liquidity to banks in need. In the model, each bank is composed by two types of agents, depositors and shareholder. Each bank might invest into a risk-free or a risky asset. Both investments provide the same expected value, but the latter provides a private benefit to shareholders, thus inducing moral hazard. Investment projects may be affected by liquidity shocks, making them more costly. In this framework, interbank relationships are credit lines able to insure banks against liquidity shocks. When financial institutions have to decide whether to participate in a credit line, they weigh the benefit of the insurance with the cost of counterparty risk. To determine the network structure, the authors introduce the notion of Investment Nash Equilibrium (INE). Formally, an allocation $(K; x; s)$

---

5. See Acemoglu et al. [2] for a model of Bayesian learning and information aggregation on a social network.

6. The authors identify two other important situations in which the network structure may play a role in reducing systemic stability: firesale of assets [40] and withdrawal of liquidity.

is an Investment Nash Equilibrium (INE) for a given economy $(N; e)$ with $x = (x_i)$, $i \in N$, if

$$m_i(K; x_i; s) \geq m_i\big(K; x_i; (s_{-i}; \tilde{s}_i)\big) \; \forall i \in N, \qquad (10.3)$$

where K represents the financial network, x is the bank capital, s is the investment strategy profile, e is the bank endowment, N is the set of banks, and $m_i(\cdot)$ is the bank profit. An equilibrium is obtained when the arising network structure is both an INE and pairwise stable. For low value of the counterparty risk, the fully connected network arises. However, by increasing the level of counterparty risk the network structure becomes more sparse. Additionally, a decentralized equilibrium presents a core–periphery structure with banks in the core investing in safe investments. The authors show that when the risk associated with lending is too high, connections become too costly, and they are consequently severed. Nonetheless, the liquidity insurance mechanism does not disappear completely as safer banks keep on insuring each other. This result shows that, during financial distress periods, the structure of interbank relationships does not disappear completely.

Last but not least, Aymanns and Georg [18] develop a model of synchronization of bank's investment strategies. Banks' network structure endogenously emerges via a pairwise stability mechanism. Banks receive both a private and a social signal. The investment strategy synchronization in the network evolves accordingly to the weight that agents assign to the private and the social beliefs. Following Acemoglu et al. [1], the authors show that the strategy decision of bank i, $x_t^i = \sigma_t^i(I_t^i)$, is given as

$$x^i = \begin{cases} 1 & \text{if } \mathbb{P}_\sigma(\theta = 1|s_t^i) + \mathbb{P}_\sigma(\theta = 1|x_{t-1}^j, j \in K_{t-1}^i) > 1, \\ 0 & \text{if } \underbrace{\mathbb{P}_\sigma(\theta = 1|s_t^i)}_{\text{private belief } p} + \underbrace{\mathbb{P}_\sigma(\theta = 1|x_{t-1}^j, j \in K_{t-1}^i)}_{\text{social belief } q} < 1, \end{cases} \qquad (10.4)$$

and $x^i \in \{0, 1\}$ otherwise. Agents better weigh the social belief if their neighborhood constitutes a larger fraction of the overall network.

To obtain realistic network architectures, the authors assume that agents are heterogeneously informed on the state of the world. In this way, the model detects two empirically relevant sources of systemic risk, common shocks and interbank market freezes. If agents internalize the positive externality of social learning in their strategic decisions mechanism, then the probability of contagious synchronization is substantially reduced.

10.3.2   Empirical Network Analysis

The empirical analysis of credit networks explores the topology of real-world banking sectors to identify stylized facts and network properties. These studies provide important insights on differences and similarities of credit markets across several countries and different time spans.

The work of Blåvarg and Nimander [30] is among the first studies to analyze the correlation, in the Swedish interbank market, between exposures and systemic risk. The authors show that Swedish banks are heavily exposed to each other, and, consequently, the market exhibits a high probability of contagion.

A similar analysis on the Austrian interbank market exposures is presented by Boss et al. [32]. Looking at the credit market data from 2000 to 2003, the authors reconstruct the adjacency matrix of interbank network liabilities via a maximum entropy approach. Thanks to this methodology, the authors show that the distribution of banks' liabilities is power law, and this distribution is driven by the banks' wealth distribution, which displays a similar power exponent. Moreover, by looking at the values of the scaling exponents the authors identify a highly hierarchical system.

Many empirical studies deal with the Italian overnight interbank market e-Mid. This market presents high levels of heterogeneity among participants, with a small number of large borrowers and a large number of small lenders; see [67,69,65]. In addition, the topology of the Italian market does not seem to be affected by the current crisis. In fact, the network density, the persistency of bilateral relationships, and the total amount of outstanding interbank deposits remain fairly unchanged during the pre- and post-crisis periods (see [78,55]). The absence of structural breaks on the Italian overnight market confirms the empirical findings of Affinito [8], Cocco et al. [41], and Bräuning and Fecht [34] and the theoretical analysis of Castiglionesi and Navarro [39], showing the stability of interbank relationships during the crisis.

A detailed analysis of the topology of the Italian overnight market is in [51]. The main goal of the authors is to shed light on the hierarchical structure of the banking system. To test this phenomenon, they estimate different versions of a core–periphery model,[7] finding that this structure provides a better fit for e-Mid than alternative network models. Moreover, the authors find a quite stable core over the investigated time span, where the majority of banks can be classified as intermediaries. The authors also find that core banks were mainly borrowers during the crisis. This proves that the reduction of interbank lending during the

---

7. Core–periphery network models were firstly proposed by Borgatti and Everett [31]. This topology identifies densely connected core nodes and sparsely connected periphery nodes. In contrast with network "communities," the nodes in the core are also reasonably well connected to those in the periphery.

financial crisis of 2008 was mainly due to the activity of core banks, which reduced their numbers of active outgoing links.[8]

Similar studies on the empirical properties of credit networks have also been conducted on non-European markets. For instance, the Federal Funds market, analyzed by Bech and Atalay [26], is sparse and disassortative and exhibits small world phenomena. As for the Italian market, banks can be divided between net borrowers, net lenders, and intermediaries. Moreover, lenders are more numerous than borrowers and smaller in size.[9]

Before concluding this session, it is important to mention the works on multi-layered network models; see [79,21]. A multilayered network is a system where the same set of nodes belong to different layers and each layer is characterized by its own features in terms of network topology, systemic risk, and resilience.

The introduction of this particular network configuration allows the study of domino effect. In fact, when a shock hits a bank in a particular layer, this may not be confined to that layer, but may be amplified through the interaction among the various layers composing the interbank system so generating contagion.

10.4 SIMULATION TECHNIQUES

10.4.1 Computational Approaches

A considerable number of studies adopt simulation techniques to estimate the possibility of contagion via credit interlinkages starting from the analysis of real data. The aim of this line of research, efficiently reviewed by Upper [88], is to estimate the possibility and the impact of contagion when banks face different kinds of shocks.

Sheldon and Maurer [82] are among the first to apply this methodology. The authors check for systemic risk by looking at interbank transactions in the Swiss credit market. They find a small probability of contagion in the interbank market via banks' liability side. The reconstruction of interbank relationships is obtained by looking at the banks' balance-sheets data and replacing the missing values of the adjacency matrix through the maximization of entropy approach.

In a similar framework, Eisenberg and Noe [49] analyze the spread of contagion in an interlinked financial system by developing a simulation model of a clearing mechanism. In their model, the clearing vector, which satisfies the standard conditions imposed by the bankruptcy regulation, is obtained via a computational sequential default algorithm. According to this algorithm, an initial clearing vector is computed. If the clearing vector induces the default of

---

8. A similar core–periphery structure is found also in the German interbank market; see [43].
9. We also remind the empirical studies on the Mexican banking network (see [76]) and the Indian one [70].

at least one agent, then a new clearing vector is computed. The process termi-
nates when no more agents default. This mechanism, by allowing for different
rounds of defaults, is able to detect financial contagion. The authors find that
the diversification of obligations among agents increases the aggregate value of
agents in the system. Additionally, an increase in the unsystematic volatility of
the exogenous shock lowers the value of all agents in the system.

Other studies use simulated repayment mechanisms to analyze indirect
sources of financial contagion via variations in asset prices. Specifically, Cifuentes et al. [40] develop a model of a banking sector where the sale of asset
by distressed institutions may reduce the assets' value of other institutions. The
authors show that the adoption of a mark-to-market accounting may generate a
second round of asset sales and increase the effect of the original shock, thus
creating systemic risk. According to this mechanism, a small shock on the asset
value may lead to a systemic event. Moreover, the authors highlight that systemic risk may in fact be higher than the risk provided by the original shock.
Cifuentes et al. [40] test their model under different market structures by varying the interbank topology. They notice that the system presents a nonmonotonic
relationship between the number of banks' connections and the liquidity threshold, which might lead to contagion.

Many papers analyze contagion in credit systems starting from the observation of real data on interbank liabilities. The aim of these studies is to understand
the system resiliency to different shocks. The methodologies adopted in these
models were initially introduced by Anderson et al. [16] and Albert et al. [11]
in epidemiology studies.

Furfine [52] is one of the first authors adopting simulation methodologies
to analyze the probability and the effect of contagion starting from the chain
of liabilities of a real-world interbank market. Starting from the American payment system data, Fedwire, from February to March 1998, the author rebuilds
the amount of overnight interbank transactions via a computational algorithm.
Once obtained the matrix of interbank transactions, the author simulates the default of the biggest (or the tenth biggest) borrower to test for the probability of
contagion. The author finds that the contagion effect in this market is relatively
limited, and this is not extended to the entire system. Specifically, the exogenous
default of the biggest borrower produces a loss of 4% of the asset value of the
banking system. The loss induced by the tenth biggest borrowers is lower, indicating the strong weight of the biggest agent. Surprisingly, the author finds that
the effect of contagion is magnified if one introduces a rumor preventing lenders
to provide capital at the biggest borrower. The effect of the introduction of this
simple behavioral reinforcement induces a liquidity effect, which increases the
total losses due to contagion to 9% of total assets of the banking system.

In a similar spirit, Boss et al. [33] analyze the stability of the Austrian interbank market by simulating the default of individual banks. Differently from Furfine [52], the authors perform their analysis on the banking system stability by removing a single bank in each separate simulation. The result of this exercise indicates a high stability of this highly connected market. Similar simulation analysis is performed for the UK, the Hungarian, and the Belgian interbank market, by Wells [91], Lublóy [75], and Degryse et al. [45], respectively. All these studies indicate that the default of a single bank rarely induces systemic events. However, the default of highly connected banks may substantially weaken the capital holding of other institutions, thus highlighting the importance of interbank connections.

Different results are found in the German interbank market. Upper and Worms [89], in fact, show that the failure of a single bank can lead to the breakdown of the 15% of the total assets of the banking system.

Even if several simulated mechanisms to generate contagion have been proposed, they are not free from criticism. These critiques refer to the default algorithms, to the naive definition of the behavioral rules, and to the adoption of the maximum entropy principle; see [88,78] for more details.

10.4.2 Agent-Based Models of the Credit Market

The papers reviewed so far consider the effects of single sources of contagion on credit systems. Agent-based models, instead, analyze economic systems from the point of view of the "complexity." This methodology, in fact, is able to jointly replicate plausible agents' behavioral rules, market microstructure, and interactions between components. Moreover, given its varied prospectives, this approach helps in defining the best policies able to mitigate systemic risk; see [64].

Agent-based literature has revealed a wide variety of sources of systemic risk, ranging from agents heterogeneity to network topology. Some studies have analyzed the relationship between the credit network topology and the resilience of the financial system; see [68,25,74,60,28].

Other studies have focused on the effect that agents' strategic choices have on the systemic stability. In this regard, the literature has focused on optimizing behaviors, such as portfolio maximization or risk and costs minimization; see [36,15].

Last but not least, additional studies have considered possible feedback loops between the macroeconomy and the financial sector [14,86,62,61].

The above-mentioned paper of Allen and Gale [13] has shown that modeling the credit system as a random graph, when increasing the degree of connectivity of the network, the probability of bankruptcy avalanches decreases. However, when the credit network is completely connected, these authors have proven that the probability of bankruptcy cascades goes to zero. The explanation for this result is that, in credit networks, two opposite effects interact. On the one hand, increasing the network connectivity decreases the banks' risk, thanks to risk sharing. On the other hand, increasing the connectivity rises the systemic risk due to the higher numbers of connected agents, which, in case of default, may be compromised. According to this model, the impact of the risk sharing plays a leading role. So, in this model, there is a benefit in creating links between agents because they allow to diversify risk. Notwithstanding, the global financial crisis, burst in August 2007, has shown the dark side of interbank connections. In the light of this empirical evidence, many studies have tried to understand the real effect of the connectivity on the stability of the credit system. Specifically, many agent-based models have shown that the introduction of a trend reinforcement in the stochastic process, describing the fragility of the nodes, generates a trade-off. Rising the connectivity, the network is less exposed to systemic risk in the beginning, thanks to risk sharing. However, when the connectivity becomes too high, the systematic risk eventually increases.

A forerunner of this trade-off between risk sharing and systemic risk is already present by Iori et al. [68], who show that, in the presence of heterogeneity, a nonmonotonic relationship between connectivity and systemic risk exists. The authors consider a system of commercial banks whose objective is to maximize their expected profits given exogenous investment opportunities. In the model, banks exchange capital in the overnight interbank market to counteract exogenous deposit fluctuations and satisfy their reserve requirements. The authors show the importance of agents' heterogeneity in explaining the ambiguous effect of interbank linkages on systemic risk. Specifically, in case of homogeneous banks, an increase in the connectivity always increases the stability, whereas in the presence of heterogeneous banks, an increase in the connectivity produces a nonmonotonic effect on the market stability.

Similar results are shown in Nier et al. [80]. The authors develop a simulated banking system to analyze the relationship between interbank linkages and systemic risk by including a feedback effect via assets' fire-sale. In their comparative static exercise, the authors recognize an increasing, but nonmonotonic, relationship between the size of interbank exposures and the number of defaults. Similarly, the authors recognize an M-shape relationship between the number of defaults and the Erdős–Rényi connection probability. Hence, a small increase in interbank linkages initially reduces the system stability, however, further increases in the connectivity unambiguously decrease contagion.

The authors also run an additional experiment. By including cash-in-the-market prices, they investigate the effect of the liquidity in the system. Cash-in-the-market prices occur when there is limited liquidity to buy the assets of failed banks. Limited liquidity further reduces the price of those assets, thus inducing a positive feedback loop in the system. The introduction of this illiquidity effect increases contagious defaults for any level of connectivity. In addition, illiquidity smoothes the M-shape relationship between contagion and connectivity. More concentrated systems are fragile, in particular, when markets are illiquid.

The effect of the connectivity in an Erdős–Rényi credit network is also investigated by May and Arinaminpathy [77]. The authors consider a very simplified banking system with no liquidity effects. Similarly to the epidemiology studies, each time step, one single bank faces an exogenous shock. In their simple framework, the authors find a nonmonotonic relationship between the number of defaults and the Erdős–Rényi connection probability p. Moreover, in an other experiment, the authors introduce an illiquidity effect modeled as an asset price depression. The introduction of this effect reduces the stability of the system measured in terms of number of agents' defaults.

The trade-off between connectivity and systemic (in)stability is also given by Battiston et al. [25]. This phenomenon is generated by the joint effect of *interdependence* in banks financial conditions and *financial accelerator*. The authors develop a system of differential equations of the creditworthiness, or distance from default, $\rho_i \in [0, 1]$ of bank i over time. In its extended form, the law of motion of robustness is described by a *time-delayed* stochastic differential equation (SDE)

$$d\rho_i = \left[\sum_j W_{ij}\rho_j(t) + h\big(\rho(t), \rho(t')\big) \right] dt + \rho \sum_j W_{ij} d\epsilon_j, \qquad (10.5)$$

where the first element represents the dependence on the exposure of other banks' credit worthiness (W_{ij} represents the exposition of bank i to bank j), the second term represents the dependence on previous periods' credit worthiness, whereas the last term represents the shock coming from independent Wiener processes. In the model, an increase in the network connectivity may reduce the risk associated to individual banks; however, at the same time, it may increase the system instability. The result of this trade-off is that the relationship between systemic risk and interbank connectivity is initially increasing for low values of connectivity and then decreasing for high values of connectivity. The negative relationship between high connectivity and systemic stability is magnified if a stylized behavioral rule is introduced. In fact, when banks are less willing to lend capital in case of their neighbor default, the authors observe that systemic crisis becomes not only more severe, but also more frequent.

Some models indicate that agents' heterogeneity contribute to instability. An intuition of why the degree of heterogeneity may generate contagion is as follows. When the agents' balance sheets are heterogeneous, banks are not uniformly exposed to their counterparty. Therefore, if the contagion is triggered by the failure of a big bank, which represents the highest source of exposure for its creditors, the situation is certainly worse than when agents are homogeneous. In line with this view, Gai and Kapadia [57] show that heterogeneous credit networks are very fragile in case of failure of the most connected agent but robust to random attack. Caccioli et al. [36], by extending the model of Gai and Kapadia [57], show that a heterogeneous distribution of assets increases the probability of contagion even with respect to random failures.

Another important source of infection depends on the nature of the shock hitting the system. In this regard, Ladley [72] develops a partial equilibrium model with heterogeneous interacting banks, with the aim to analyze the resilience of alternative market structure with respect to different exogenous shocks. Ladley recognizes that when shocks are "economy-wide," interbank linkages spread systemic instability. On the contrary, when shocks are limited, interbank linkages improve the systemic stability.

In the proposed framework, banks are profit-maximizer agents that invest their deposits into risky investment opportunities. Banks interact with each other in the interbank market in order to exchange capitals. Specifically, financial institutions with excess funds lend capital, whereas banks with excess investment opportunities may borrow in the interbank market. Banks' investment decisions are influenced by five parameters, namely the reserve and equity ratios, the lending and deposit interest rates, and the repayment probability. Interestingly, the parameters' value are updated via a genetic algorithm. Specifically, at each period, two banks are selected: the worst performing bank substitutes its parameters' values with those of the other institution plus an innovation term. This upgrade continues until reaching a steady state, where, in line with the empirical literature (see [41]), large banks are net borrowers, and small banks, constrained in their level of equity, lend small amounts to few large financial institutions.

In his model, Ladley shows that the frequency of bankruptcies decreases when external shocks are low, whereas it increases when external shocks are high. This result suggests that there exists no optimal network structure able to resist to each attack.

Furthermore, the author introduces a "confidence effect," where banks consider all their counterparties riskier in case of one of their borrowers' default. This negative externality, by reducing the volumes of exchanges and increasing the volatility of the interbank rate, increases interbank contagion ceteris paribus.

The works presented so far consider fixed credit network topologies. However, some papers analyze the effect of contagion on different or evolving network architectures. An interesting contribution in this direction is made by Georg [60], who analyzes the effects of alternative network structures on the interbank market stability. This model includes both commercial and central banks. Commercial banks maximize a Constant Absolute Risk Aversion utility function (CARA) to allocate their portfolio between risky investments and riskless excess reserves. By varying the agents' connection probability the author obtains different interbank network structures, ranging from the random to the small-world and scale-free one. The network structure plays little role in influencing systemic stability in normal times, whereas it becomes crucial in periods of financial distress. Moreover, the degree of interconnectedness has a nonmonotonic effect on financial contagion: systemic risk tends to be larger in random networks than in small-world and scale-free networks.

Last but not least, the author studies the role of the central bank in providing liquidity. Georg shows that the liquidity provision presents a nonlinear stabilizing effect on the stability of the system. Low levels of liquidity injection increase the network stability, whereas high levels produce a crowding-out effect by reducing volumes in the interbank market.

In a similar spirit, Lenzu and Tedeschi [74] develop an agent-based interbank network, where credit relationships evolve endogenously via a fitness mechanism. In the proposed framework, the economy is populated by banks that review their lending agreements every period. Specifically, each period t, each agent i cuts its ongoing link with agent j and forms a new link with a randomly chosen agent k with probability

$$Pr_i^t = \frac{1}{1 + e^{-\gamma(\phi_j^t - \phi_k^t)}},$$ (10.6)

where ϕ_l^t is a measure of agent's attractiveness expressed as a function of a microfounded bankruptcy probability. The lower the probability, the higher the expected profit, the higher the probability that the lender enters into a lending agreement with borrower. The parameter $\gamma \in [0, \infty]$ represents the signal credibility and indicates the trust of agents on the performance of their counterparties. By changing the trust parameter the system results in very different network architectures, ranging from random to scale-free networks. The authors study how the different networks structures respond to external liquidity shocks. Specifically, they show that a random financial network is more resilient to random liquidity shocks than the scale-free one in case of agents' heterogeneity.

The articles considered so far focused on the effect of the network architecture in spreading contagion via liquidity shocks and/or counterparty risk. However, additional sources of instability have been recognized during the 2007 financial crisis. Specifically, agents' strategic behavior seems to have played a key role in generating financial distress [42]. In this regard, the agent-based literature mainly focuses on two behavioral mechanisms: the roll-over risk of credit lines [15] and the portfolio rebalancing [37].

About the first mechanism, Anand et al. [15] develop a model in which the arrival of bad news on a financial institution leads its creditors to lose confidence in it. Using a game-theoretical network framework, where creditors must decide whether to withdraw their funds (foreclose) or roll over to maturity, the authors find the conditions under which markets "freeze" and highlight how the reestablishment of normal credit conditions can take a prolonged time.

With respect to the second mechanism, namely a strategic portfolio rebalancing, Caccioli et al. [37] analyze the effect of the assets' price variation, which follows a fire-sale, on the systemic stability. By considering a system composed by a set of N banks and M assets, the authors generate contagion via common asset holdings, that is, overlapping portfolios. An intuition of how this mechanism may generate contagion is as follows. In the event that an asset price fluctuation causes an institution to fail, the resulting fire sale of assets by that institution further depresses prices, which in turn may cause other institutions to fail, causing a spiral of selling and further asset price decreases.

The fundamental assumption of the model is that, in the period of crisis, banks have no time to rebalance their portfolios before default, but their assets are immediately liquidated. The authors analyze the circumstances under which systemic instabilities are likely to occur as a function of some model parameters such as leverage, market crowding, diversification, and market impact. Although diversification may be good for individual institutions, it can create dangerous systemic effects, and, as a result, financial contagion gets worse with too much diversification. Moreover, the authors identify a critical threshold for leverage; below it, financial networks are always stable, and above it, the unstable region grows as leverage increases.

A number of agent-based models considered the interrelation occurring between the financial market and the real economy. Specifically, these studies consider possible feedback loops between the two systems, with the credit market affecting economic growth and the firms' performance influencing the stability of the banking system.

One first contribution in this direction is made by Tedeschi et al. [86]. The authors develop an agent-based model to understand the relationship between business cycles, economic growth, and systemic stability. The framework considers the simultaneous presence of three sectors: goods, credit, and interbank market. The authors study the effect of a demand shock, which affects firms by increasing the connectivity in the interbank system. Their results show that a higher banks' connectivity not only increases the agent's financial fragility, but also generates larger bankruptcy cascades due to the larger systemic risk. Interestingly, high interbank linkages have no effect on economic output, even during bust/boom. The interbank market, in fact, just has a marginal effect on firms' investments and on the granted loans. In contrast, higher bank reserve requirements stabilize the economic system, not only by decreasing financial fragility, but also by dampening avalanches. However, holding in reserve a larger percentage of banks' equity affects the aggregate output growth by reducing credit to companies.

Grilli et al. [62,61] extend the previous paper by including a supply shock on firms and microfounded behavioral rules. They show that these mechanisms generate a nonmonotonic relation between bank connectivity and micro- and macro-performances. Indeed, agents performance and macroactivities increase with the level of the connectivity up to a threshold, which can be dubbed as pseudo-optimal. On the contrary, the net effect in terms of micro- and aggregate outputs is negative for any level of the connectivity exceeding the optimum threshold. Moreover, the level of the optimal connectivity depends critically on the emergence of a phase transition in the modeled random network. When the interbank market reaches the phase transition, the presence of many interconnected banks suggests that the credit network is more susceptible to the domino effect. In this case, when failures occur, many agents are potentially compromised.

Before concluding this section, it is important to remind that other agent-based models focus attention on the firm–bank or firm–firm credit relationships [66,58,59]. The results of these important studies are in line with the previous ones.

10.5 CONCLUDING REMARKS

In the last thirty years, most of advanced and developing economies have undertaken a deep transformation that is usually named as financialization of the economy. Major changes can be identified in the deregulation of financial markets, liberalization of capital transfers and in the privatization of the banking system. The financial sector has then assumed an increasing relevance with respect to the production sector; furthermore, the role of the banking system has gradually shifted from the loan-based financing of nonfinancial corporations to more market-based activities and speculative operations, whereas nonfinancial corporations have been increasingly involved in financial activities.

Financial innovation and easy credit have created asset bubbles and debt-induced economic booms, with the consequent rising of household debt–income ratios, corporate debt–equity ratios, and bank leverage, which have made the economy increasingly financially fragile and potentially unstable. Following the severe financial and economic crises that started in 2007 in US, the phenomenon of the financialization is increasingly under critical discussion as some of the major causes of the crisis.

Based on the lessons taken from these crises, many scholars have begun to seriously consider the effect of the interaction on the (in)stability of financial systems. The aim of this review has been, therefore, to illustrate the Journey, made by the Economic literature, down the Right Road, where heterogeneous agents interact. A careful analysis of the dynamic relationships that govern the interaction among individuals at the microlevel and economic sectors at the macrolevel has been indicated as the key element to explain real and financial cycles. Moreover, the analyzed papers have shown that the network of credit relationships may lead to systemic risk, that is, the risk of an epidemic diffusion of financial distress and eventually to a fully fledged financial crisis. In this regard, on the one hand, our review has shown that idiosyncratic shocks can well be the source of an epidemic diffusion of financial distress. In other words, in a financial network, idiosyncratic shocks usually do not cancel out in the aggregate, especially, if they hit crucial nodes (hubs) of the network. On the other hand, the revised literature has proven that, in credit networks, the interaction itself can lead to avalanches of bankruptcies. An intuition of how to trigger domino effect in a networked economy is as follows. Suppose, for instance, that a firm goes bust. Both the suppliers and the banks which made business with the bankrupt firm will bear the brunt of the default. In other words, the default creates a negative externality for connected agents. The deterioration of the bank's financial condition due to the borrower's bankruptcy may be absorbed if the size of the loan is small and/or the bank's net worth is high. If this is not the case, then also the bank goes bankrupt. If the bank survives, however, then it will restrain credit supply and/or make credit conditions harsher—raising the interest rate on loans across the board—for all its borrowers. Therefore, the default of one agent can bring about an avalanche of bankruptcies. Whereas the proximate cause of the bankruptcy of a certain firm in the middle of the avalanche is the interest rate hike, the remote cause is the bankruptcy of a firm at the beginning of the avalanche that forced the banks to push interest rates up. The interest rate hike leads to more bankruptcies and eventually to a bankruptcy chain: "the high rate of bankruptcy is a cause of the high interest rate as much as a consequence of it" [84]. An avalanche of bankruptcies therefore is due to the positive feedback of the bankruptcy of a single agent on the net-worth of the "neighbors," linked to the bankrupt agent by credit links of one sort or another.

Using Mr. Trichet's words: "the key lesson we would draw from our experience is the danger of relying on a single tool, methodology or paradigm. Policy-makers need to have input from various theoretical perspectives and from a range of empirical approaches. ... we need to develop complementary tools to improve the robustness of our overall framework. ... In this context, we would very much welcome inspiration from other disciplines: physics, engineering, psychology, biology. Bringing experts from these fields together with economists and central bankers is potentially very creative and valuable. Scientists have developed sophisticated tools for analyzing complex dynamic systems in a rigorous way. These models have proved helpful in understanding many important but complex phenomena: epidemics, weather patterns, crowd psychology, magnetic fields. Such tools have been applied by market practitioners to portfolio management decisions, on occasion with some success".

Our contribution has sought to do exactly what Mr. Trichet was calling for. To foster our understanding of the economic dynamics, this review has proposed the use of new tools to reconstruct the dependence among agents at the microlevel, with strong stress on the network properties of the economy as a whole.

REFERENCES

[1] D. Acemoglu, M.A. Dahleh, I. Lobel, A. Ozdaglar, Bayesian learning in social networks, The Review of Economic Studies 78 (4) (2011) 1201–1236.

[2] D. Acemoglu, A. Ozdaglar, A. Tahbaz-Salehi, Systemic risk and stability in financial networks, The American Economic Review 105 (2) (2015) 564–608.

[3] V.V. Acharya, D. Gromb, T. Yorulmazer, Imperfect competition in the interbank market for liquidity as a rationale for central banking, American Economic Journal: Macroeconomics 4 (2) (2012) 184–217.

[4] V.V. Acharya, O. Merrouche, Precautionary hoarding of liquidity and interbank markets: evidence from the subprime crisis, Review of Finance (2012) rfs022.

[5] V.V. Acharya, D. Skeie, A model of liquidity hoarding and term premia in inter-bank markets, Journal of Monetary Economics 58 (5) (2011) 436–447.

[6] V.V. Acharya, T. Yorulmazer, Cash-in-the-market pricing and optimal resolution of bank failures, The Review of Financial Studies 21 (6) (2008) 2705–2742.

[7] V.V. Acharya, T. Yorulmazer, Information contagion and bank herding, Journal of Money, Credit, and Banking 40 (1) (2008) 215–231.

[8] M. Affinito, Do interbank customer relationships exist? And how did they function in the crisis? Learning from Italy, Journal of Banking & Finance 36 (12) (2012) 3163–3184.

[9] G. Afonso, A. Kovner, A. Schoar, Stressed, not frozen: the federal funds market in the financial crisis, The Journal of Finance 66 (4) (2011) 1109–1139.

[10] P. Aghion, P. Bolton, M. Dewatripont, Contagious bank failures in a free banking system, European Economic Review 44 (4) (2000) 713–718.

[11] R. Albert, H. Jeong, A.-L. Barabási, Error and attack tolerance of complex networks, Nature 406 (6794) (2000) 378–382.

[12] F. Allen, A. Babus, Networks in Finance, Wharton Financial Institutions Center Working Paper (08-07), 2008.

[13] F. Allen, D. Gale, Financial contagion, Journal of Political Economy 108 (1) (2000) 1–33.

[14] K. Anand, P. Gai, S. Kapadia, S. Brennan, M. Willison, A network model of financial system resilience, Journal of Economic Behavior & Organization 85 (2013) 219–235.

[15] K. Anand, P. Gai, M. Marsili, Rollover risk, network structure and systemic financial crises, Journal of Economic Dynamics and Control 36 (8) (2012) 1088–1100.

[16] R.M. Anderson, R.M. May, B. Anderson, Infectious Diseases of Humans: Dynamics and Control, vol. 28, Wiley Online Library, 1992.

[17] P. Angelini, G. Maresca, D. Russo, Systemic risk in the netting system, Journal of Banking & Finance 20 (5) (1996) 853–868.

[18] C. Aymanns, C.-P. Georg, Contagious synchronization and endogenous network formation in financial networks, Journal of Banking & Finance 50 (2015) 273–285.

[19] A. Babus, The formation of financial networks, The Rand Journal of Economics 47 (2) (2016) 239–272.

[20] A. Babus, T.-W. Hu, Endogenous Intermediation in Over-the-Counter Markets, CEPR Discussion Paper No. DP10708, 2015.

[21] L. Bargigli, G. Di Iasio, L. Infante, F. Lillo, F. Pierobon, The multiplex structure of interbank networks, Quantitative Finance 15 (4) (2015) 673–691.

[22] L. Bargigli, G. Tedeschi, Major trends in agent-based economics, Journal of Economic Interaction and Coordination (2013) 1–7.

[23] L. Bargigli, G. Tedeschi, Interaction in agent-based economics: a survey on the network approach, Physica A: Statistical Mechanics and its Applications 399 (2014) 1–15.

[24] S. Battiston, D.D. Gatti, M. Gallegati, B. Greenwald, J.E. Stiglitz, Default cascades: when does risk diversification increase stability?, Journal of Financial Stability 8 (3) (2012) 138–149.

[25] S. Battiston, D.D. Gatti, M. Gallegati, B. Greenwald, J.E. Stiglitz, Liaisons dangereuses: increasing connectivity, risk sharing, and systemic risk, Journal of Economic Dynamics and Control 36 (8) (2012) 1121–1141.

[26] M.L. Bech, E. Atalay, The topology of the federal funds market, Physica A: Statistical Mechanics and its Applications 389 (22) (2010) 5223–5246.

[27] M.L. Bech, R.J. Garratt, Illiquidity in the interbank payment system following wide-scale disruptions, Journal of Money, Credit, and Banking 44 (5) (2012) 903–929.

[28] S. Berardi, G. Tedeschi, From banks' strategies to financial (in)stability, International Review of Economics & Finance 47 (2017) 255–272.

[29] M. Billio, M. Getmansky, A.W. Lo, L. Pelizzon, Econometric measures of connectedness and systemic risk in the finance and insurance sectors, Journal of Financial Economics 104 (3) (2012) 535–559.

[30] M. Blåvarg, P. Nimander, Interbank exposures and systemic risk, in: Proceedings of the Third Joint Central Bank Research Conference on Risk Measurement and Systemic Risk, BIS, March 2002, 2002, p. 287.

[31] S.P. Borgatti, M.G. Everett, Models of core/periphery structures, Social Networks 21 (4) (2000) 375–395.

[32] M. Boss, H. Elsinger, M. Summer, S. Thurner, Network topology of the interbank market, Quantitative Finance 4 (6) (2004) 677–684.

[33] M. Boss, M. Summer, S. Thurner, Contagion flow through banking networks, in: International Conference on Computational Science, Springer, 2004, pp. 1070–1077.

[34] F. Bräuning, F. Fecht, Relationship Lending in the Interbank Market and the Price of Liquidity, Discussion Papers 22/2012, Deutsche Bundesbank, Research Centre, 2012.

[35] M.K. Brunnermeier, Deciphering the liquidity and credit crunch 2007–2008, The Journal of Economic Perspectives 23 (1) (2009) 77–100.

[36] F. Caccioli, T.A. Catanach, J.D. Farmer, Heterogeneity, correlations and financial contagion, Advances in Complex Systems 15 (supp02) (2012) 1250058.

[37] F. Caccioli, M. Shrestha, C. Moore, J.D. Farmer, Stability analysis of financial contagion due to overlapping portfolios, Journal of Banking & Finance 46 (2014) 233–245.

[38] N. Cassola, C. Holthausen, M.L. Duca, The 2007/2008 turmoil: a challenge for the integration of the euro area money market, in: Conference on Liquidity: Concepts and Risks, CESifo Conference Centre, Munich, 2008, pp. 17–23.

[39] F. Castiglionesi, N. Navarro, Optimal Fragile Financial Networks, 2008 Meeting Papers 658, Society for Economic Dynamics, 2008.

[40] R. Cifuentes, G. Ferrucci, H.S. Shin, Liquidity risk and contagion, Journal of the European Economic Association 3 (2–3) (2005) 556–566.

[41] J.F. Cocco, F.J. Gomes, N.C. Martins, Lending relationships in the interbank market, Journal of Financial Intermediation 18 (1) (2009) 24–48.

[42] F.C.I. Commission, The Financial Crisis Inquiry Report: Final Report of the National Commission on the Causes of the Financial and Economic Crisis in the United States, PublicAffairs, 2011.

[43] B. Craig, G. Von Peter, Interbank tiering and money center banks, Journal of Financial Intermediation 23 (3) (2014) 322–347.

[44] A. Dasgupta, Financial contagion through capital connections: a model of the origin and spread of bank panics, Journal of the European Economic Association 2 (6) (2004) 1049–1084.

[45] H. Degryse, G. Nguyen, et al., Interbank exposures: an empirical examination of contagion risk in the Belgian banking system, International Journal of Central Banking 3 (2) (2007) 123–171.

[46] D.W. Diamond, P.H. Dybvig, Bank runs, deposit insurance, and liquidity, Journal of Political Economy (1983) 401–419.

[47] D.W. Diamond, R.G. Rajan, Liquidity shortages and banking crises, The Journal of Finance 60 (2) (2005) 615–647.

[48] D. Duffie, N. Gârleanu, L.H. Pedersen, Over-the-counter markets, Econometrica 73 (6) (2005) 1815–1847.

[49] L. Eisenberg, T.H. Noe, Systemic risk in financial systems, Management Science 47 (2) (2001) 236–249.

[50] X. Freixas, B.M. Parigi, J.-C. Rochet, Systemic risk, interbank relations, and liquidity provision by the central bank, Journal of Money, Credit, and Banking (2000) 611–638.

[51] D. Fricke, T. Lux, Core–periphery structure in the overnight money market: evidence from the e-mid trading platform, Computational Economics 45 (3) (2015) 359–395.

[52] C. Furfine, Interbank exposures: quantifying the risk of contagion, Journal of Money, Credit, and Banking 35 (1) (2003) 111–128.

[53] C.H. Furfine, Banks as monitors of other banks: evidence from the overnight federal funds market, The Journal of Business 74 (1) (2001) 33–57.

[54] S. Gabrieli, The Functioning of the European Interbank Market during the 2007–08 Financial Crisis, CEIS Research Paper 158, Tor Vergata University, CEIS, 2010.

[55] S. Gabrieli, Too-Connected Versus Too-Big-to-Fail: Banks' Network Centrality and Overnight Interest Rates, Working papers, Banque de France, 2012.

[56] P. Gai, A. Haldane, S. Kapadia, Complexity, concentration and contagion, Journal of Monetary Economics 58 (5) (2011) 453–470.

[57] P. Gai, S. Kapadia, Contagion in financial networks, in: Proceedings of the Royal Society of London A: Mathematical, Physical and Engineering Sciences, The Royal Society, 2010.

[58] D.D. Gatti, M. Gallegati, B. Greenwald, A. Russo, J.E. Stiglitz, The financial accelerator in an evolving credit network, Journal of Economic Dynamics and Control 34 (9) (2010) 1627–1650.

[59] D.D. Gatti, M. Gallegati, B.C. Greenwald, A. Russo, J.E. Stiglitz, Business fluctuations and bankruptcy avalanches in an evolving network economy, Journal of Economic Interaction and Coordination 4 (2) (2009) 195–212.

[60] C.-P. Georg, The effect of the interbank network structure on contagion and common shocks, Journal of Banking & Finance 37 (7) (2013) 2216–2228.

[61] R. Grilli, G. Tedeschi, M. Gallegati, Bank interlinkages and macroeconomic stability, International Review of Economics & Finance 34 (2014) 72–88.

[62] R. Grilli, G. Tedeschi, M. Gallegati, Markets connectivity and financial contagion, Journal of Economic Interaction and Coordination 10 (2) (2015) 287–304.

[63] S.J. Grossman, J.E. Stiglitz, On the impossibility of informationally efficient markets, The American Economic Review 70 (3) (1980) 393–408.

[64] A.G. Haldane, R.M. May, Systemic risk in banking ecosystems, Nature 469 (7330) (2011) 351–355.

[65] V. Hatzopoulos, G. Iori, R.N. Mantegna, S. Miccichè, M. Tumminello, Quantifying preferential trading in the e-mid interbank market, Quantitative Finance 15 (4) (2015) 693–710.

[66] U. Holmberg, The Credit Market and the Determinants of Credit Crunches: An Agent Based Modeling Approach, Tech. rep., Umeå University, Department of Economics, 2012.

[67] G. Iori, G. De Masi, O.V. Precup, G. Gabbi, G. Caldarelli, A network analysis of the Italian overnight money market, Journal of Economic Dynamics and Control 32 (1) (2008) 259–278.

[68] G. Iori, S. Jafarey, F.G. Padilla, Systemic risk on the interbank market, Journal of Economic Behavior & Organization 61 (4) (2006) 525–542.

[69] G. Iori, R.N. Mantegna, L. Marotta, S. Micciche, J. Porter, M. Tumminello, Networked relationships in the e-mid interbank market: a trading model with memory, Journal of Economic Dynamics and Control 50 (2015) 98–116.

[70] R. Iyer, J.-L. Peydro, Interbank contagion at work: evidence from a natural experiment, The Review of Financial Studies 24 (4) (2011) 1337–1377.

[71] M.O. Jackson, A. Wolinsky, A strategic model of social and economic networks, in: Networks and Groups, Springer, 2003, pp. 23–49.

[72] D. Ladley, Contagion and risk-sharing on the inter-bank market, Journal of Economic Dynamics and Control 37 (7) (2013) 1384–1400.

[73] R. Lagos, G. Rocheteau, P.-O. Weill, Crises and liquidity in over-the-counter markets, Journal of Economic Theory 146 (6) (2011) 2169–2205.

[74] S. Lenzu, G. Tedeschi, Systemic risk on different interbank network topologies, Physica A: Statistical Mechanics and its Applications 391 (18) (2012) 4331–4341.

[75] Á. Lublóy, Domino effect in the Hungarian interbank market, Hungarian Economic Review 52 (4) (2005) 377–401.

[76] S. Martinez-Jaramillo, B. Alexandrova-Kabadjova, B. Bravo-Benitez, J.P. Solórzano-Margain, An empirical study of the Mexican banking system's network and its implications for systemic risk, Journal of Economic Dynamics and Control 40 (2014) 242–265.

[77] R.M. May, N. Arinaminpathy, Systemic risk: the dynamics of model banking systems, Journal of the Royal Society Interface 7 (46) (2010) 823–838.

[78] P.E. Mistrulli, Assessing financial contagion in the interbank market: maximum entropy versus observed interbank lending patterns, Journal of Banking & Finance 35 (5) (2011) 1114–1127.

[79] M. Montagna, C. Kok, Multi-Layered Interbank Model for Assessing Systemic Risk, Tech. rep., Kiel Institute for the World Economy (IfW), 2013.

[80] E. Nier, J. Yang, T. Yorulmazer, A. Alentorn, Network models and financial stability, Journal of Economic Dynamics and Control 31 (6) (2007) 2033–2060.

[81] J.-C. Rochet, J. Tirole, Interbank lending and systemic risk, Journal of Money, Credit, and Banking 28 (4) (1996) 733–762.

[82] G. Sheldon, M. Maurer, Interbank lending and systemic risk: an empirical analysis for Switzerland, Revue Suisse d'Economie Politique et de Statistique 134 (1998) 685–704.

[83] H.S. Shin, Financial Intermediation and the Post-Crisis Financial System, BIS Working Papers 304, Bank for International Settlements, 2010.

[84] J. Stiglitz, B. Greenwald, Towards a New Paradigm in Monetary Economics, Cambridge University Press, 2003.

[85] G. Tedeschi, G. Iori, M. Gallegati, Herding effects in order driven markets: the rise and fall of gurus, Journal of Economic Behavior & Organization 81 (1) (2012) 82–96.

[86] G. Tedeschi, A. Mazloumian, M. Gallegati, D. Helbing, Bankruptcy cascades in interbank markets, PLoS ONE 7 (12) (2012) e52749.

[87] A. Temizsoy, G. Iori, G. Montes-Rojas, The role of bank relationships in the interbank market, Journal of Economic Dynamics and Control 59 (2015) 118–141.

[88] C. Upper, Simulation methods to assess the danger of contagion in interbank markets, Journal of Financial Stability 7 (3) (2011) 111–125.

[89] C. Upper, A. Worms, Estimating bilateral exposures in the German interbank market: is there a danger of contagion?, European Economic Review 48 (4) (2004) 827–849.

[90] M. van der Leij, J. Kovářík, Risk Aversion and Social Networks, Working papers, serie ad, Instituto Valenciano de Investigaciones Económicas, S.A. (Ivie), 2012.

[91] S. Wells, Financial Interlinkages in the United Kingdom's Interbank Market and the Risk of Contagion, Tech. rep., Bank of England, 2004.

Index